APR 1 3 2006

EAST MEADOW PUBLIC LIBRARY

D1431199

East Meadow Public Library
1886 Front Street
East Meadow, L.I., N.Y. 11554-1700

BAKER & TAYLOR

Believeniks!

ALSO BY IVAN FELT

The Jargon of Inauthenticity: TV Guide and the TeleLiterate Public (1978)

The Stiff-Necked Adversary of Thought (1984)

Somnambulists, Nerds, Republicans: American Persiflage (1992)

Lost & Found Referentials: Commercials and Koans (2005)

ALSO BY HARRIS CONKLIN

Poetry

Smudged Moral Maps (1979)

The Ghost of My Appetite (1982)

Antithetical Avenues (1989)

Horn of Empty (1995)

Novellas

Nowhere/Near (1983)

ALSO BY IVAN FELT & HARRIS CONKLIN

Believeniks! Go to the Movies (forthcoming)

Believeniks!

------------------ **2005:** ------------------

The Year We Wrote a Book About the Mets

IVAN FELT

&

HARRIS CONKLIN

DOUBLEDAY

New York   London   Toronto   Sydney   Auckland

PUBLISHED BY DOUBLEDAY

Copyright © 2006 by Ivan Felt and Harris Conklin

All Rights Reserved

Published in the United States by Doubleday, an imprint of
The Doubleday Broadway Publishing Group, a division
of Random House, Inc., New York.

www.doubleday.com

DOUBLEDAY and the portrayal of an anchor with a dolphin
are registered trademarks of Random House, Inc.

Photograph on page iv by Lee Friedlander.
Courtesy of Fraenkel Gallery, San Francisco.

Book design by Michael Collica

Library of Congress Cataloging-in-Publication Data
Felt, Ivan.
Believeniks! : 2005, the year we wrote a book about
the Mets / Ivan Felt and Harris Conklin.—1st ed.
p. cm.
ISBN 0-385-51716-5
1. New York Mets (Baseball team). 2. New York Mets
(Baseball team)—Anecdotes. I. Conklin, Harris. II. Title.
GV875.N45F45 2006
796.357'64097471—dc22
2005057235

ISBN-13: 978-0-385-51716-4
ISBN-10: 0-385-51716-5

PRINTED IN THE UNITED STATES OF AMERICA

1 3 5 7 9 10 8 6 4 2

First Edition

TO JERRY KOOSMAN

". . . to play meaningful games in September . . ."

—Fred Wilpon, Mets owner

"The Mets would finish in last place again, and no one would suffer."

—Paul Auster, *City of Glass*

"The Mets is a good thing. They give everybody jobs. Just like the WPA."

—Billy Loes, journeyman extraordinaire, purchased by Mets during expansion; retired rather than reporting

Ivan Felt—The Critic

Harris Conklin—The Poet

Willie Randolph—The Skipper

Carlos Beltran—The Franchise

Pedro Martinez—The Savior

Cliff Floyd—The Trouper

David Wright—The Kid

Jose Reyes—The Flash

Braden Looper—The Goat

The Mink—The Mink

Mesch—The Uscher

Filthy Pierrot—The Frog

Also see: The Encyclopedia Metsiana, page 263

Believeniks!

- -

Hot Stove

November 11, 2004

Harris,

At this point I have recourse to what the first Mrs. Ivan Felt might have had to say about the Mets this off-season: "With Pluto in the Twelfth House, consciousness is opening up to a power which can *will into being* that which you most desire."

(That's as far as I rode on the spiritual railroad with her. I wanted to get off someplace where you could still get a good steak.)

Now, when the Mets need something, desire something, declare their yearning for something, strive to obtain something—what it usually means is that they end up getting Joe Foy, Jim Fregosi, or Shawn Abner.

(A Mets fan does not necessarily have to be a Mets historian, and so I will only mention, briefly and in passing, such exceptions to this observation as Donn Clendenon [for Steve Renko and Kevin Collins], Rusty Staub [Tim Foli, Mike

Jorgensen, and, admittedly, Ken Singleton], or Keith Hernandez [Neil Allen].)

It's not that I don't feel good about Minaya being in the GM job. I always figured that when Steve Phillips got canned—and that always seemed to me to be a matter of time—Minaya would replace him, and so my heart sank when he moved into the lonely caretaker's cabin atop Olympic Stadium a couple of years ago. It's the Wilpons that I'm not sure about. As field managerial candidates go, Willie Randolph has *got* to be our man, and I am not entirely certain that Fred 'n' Jeff are 100 percent free of misconceptions, shall we say, concerning certain candidates for supervisory positions. I have this great fear that the Mets will hire an older manager; some white-haired, pallid martinet who'll have the players scrambling for the parking lot ten minutes after the final out of each game; a combination of the worst of both worlds: the polymathic computer whiz whose best pal is his PowerBook (I should talk) and the garden-variety tyrant who imposes a ten PM curfew and bans beer from the postgame spread. The presence of such a despot, along with the daily late-inning emergence from the dugout of Rick Peterson's unfortunate hair along with the man attached to it, might just drive me away from our team.

I've been rooting for Willie for years anyway. Yankee or not. I always viewed him as fulfilling the Push Me, Pull You role of the neglected and/or abused middle child in the Yankees' dysfunctioning clan. And now his travails over the last few years, seeking a managerial job. That marvelous insouciance of his, claiming not to be able to remember the number of times he's been interviewed for the manager's spot. You buy that? I don't buy it for one minute. You know the guy

can quote chapter and verse from any one of those phony
interviews.

Hopefully,
Ivan

- -

December 5, 2004

Ivan,

You may not recognize me on opening day, since I'm
growing a beard to protest the election. My freak flag shall
fly, though I forecast a Santa Clausian hue. Speaking of Santa
Claus, we've been given our early gift: defying front-office
precedent and your dire and appropriate premonitions, we
hired Randolph. Now a body can begin to rouse itself from
the autumn of its discontent to don the blue and orange, to
start listening to WFAN, to root, a word that reminds me of a
plate of winter vegetables, of comfort food. Needless to say,
I share your relief at our swapping Steve Phillips for Omar
Minaya. Yet I draw the line at any fannish romance with a
team's executives. They're executives. Suits. With a manager—a young, black, first-time manager from Brooklyn, and
a refugee from Steinbrenner's gulag—there I can permit myself to begin. A manager or coach, like a player, like a fan, is
a not-so-secret boy. That's why they keep them dressed up in
tights as if they're about to rush onto the field at any moment
and take up a glove or bat, even when they're dragging an
oxygen tank on wheels behind them.

And Willie Randolph's particular boyishness touches me,
because, as you say, it is a stunted thing. So many of those

longtime Yankees forged in the emasculating furnace of George Steinbrenner's vulgarian rages, never permitted to grow facial hair (a theme emerges!), second-guessed and undercut in the pages of the *Post*. These always have a certain crushed look behind their eyes, as if they've been told it all went as it should but can't find voice to say it doesn't feel as good as it was meant to. Think of Dave Righetti, Don Mattingly, Andy Pettitte, Bernie Williams. (I once read an interview in which Williams mused on how he might rather have gone to law school!) Randolph strikes me as the earliest example of the type, and the noblest. The middle child, indeed—but when will he rebel? Leading the Mets to the promised land would qualify, wouldn't it?

Yes, a manager is good. Players would be even better.

Fondly,

Conklin

December 25, 2004

Dear Harris,

Hope this hasn't caught you in the middle of some arcane Papist ritual. "Squeezing the stocking," are you? "Plugging in the lights"? I'm being a little disingenuous; you know I married outside my ancestral faith at least once; was coerced into the Christian fold on more than one holiday occasion. Think of Nathan Zuckerman, in *The Counterlife*, seated uncomfortably amid the Westminster pews, thinking not of the horrors visited upon his people but of those to be visited upon himself at the Christmas dinner that is to follow.

I do appreciate the Christmas gift we received from Minaya, Randolph, Wilpon, and Co., one Pedro Jaime Martinez. Are you excited? At last, a pitcher who won't make me want to stick my head in the oven every time he takes the mound. In their online fan forums, the citizens of Red Sox Nation are playing their particularly acid version of sour grapes—pure vinegar. Pedro is done, according to them. We'll be sorry. He won't win ten games for the Mets. He's laughing all the way to the Bank of the DR with our big American dollars. Poor Boston. Views everything through that New York lens, much like San Francisco does with L.A. I stood in a bar, Milady's on Thompson, and cheered along with the crowd when the Red Sox finished their sweep of St. Louis, completing that unnameably great comeback—can you even imagine Boston fans reciprocating so good-natured a sentiment?

Before I put on my coat and head out for my Christmas ale and burger at Fanelli's, let me add this: Pedro wears number 45, the same number as the late, great Tug McGraw, but also the same as the current, pretty good, John Franco, aka the Man Who Came to Dinner—I'm beginning to think that we'll have to start flicking the lights on and off to make him get the message. I hope Pedro insists on keeping the number, paying Franco off with a Rolex or Hummer or whatever the petty tax is these days.

Petty, he says. Like a real academic, always spending someone else's money.

Though I've always viewed the Mets' reluctance to retire numbers with a certain dismay. McGraw was the man, after all, who gave the Mets their most persistent, and somehow most genuine, rallying cry. Why not have retired number 45 in his honor? Though these reflections tend to become maundering after a while. If you want to retire number 45, then you need to retire Koosman's 36. Who's a more emblematic Met pitcher, after Seaver, than Koos? And what about the man who caught them both, as well as Ryan, Matlack, Gentry, etc.—Jerry Grote. Ave atque vale #15. What about the original Met, Ed Kranepool (my old favorite)? Put a big number 7 on the left-field wall. Bud Harrelson was the best defensive shortstop in the league, as well as being a spark plug on the '69 and '73 teams. Hang up #3. And what about Cleon? 21 should be off-limits evermore. The Mets would have been out of the '69 series if not for Tommie Agee's two great catches—there goes #20. Of course, Howard Johnson wore #20, too. HoJo!

Hmmm. What about Swoboda, speaking of '69. There is no more articulate and thoughtful alumni of the Mets—he wore #4. But then, so did Rusty Staub. And Lenny Dykstra. And Robin Ventura. Four number 4s, quadruply retired, stretched nobly across the left-center fence.

Back to #7—already spoken for, as we have seen, by Ed Kranepool. Yet, who kept the Mets' hopes alive in game six— the *only* game six? Kevin Mitchell, that's who. But then, Todd Pratt saved the Mets from facing Randy Johnson in a prospective game five, in Arizona, by lofting his mighty homer in the '99 division series. And we might as well just skip the career and send Jose Reyes straight to Cooperstown. So, four numbers S E V E N across the royal-blue outfield wall.

Eight? The Kid! Who else? A genuine Hall of Famer! But then again, so was Yogi Berra.

At this rate I'm going to miss last call—let me wrap this up: seriously, #16. Gooden. No one should have it but him. To quote the man himself, on Frank Viola's arrival in Flushing: "He can have my wife, but he can't have my number."

Seventeen. Fan of Felix "The Cat" Millan though I may be, I cannot—and I really mean this, now, Conklin—imagine what the Mets are thinking about by not retiring Keith Hernandez's number.

Finally, because I can go on all night, #18. Darryl Strawberry (though George "The Stork" Theodore comes to mind). The Mets showed Strawberry exactly what they thought of him by giving his number to Bret Saberhagen immediately after his departure for Los Angeles.

Adeste Fideles,
Ivan

P.S. Can't resist: #40; why would they have stuck poor Pat Zachry with this one? To suggest that he was "almost" as good as Seaver, #41?

January 1

Ivan,

Spellbound by your disquisition on retiring Met numbers. And persuaded. My suggestion, in light of your rhetoric, is that the Mets should just retire "numbers," and move on to a whole new approach—punctuation marks.

Reyes, for instance could wear "?" on his jersey. Is he the beginning of a glorious future? Or nothing at all?

Or no—give the standard question mark to Wright, that's better. Then give Reyes the upside-down "Latino" question mark. And my keyboard can't handle it, but Kaz Matsui can wear a Japanese question mark—our infield's all unknowns. The Future Is Now??? (Maybe the whole team could change its name to "? and the Mysteriopolitans.")

That leaves "!" for Pedro, and "$" for Beltran. (God knows we'll need it.) Give the bracket marks to Cameron and Floyd, and our outfield looks like this:

{$}

Yours in concrete poetry,
Harris

P.S. Yes, I'm excited.

January 27

H.,

Party's over. We nail down Pedro and Beltran, but Delgado gets away. Rumor is, that Republican Leiter talked him into it. Isn't Doug Mienkiewicz (oh, I give up . . . the paper's downstairs with the correct spelling) the perfect Mets fallback, though? Classic move: everything, or something sort of OK.

Classic press release, too: since we called the Red Sox's defensive backup "our number-two option after Delgado" we'll pretend that puts them in the same universe: "Hey, we got our number-two option!" If I recall my SAT math exercises involving extending a numerical series, that means our third option for first base in 2005 was the Atlanta Braves' batboy. Or: "Our third option for first base was Mr. Met." Humor's how we'll salve this indignity, Conk. Work with me. I'm testing lines aloud, like the Marx Brothers. "Our third option for first base was 'Who'?" Say it with me: Doug Who. But no, that's untenable. Mientkiewicz has done nothing wrong. I say we dub him "The Mink."

I.

February 28

Dear Ivan,

Here's why I love Felipe Alou. Did you catch his quote yesterday? The first sane words I've heard spoken on the subject of the McCarthyite steroids purge. Here he is, baseball's Edward R. Murrow: "If you're good, you're good—whether it is the era of the steroids, or the cigars, or the hot dog, or the beer, or the amphetamine, or the red juice or the whiskey."

What I love, apart from the sense of perspective tangible in Alou's use of the word "era" (i.e., the understanding—so dim in contemporary consciousness, which tends to believe all pasts are benighted and innocently sepia while only our present is full-color and self-aware—that we are, in fact, also living in an "era"), is his delicious distending of his list of substances, long beyond where he'd made his point, just for the sheer pleasure of hearing the words assembled. Ah, the red juice—now *that* was an era. I could imagine the quote going on even longer, Alou relentlessly tabulating baseball's lapses and implicating the men who seemingly played under their various signs: ". . . or the era of the bar fight, or the polyester shirt, or the ugly charter, or the married hostesses, or spare ribs with McCovey, or nude Ping-Pong in Concepcion's basement . . ."

Herewith, the Alou history of baseball:

The Whiskey & Cigars Era

Ford C. Frick, Kenesaw Mountain Landis, and the McPhails are whiskey/cigar figures—the true whiskey/cigar adherents, not the ones such as those you see nowadays. They were joined by their special friends Hack Wilson (whiskey), Babe Ruth (whiskey, cigars, women), Jimmie Fox (whiskey, cigars, women, farming implements), Ralph Kiner (whiskey, kielbasa), Earl Torgeson (whiskey, cigars, fistfights)—this congenial list goes on and on. And don't forget Hank Greenberg (Manischewitz, potato pancake).

Hot Dogs & Beer

These are the big guys. Almost all played for the Detroit Tigers. Freehan, Cash, Gates Brown, Mickey Lolich—each of these men lost a good portion of his career to hot dogs and beer. And the great throwback, Boomer.

Amphetamine

Leo Durocher, Eddie Stanky, and Billy Martin each play three positions. Each inning ends with an intramural brawl.

Though St. Louis has a whole amphetamine tradition of a different sort—a speedy type who falls off a weird mid-career cliff—Curt Flood, Garry Templeton, Vince Coleman. Maury Wills is also an amphetamine player of this type.

Red Juice

The red juice era is actually an era involving players more known for their escapades off the field. Bo Belinsky, Jim Bouton, and Joe Pepitone are the avatars of the red juice era. And then there's the Cincinnati Reds: Pete Rose, Pete Rose, Pete Rose (Gertrude Stein).

Coq au Vin

This era nudges up against the present day, and includes some favorite Mets. Rusty Staub a preeminent coq au vin player. Keith Hernandez also in this category. And, needless to say, Wade Boggs. Maybe David Cone and Ron Darling too. Tony "Gourmet Ghetto" La Russa would probably be the representative manager for this type of player.

The point, Ivan? My point, and Alou's? EVERYONE'S ON SOMETHING. Every outcome, every twitch of life on this planet, is chemically rigged, because we're chemical animals. Jacked up and slowed down, morphed and melded, becalmed with large meals and rekindled with nicotine and martinis. We're a species of shameless hypocrites, our journalists bleeding Starbucks and Prozac from their eyeballs as they pound toward deadlines on pieces denouncing impure athletics. Balzac had his coffee—killed himself with it. Greatest novelist who ever lived, long as you don't have to read him. Coleridge needed to trip his way to Xanadu. Sherlock Holmes had his cocaine—would we still want Moriarty on the prowl? And, I freely confess, this letter is written under the influence of Dewar's (White Label) and Breyers (Butter Pecan). I don't regret a thing.

Compromised at birth,
Harris

March 3

H—

But didn't David Wells cut his pitching hand on a wineglass during a playful tussle with a male friend at his house in San Diego? Maybe you need to shift Boomer over to Coq au Vin.

And then there's Dock Ellis, a one-man Acid Era. Threw a no-hitter while mentally leafing through Timothy Leary's *Tibetan Book of the Dead*. I would have secured about a thousand hits for my staff after that. Maybe that was the secret of the 1970 Pirates.

Never forget Jimmy Piersall, surely the best player of the Thorazine and Shock Treatment Era.

I.

P.S. *Spare Ribs with McCovey*—isn't that the name of an early
Tom Waits record?

- -

March 17

Ivan,

I couldn't help noticing a certain small headline in the
sports pages today, as I sought for more Met reports, tobacco
with which to fuel my pipe dreams. The headline read: "Radatz Dies from Fall at Home." No disrespect to Dick Radatz, a
memorable player, but my spider-sense began throbbing,
alerted by the assonance of "fall at home" to "Hall of Fame"
(an honor denied Radatz): might there be some occult message secreted therein? So I wasted a morning, and now I
waste a portion of yours. Here, according to the sheaf of ana-
grams I scribbled and crumpled at my writing desk, the site
where I ordinarily attempt to foster lucidity and value, are the
stealth candidates—the bizarro candidates, if you will—who
seem to have crept in ahead of Radatz: "Hall of Fame Admits
Oz Darter." "Hall of Fame Admits Rat Dozer." "Hall of Fame
Admits Dr. Art Zoe." Or, this pair of players, apparently voted
in on the same ballot: "Itz Sartre, Oz Dam, Hall of Fame." (Itz
Sartre must certainly have been in the Mets system at one
point, a prospect tossed in on some disastrous trade.)

Alternately, here are the still-denied players for whom
this mysterious message advocates: "Hall of Fame, Admit
Sad Terroz." "Hall of Fame, Admit Ted Razors." (Ted Razors,
now there was a fielder. I can still picture him, floating high
above Wrigley's ivy to rob a home run.)

Perhaps, Ivan, you and I ought to consider opening a business under this name: "Ted Mozart's Arid Hall of Fame"? Or consider this claim: "Me is Dar, Hall of Fame Tzar."

Needless to say, I was most compelled by those messages pertaining to our boys: "Oz Met Darts Hall of Fame Raid." "Mets Adz Raid Hall of Fame Rot." "Dr. Met Oz Raids at Hall of Fame." As you see, I could never manage to work "Met" in without also using the word "raid." What this tells us, I don't know. Possibly a spur to quasi-military bravery in the coming season. Or it could refer to a bug spray.

Fingers cramped,

Harris

- -

March 18

Harris,

Despair, or merely a resigned shrug as an unnamed spokesman for the Mets' front office concisely sums up the team's philosophy (and dilemma)?

"The person acknowledged this is the least opportune time to try to deal for a quality pitcher, but said many lesser pitchers—pitchers not comparable to Trachsel—will become available as teams cut their rosters down before Opening Day."

What ever will we do without Mr. Freeze, the King of Boredom? I realize suddenly that like Craig Swan, Bobby Jones, and other hapless pitchers before him, Trachsel's become the mainstay of a shaky team. And shaky the Mets still are, if they're scrambling around looking for "lesser pitchers," those "pitchers not comparable to Trachsel." Well, these guys should be very handy just in case the Mets get into any games with roving bands of hitters also cut from other teams' rosters before Opening Day.

Keeping the label up,
I.F.

- -

March 27

Ivan,

Here's a recipe for fourth place:

1. Trade excellent defensive backup catcher in off-season.
2. Release emergency backup catcher two days before number-three starter undergoes surgery for herniated disk, necessitating minimum three-month convalescence.
3. Sift for possible substitutes for number-three starter among usual suspects before deciding that the most compelling choice lies in Los Angeles.
4. Trade remaining backup catcher (and player with highest springtime BA) for said Dodger, a left-hander of Japanese descent and dubious merit.
5. Allow to rest for two weeks before starting catcher sustains concussion.

Kaz Ishii's a strange creature, isn't he? How do you walk that many people if you don't have "stuff" that also generates strikeouts? How do you win thirteen games—in any season, in any stadium—with those stats? I fear we're looking at a statistical oddity and that his record should rightly have been 4–16. And will be, this year.

Ticket opportunities are looking brighter and brighter.

But the Mink's gonna catch everything hit his way!

Springily,

Harris

1

Ugly Uniforms

[*April*]

April 5

Conk,

You know I've never been an Opening Day kind of person. It's not in my nature to aggressively court physical discomfort. Opening Day is cold, nasty, often wet—yet draped in ritual and ceremony. That is to say that it's not subject to cancellation. It's on this day (as on any given day in the Sun Belt) that one most fully appreciates the extent to which seasons are an intellectual construct. "Spring" has begun.

Opening Day is a day for masochists and physical stalwarts and for children, who would rather do anything than attend school. You remember we went to Shea on Opening Day in 1970? Forty degrees. We played the Pirates. Clemente, Stargell, Mazeroski. Al Oliver. Little bitty Freddie Patek. Place wasn't full to watch the new World Champs, much less an opponent with three Hall of Famers (and you can make a case for Oliver, too) in the starting lineup. I prefer now to think of the thin crowd as having more to do with the unobtrusive marketing style of the day than with lack of interest, though perhaps the two add up to the same thing.

I hate Opening Day. Yet we nursed a pair of Rheingolds. Men wore coats, ties, fedoras. Jane Jarvis played her organ, inherently amiable. These were troubled times, yet I'm having no difficulty making them seem idyllic. Then again, it was the Pirates who introduced the major leagues to double-knit pullover jerseys and Sansabelt slacks that season, an omen.

Jerry Grote hit a triple that day, I just remembered. Imagine that.

Speaking of omens, the night before the opener at Cincinnati I dreamed I was sitting next to Yogi Berra. We were at Shea, in the loge—really good seats just behind the home dugout. I was overjoyed to see him, really I was. For some reason, nobody ever remembers how long and how closely Yogi was intertwined with the Mets. In all the incestuously convoluted dealings between the two teams, the Yankees always seem to emerge as true possessors of a given figure's provenance (except in the case of a Marv Throneberry). I know that you know that I don't wish to grant Steinbrenner a thing, but it seems that the spirit that moves him is one of rehabilitation, while it's a purgative one that moves (so to speak) the Wilpons more often than not. Anyway, I said something like, "Yogi! You're back at Shea! How great!" He looked at me, raised his sweaty Harry M. Stevens cup of beer to his lips, sipped, then spoke: "They got rid of the *ugly uniforms*."

I woke up instantly and stared at the water-stained ceiling in my bedroom. *Ugly uniforms?* What did Yogi mean? Something along the lines of the proverbial *empty suit*? E.g., Art Howe, Mo Vaughn, Roberto Alomar? Steve Phillips, the architect of 2002–04? Jason Phillips's goggles, which no man batting under .200 has any business wearing (or maybe I've got it backward; maybe every man sweating under the Mendoza Line ought to be wearing them)? By *ugly* did Yogi mean Tom Glavine's run support? John Franco in his dotage? The spectacle of Mike Piazza at first base looking like a man awkwardly sliding pizzas into a brick oven with a paddle? Were these the *ugly uniforms* Yogi had referenced? Had they been banished forever?

Take one ugly uniform: the emergence of Steve Trachsel as the implacable stopper a couple of seasons ago. Not only is Steve Trachsel the number-three starter on just about any other team—he's the number-three starter on the Mets! So you'll understand when I say that when I viewed a fuzzy montage on MLB.com of Martinez's twelve strikeouts against the Reds in the opener, my heart swelled. Now, you really can't tell shit from such a display, but, watching Pedro mow them down in abbreviated time, it struck me how long it's been since a pitcher about whom I didn't entertain grave doubts took the mound for the Mets. It's been several years of cringing and peeking through fingers. OK, so we lost. Big deal. It serves tradition. Disdain April. April is overrated. So the bullpen blew it. At least we can thank Christ that John Franco didn't have the chance to blow it. I have hopes for Looper this season. The hitters hit. The runners ran. The fielders fielded.

All this anticipation (and accompanying desire) is motivating me to violate the two principal directives embedded in me throughout my childhood by Mrs. Sophie Felt, namely (1) DON'T UNDER ANY CIRCUMSTANCES WATCH THAT IDIOT TELEVISION, IT WILL ROT YOUR BRAINS OUT, and

(2) SAVE YOUR MONEY, YOU CAN NEVER TELL WHEN THE WOLF WILL BE AT THE DOOR. That is, for the first time in my unmarried life I'm going to call to see about having cable TV installed in here. So hopeful am I that the Mets will win (i.e., come in third—I'm not a complete idiot), that I'm willing to pay to watch car commercials, deodorant commercials, beer commercials, and the occasional inning of New York Mets baseball. I know that the dispute between Cablevision and Time Warner will have to come to an end sooner or later.

Yours,
Ivan

April 10, 2005, 9 PM

Ivan,

I hadn't realized how deeply the oh-and-five start had affected—almost wrote afflicted—me, until this afternoon. It was over when Pedro Martinez threw the two-hitter. And what glorious words those are, so I'll type them again: Martinez, two-hitter. I'd been wallowing all week. After Braden Looper blew that ninth inning we seemed in a kind of trance, hell-bent on becoming, I insist, the most talented roster ever to be the last team in the league without a victory a week into the season. I mean, was all the off-season fuss really an absolutely empty balloon going up? Can you and I be wearing such blinders, Ivan? Is that not a formidable lineup, at least until you get to Minkiewicz? Going without a win this week when even the Rockies and the Pirates were able to collect one was, to speak of nighttime dreams (instead of these day-light dreams we fans call hope, which plague me far worse than any nocturnal terror), much like those dreams of early adolescence in which one is walking around the family home or the classroom without any pants on. Everyone will see, I find myself thinking in a panic. Everyone will open up the newspaper and look at the standings and see that the Mets are without a win, and I am without pants. Everyone will judge my pathetic endowment, my sad dwindled Mr. Met.

Of course it had to be Martinez, who on the one hand barely seems a Met yet, is only six days old, and yet on the other hand seems a kind of ur-Met, almost either a Cro-Magnon or post-nuclear-holocaust Met, who seems to have had his uniform tattooed onto his flesh as though by a radiation blast, and to occupy the mound with a fury that indicts those others who've dishonored Metsitude by acting as though it is an optional or provisional identity—the Roberto Alomars and Mo Vaughns, say—rather than the life-or-death struggle he apparently knows it is, so of course it was Martinez who had to carry us there on his sloped shoulders.

Did you know that there's only one pitcher shorter than six feet in the Hall of Fame? I won't play trivia games with you, it's Whitey Ford of whom I speak. Pedro Martinez stands to be the second. (That is unless they take John Franco first, and with his alleged mob connections, who knows?)

And then, of course, it ends, and we're merely one and five. Though, better not to say one and five. We're three games out of first place, that's what we are.

This is the miracle (or had I better not use that word?) and jest of a baseball season, its indomitably petlike component, its resemblance to the springy existence of a young spaniel or dachshund: it swallows trauma like licking poison off the sidewalk and keeps going. A team's season is like a puppy, yes—follow me here, trust me for once, Ivan—in that it cannot know tragedy until it is far too late. You and I and other sufferers, we're the pet owners, who recall the puppies of the past, the ones flattened in July or August on the six-lane highway that was built too close to our street, or the others who showed signs of canine leukemia (don't correct me if there is no such thing) in May or June yet went on flouncing as though healthy, and there's no way to tell a puppy it's got leukemia, so we go on cavorting with those, trying not to notice their weakened condition, until in September they're looking for a cool place on the basement floor to lie so as to soothe feverish, dying tremors, while indicting our more worldly glances with their helpless, foolish, dewy eyes—what happened to me, for god's sake? I was a puppy!

And tomorrow's the home opener, which phrase always makes me think of the can opener. Hope springs eternal. Choke sweeps infernal. Hang me for an infidel.

Yours,
Harris

April 11

Harris,

Let me correct you about this puppy business. You forget that I worked for Dr. Sullivan's Cat & Dog abattoir for two sweaty dollars an hour, trying to prove something to my father before capitulating and allowing myself to be enrolled at NYU. I don't remember exactly what I was trying to prove. Possibly that I could be the most bad-tempered, unfriendly, rude, and somewhat threatening person ever to appear—late, invariably—at his family's dinner table. This was when the problems were happening with my sister. You remember my sister, right? At that time her name was Zeenat. She was living in an engineered community near Death Valley with Raj Mandelbaum, her boyfriend from Purchase. The residents were required to phone home and shake the money tree about twice a week. My mother spent about six months literally on the verge of tears. Slam a door, she cried. Tear an envelope in two, she wept. The teakettle whistled too stridently for her nerves; great heaving sobs were the result. So I'm walking in the door around six o'clock every night, fresh from a day spent shoveling kitty litter and watching animals get their reproductive organs removed by the always spectacularly inebriated Sullivan, spoiling for a fight. Albert would be right behind me, seething over the really quite enormous quantities of cash that were disappearing from Amalgamated's coffers due to "entertainment" and "organizing" expenses. His beloved union was crooked, my sister was making the desert bloom with his hard-earned cash, and I was declining to attend a first-rate second-rate school—with my grades!—to work for a drunken goy vet. In retrospect, my transgression seems least offensive among the three, but I was the only available target, so every night we went at it over the pot roast.

Where was I? The point I was going to make, actually, has little to do with anything I can draw from my vast experience with veterinary medicine. The point has to do with the several subtle differences between men and dogs. A sick dog you can tell nothing to, I agree with you there. But what men and Mets alike have stitched into the fabric of the cerebral cortex is a foreknowledge of doom, both of its absolute certainty and of its imminence. In baseball terms this adds up to fatalism. The Mets are a team strangely inclined to fatalism. The drama has to build; a team has to be composed of, you know, Jerry Bucheks and Craig Swans and Ryan Thompsons, guys humming along and, following Satchel's advice, rarely casting a glance over their shoulders to see what's gaining on them, the guys the team settles upon once the bitterness of defeated expectations has passed and the team has dug in for a long stretch of incompetence the way another franchise might settle for mere mediocrity (the Fosters, the Bonillas, the Colemans, the Vaughns—the substance, in short, of such expectations, are another species of story entirely. And then there's the tragic genre, sui generis, called Pat Zachry). The general idea is: What's the use. And then suddenly a strange apostatic figure turns up. A Seaver. A Hernandez. They gather disciples around them, the Grotes and Backmans. They convert key holdovers. They mold up-and-coming talent. Their skills enable an imaginative manager to take risks. The right conditions, in other words, for intelligent life to appear.

This to me is Pedro. Pedro is a man uninterested in the opulent history of the team's losing ways. He sees nothing funny about it. He will not sit still while you explain to him that the Mets are proudly squatting on some bogus statistic like, say, entering the eighth with a one-run lead they are four times as likely as the Devil Rays to hit the leadoff batter with the first pitch and then give up a home run. And there is an element of reprimand involved: the Red Sox determined that it was not worth paying the freight for two years of steady deterioration in exchange for two years of brilliance. I may be proven wrong, but it seems to me to be penny-wise. Come October—come September—the Red Sox will be wishing they'd coughed up the dough. I wouldn't bet on Schilling over Pedro. Not to mention the fact that Schilling is a man I strongly suspect would secretly harbor John Rocker–like feelings about the 7 train and environs, whereas Pedro *is* the number 7 line. I love the arrogance—always have loved it—of the justified hot dog. Give me arrogance over fake-o modesty every time. What did he say after his second start? "They needed me, *or someone like me*." [Emphasis added.] Classic paralepsis, immediately encouraging the listener to conclude: Who could possibly be like Pedro? Nobody.

Now the trick is to see whether Tommy Glavine has stepped up; stopped bitching about the loss of his canasta partners and started pitching. He had all winter to talk about golf. Between him and Pedro, the Mets should be good for thirty-six victories. Stop laughing, Conklin. I can see you snickering up your sleeve; that way you used to blow milk out your nose. Eighteen apiece—that's too much to ask?

Look, I'll pick you up if you like. I still have my Town Car, which, as the lawyers plotted the dissolution of our union, the fourth Mrs. Felt, herself somewhat dissolute, ceded to me, favoring boring old cash and a chunk of my TIAA-CREF retirement fund. We'll go out early and catch BP—visitor's BP, anyway.

Yours,

Ivan

P.S. I've seen you without your pants, and in high school. I remember your Mr. Met as being ripe, taut, buoyant.

P.P.S. Are you as disappointed as I to learn that Minkiewicz pronounces his name "Man KAY Vitch"? I must have forgotten this over the winter. It seems to me that he is not asserting a correct pronunciation so much as some kind of a perverse personal preference (much like the man's archaic refusal to wear batting gloves), the sort of beanball ballplayers like to toss at reporters and broadcasters to fuck them up real good. Remember Jim Beauchamp? A good old boy, one of those lifetime minor leaguers who got carried around on the relatively light-hitting big-league rosters of the late '60s–early '70s. Perfect Met, really. First baseman, like the Mink. But he pronounced his name BEECH-um. Bruce Boisclair was another. That's bow-CLARE to you. Could it be possible that such blinkered francophonics spawned the ardor of our friend in section 101, Filthy Pierrot?

P.P.P.S. I know, I know: you think Pierrot is a closet Expos fan. But the Expos are no more. No more blue road uniforms. No more serif-typeface team name and uniform numbers. No more leaky billion-dollar Olympic Stadium, or Jarry Park, either, for that matter. No more Peter Max "M." (I didn't know that was supposed to be an "M" until I was twenty-five, Harris. I thought it was some sort of pop-art wave, cresting and about to break over the bill of their tricolor cap.) The Expos are no more, yet there he was, back in section 101, and to see Houston. Not even Washington. A fan! A compatriot! Give him a chance! The opening bars of the "Marseillaise" are not *just* the beginning of "All You Need Is Love." Give the guy a chance.

P.P.P.P.S. Speaking of "All You Need Is Love," the song's very fitting in your case. Did you ever ring up Marcie Steingardner, my friend from the Humanities office? She was taken with you. Absolutely. You're just her type. She loves the Irish. She thinks of you as mystic and sagacious people. She knows her Yeats. She doesn't even care that you're not that big a drunk. Plus she gives the best head at Hunter College, Conk.

P.P.P.P.P.S. Called Time Warner Cable. Very disconcerting. Angela, the young woman to whom I spoke, advised me that she would have to put in a "serviceability order" to see whether it's possible to install cable in my apartment. My protest that every other apartment in the building subscribes to cable service fell upon deaf ears. Or bureaucratically plugged-up ears, anyway. I don't blame the kid. She was perfectly nice. She guided me through my confusion and unease without once making me feel like the 2,000-year-old man, though I managed to feel that way all by myself.

Pssssst: Lee Mazzilli is fifty. Make you feel old?

April 13

Ivan,

I wasn't so sorry to miss visitor's BP, but next time let's park Mrs. Felt IV's Town Car on my block, not a difficult or risky thing to do as the Thai and Nepalese bandits who are forever outside polishing their tires tolerate me well and will secure your chariot's safety—I realize it must be sworn to some automotive museum, the keys only still in your possession on the curator's goodwill—and just go ahead and take the 7 train two stops. Not only do I pine for the flyover walkway approach to the stadium, and the cagelike subway entrance below, both of which stir primordial memory-gunk as fiercely as the interior struts and angled walkways (and the Jerry Grote and Tom Seaver banners) within the confines, but the culture of Shea's parking lot almost took my heart away before we got inside. The same disingenuously jocular conversations you adore striking up both in our section (and perhaps we should finally restrategize—I share your fondness for 101, that rare vantage from which we can dispute balls and strikes with some authority, but Filthy Pierrot, or whatever his right name is, really may be some kind of season-ticket holder up there, much as he appears not to be able to afford new clothes or even stadium food for his bloodshot-eyed transatlantic ragamuffins) and, as I recall, on the 7 train as the stops approach the stadium and the concentration of merchandise-identified Metsians thickens, don't beguile me to the same extent in a parking lot. Nor does any genre of meat taste accurate to itself in a parking lot. If I'd been surrounded by passive-aggressively respectful adjunct professors, a check imprinted with my usual speaker's fee tucked beside my return plane ticket in my breast pocket, I couldn't have enjoyed a freebie chicken-kebob less. You know I don't even like to graze from the stadium corridors, much less in the lot. Dinner at the game comes to you where you sit in your seat, however long the wait, and is fished from a steaming aluminum sarcophagus. It is, in short, an ordinary frankfurter, sweating into its starchy cushion. We're not Americans, Felt, we're New Yorkers, and we'll ride the train.

I'll admit you're onto something with Pedro. I'd forgotten how a whole roster can seem spiritually derived from one player's psyche—think of Brett's Royals, Gibson's Cardinals, Stewart's A's, or, yes, the Seaver or Hernandez Mets. Today's weird spectacle, that scoreboard dysfunction that had Pedro's pixeled grinning visage locked into view for what seemed hours, the Astros rightly complaining that the back-drop wasn't blacked out for their at bats, and then Pedro himself committing that almost flamenco-style prance atop the dugout seemed, weirdly but absolutely, the contest's key. The team seemed to draw a rally out of themselves precisely not to disappoint a crowd unexpectedly incited by the wave of Pedromorphic resonances. What's next—will his little midget friend have to be suited up à la Eddie Gaedel? What fascinates me is that the other story which seems in-escapably to frame the season—Randolph bringing steely nativist soul and discipline to a group both youthfully impressionable and institutionally demoralized (i.e., we're Mets, after all)—finds itself in such a fascinating negotiation with the Pedro-ness of it all. Can Randolph slacken his grip so as to let the Pedroviral madness flow through the team's bloodstream? From the look of things now I'd say it could be. And to turn your notion of exile the other way, it feels to me as well that this is what Pedro came here to do. The Red Sox could never quite belong to him: no 7 train, no constituency. In a town with a fandom and tradition as white as Boston's, Pedro was an exotic ornament, but the team belonged to Curt Schilling, to the Millars and Millers and Muellers and

Mullets, the fratlike Idiots. What Pedro sensed in the Mets was a team where the whole story could be Pedro. Or "Pedro and his influence on impressionable youth."

Among whom, Ivan, count my secret heart.

Harris

April 15

Harris,

If it suits you, we never have to drive to Shea again. Anything to keep you from yanking on my sleeve and whining like a five-year-old. I know that at first blush Dominic, Tina, Rocco, Ariana, Pete, Anella, Donato, Sophia, Ralph, Florence, Carmine, and Liliana don't look like the sort of people you might want to break bread with, but they're actually a lot of fun, and you saw how quickly Ralph hustled away that cousin, Chooch, when he threatened to pull your nose out your asshole so that "when you sneeze you shit your fuckin' pants." I don't know why you had to mention that "everyone's" reviewing the Lowell letters "as if he's the only poet of the twentieth century." Chooch was probably right to call you a "fucking faggot." These people know from Lowell, Mass.—maybe. Flushing's about as far as they go. You have to roll with their unique and colorful folkways.

Anyway, grab the lever on the side of your chair and pull yourself into the upright position, just for a while longer. I don't know if you've noticed this, but you've acquired quite a television habit. A little glimpse before bedtime is one thing, as long as you're not waking up every night with a crick in your neck and a puddle of drool on your collar, but you seem to arrange things around that box to the exclusion of life. Aren't you, a poet, supposed to live life? Take a leaf from Lowell's book, live life to the fullest—throw things around! Drink more! Get married and leave your wife! I'm a mere academic, and I get out! Donato and Carmine get out, and they're not limning our reality through "vibrant and pulsatingly contemporary" verse! Have they got a file folder of rejections from *Paris Review*? The answer is no. Have I mentioned more than a dozen times recently how urgently I feel that you need to get out a little more? A baseball game is hardly a dread concession to this reality. You just have to sit there.

Your consiglieri,
Ivan

April 16

Ivan,

Watching Aaron Heilman scowl and huff his way through a one-hitter for our fifth win in a row, I was seized not with the ordinary regret a Met fan should be expected to suffer during yet another near miss in our franchise's famous and paradoxical pursuit of a no-no. There's hardly need to rehearse the absurdly exaggerated context of the chase: a pitcher's park; a pitching team; Ryan, Seaver, Matlack, Koosman, Gooden, Saberhagen, Cone, and so on; the hundreds of Met one-hitters (didn't Seaver alone pitch about twenty of the things?); and, finally and infuriatingly, the vast numbers of no-hitters and even perfect games thrown by Mets pitchers after their divorces from Flushing—Ryan's seven, Gooden and Cone for the Yanks, Seaver for the (ugh) Reds, Hideo Nomo, if I'm remembering correctly, in Coors Field (!), Mike Scott for the (ugh) Astros (our historical franchise-evil-twin, the Houstons have thrown ten of the things in the time we've failed to throw one—and, no, before you speak, only one of those ten was by Ryan). Yet, no regret there in my lonely room, Berryman's *Dream Songs* propped open but unread on my knee as I absorbed the blue cathode glow of Heilman's adamantine innings, no. In the place of regret, an eerie certainty: that April was too soon, that the chase would be spoiled if it were to be Heilman in April, but that this was the year. We'll see our no-hitter, Ivan. I rank the starter's likelihoods thus: Pedro is the best bet. Needless to say. The franchise's no-hitter drought, the no-no of no-no's, may be one of the ghosts he parachuted into Shea to dispel. Then—call me fantastical—I see Zambrano as our next best chance, his goods coalescing for one crazy night, perhaps against the Padres or the Pirates. I see Zambrano walking five, plunking a guy too, perhaps the opposing pitcher. But we'll take it. After Zambrano, our next hope, on the evidence of last night, may be Heilman himself (if we let him stay in the rotation. I have a bad feeling we may not). Not so much Glavine or Benson: their prosaic ground-ball stuff isn't enough the material of whiffs and zeros.

Even Ishii's a possibility. Picture, if you will, on an August night at Shea, Piazza walking to the mound in the ninth, Ishii having shaken off several of the catcher's signs. They stand "talking" for a long while. Nobody's even certain, due to translation difficulties, whether Ishii's aware that he's working on a no-hitter (despite several balls going to the backstop, and the three runs he walked in in the sixth). Nobody frantically Googling in the clubhouse can confirm the rumor that the kanji alphabet has a single pictogram for "no-hitter-even-though-losing"—Rick Peterson was supposed to be their specialist, but he's stumped. Reyes jogs, in his jittery, preening way, to join the conversation. The camera catches him popping his eyes and shrugging at Piazza. Piazza, summoned by the ump, at last returns to the plate, shaking his head as he reinstalls his mask. The pitch comes, and the batter, a Brewer, looking somehow both bored and frightened, tops it to Kaz Matsui. Matsui steps on second, then wheels and heaves it to a stretching Mink. Double play, and the runner dashing home from third doesn't count. No-hitter! And maybe we'll even rally in our last half inning!

Love,

Harris

April 17

Harris,

Just a quick note, now that the Mets' winning streak has ended and we can all collectively exhale. Simulated mass deflation. Or, as it's known in Metsdom, "Here we go again."

Marty Noble, on Mets.com, has a little squib about going through the Mets' clubhouse polling the players on new slogans for the team, Beltran's spontaneously coined "New Mets" apparently having fallen short less than three weeks into the regular season. The results point mostly to the hopeless lack of immunity jocks have to cliché, as defenseless against it as Indians were to smallpox, but Mike DeJean, at least, demonstrated that he has the resigned and tolerant mien to be a Met for Life. His slogan: "New Winning Mets." "Because," DeJean elaborated, "if we weren't winning, it wouldn't be new."

Ivan

April 27

Ivan,

I was driven out of the house last night, you'll be shocked to hear, by an interruption in my satellite service—some asshole screwing around on the roof of our building, apparently, trying to steal free cable or some such. By the time I'd been on the pavement shouting imprecations up at him, discovered I'd left wallet and keys inside and had therefore locked myself out of my apartment, and borrowed forty bucks from the bodega—they give me credit on milk and newspapers and charge a 5 percent interest on the monthly tab, hence are always pleased to add to the total—I figured to hop the 7 train to Shea rather than wait the hours it would likely take for my landlord to arrive with a replacement set of keys. Didn't want to miss Pedro versus Smoltz II, fifteen days after the watershed duel in Atlanta that provided the season's first ray of actual hope, our first digit in the win column.

I did conclude, however, that I couldn't bear to face Pierrot without your company. Somehow I knew he'd pry out of me the reason I was visiting Shea in a pajama top and slippers. So I bought the lousiest ticket possible from a scalper—that's, after my five-dollar MetroCard, another five bucks (you'll want to keep count, Ivan, there's a punch line coming)—leaving me with thirty in my pocket. By now we were through the anthem (I'm always happy enough to have avoided it) and I heard from the runways as I ascended Shea's inner skeleton as the crowd welcomed our hero to the mound. Alas, before I'd found my way out under the night air and jet contrails, their cheers were replaced by groans. The Braves, with a mix of seeing-eye grounders and bloop hits, glommed three almost instantaneous first-inning runs off Pedro before he'd settled into any kind of rhythm. Wincing, I carried through with my plan, covertly searching out your man Mesch without letting Pierrot or any of the other regulars from 101 spot me—the first-inning woes made a distracting cover for my espionage. I cornered Mesch deep at the base of 101's entrance tunnel, where he stood squinting crustily at the upper deck and chugging a Budweiser, his bulbously bloodshot nose and cheeks forming a kind of bright pawnbroker's sign in the gloom of the ramp. Perhaps he was reading the progress of the game, in his sagacious way, merely from the reactions of the fans—when Pedro's on the mound we actually are filling the high orange seats pretty well, Ivan.

Wasn't it you who told me the corrupt old usher's price for a stolen corporate box seat had remained set at ten bucks since 1972? He demanded twenty from me, grudgingly, gruntingly. Leaving me with ten, unless you count the three still encoded on my MetroCard. I'd need two of those three to get home, though. Pulled a ticket marked "lower box" from the recesses of that orange-and-blue apron where he keeps his greasy seat wipes. Before he let go of the ticket Mesch looked deep into my eyes.

"I remember your father," he said. He didn't elaborate, and I didn't pursue it. Rather, I wandered—padded, I guess is the word—off toward the interior ramps, to find my way to the unfamiliar, and presumably wonderful, vantage point. The game unfolding on various vendors' overhead televisions as I progressed in my wanderings—by this manner, I viewed what would be the Mets' sole accomplishment for seven innings: Floyd singling to extend his hit streak to thirteen games, Wright—lovely, mighty, unspoiled David Wright—driving him in with a double to the left-field corner.

I didn't know Shea had seats behind pillars, especially not in any section that could be termed "lower box," but indeed, there is a stand erected to support a bank of television cameras, and it was to a seat behind and nearly beneath this stand that I found myself guided, by a drunken blond twentyish usher who may have been, for all I know, Mesch's son or cousin or even his younger self, transported by time machine. I endured the rest of the game craning my neck, in misery. I wanted a sausage and beer, and settled for Poland Springs and Cracker Jack—ferry only a ten-spot inside next time, Ivan, and I believe you'll find yourself arriving at the same inevitable compromise. I didn't try redeeming the MetroCard.

Down four–one going into the ninth, we actually managed a sweet little rally, Reyes, Piazza, pinch-hitting for Ramon Castro (Pedro's personal catcher, it's beginning to seem) and Beltran stringing together hits and scoring twice before Floyd popped out to end it. The Braves have no closer, apparently, now that Smoltz has vacated the job. Small consolation, given that he's seemingly reclaimed his starter's stuff. I imagine he and Pedro, being their respective team's aces, may be reenacting this duel when it matters, in September. Let it be true.

For now, this loss drags us back to a five hundred record, at 11–11. Sobering, but if we can build from 0–5 we can build from here. I don't expect we'll linger at equilibrium too long. Nor will I visit Shea in my slippers again: they're crapped out, with a scent of stale soda and chewed gum pervading the rabbit-fur fringe. Nor will Mesch be seeing any more of my hard-borrowed cash. Tip him if you like—with me he's in the red for that seat.

Five-hundredly,

Harris

Dead in the Saddle

[*May*]

May 6

Harris,

Two prefaces:

(1) It's Willie Mays's birthday, number 74.

(2) The New York Yankees are in last place. Let's try that again.

> "Yankees in cellar."
>
> "Yankees? In cellar?"
>
> "Yankees—in cellar!"
>
> "Yankees in . . . cellar."

Feels good no matter how, and no matter how often, you say it. We have to enjoy this while we can.

Despite your own unwillingness to stiff your most boringly devoted students out of their office hours yesterday (I see you during that period, Father Conklin, as a priest in his confessional, his holy duty to counsel the doubtful, to instruct the ignorant, to admonish the sinner, to comfort the sorrowful, to forgive all injuries, to bear wrongs patiently, and to pray for the living and the dead, all of which spiritual works of mercy strike me as being shimmeringly apropos within the setting of a graduate creative-writing program.) I went undaunted to Shea to witness the second coming of Kris Benson and Mike Cameron. It was windy, but also very cold. Pierrot was there, surprisingly perhaps without his kids. He looked strangely bereft when he saw that I was alone. I believe he is aware of the effect that he has on you— enjoys it, exploits it. As usual, he brought strange food in multiple containers; occupied himself throughout the pre-game period setting his containers on the empty seat next to him, opening them, stowing the lids, putting separate serving spoons in each, ladling the food onto a Chinet plate, drinking from a wineskin. A lot of apparatus considering you can only bring into Shea a bag with the rough dimensions of a number-ten envelope. He manages, though, the peasant smuggler. Also in attendance was Mesch, eager as always to dust with his greasy cloth the seat I was about to lower my clean chinos into.

"Ready for Benson?" I asked, thinking to distract him.

He looked at me as if I were out of my mind. He looked at me as if to say that he'd been ushering people to their seats since ladies and gentlemen rode horse-drawn coaches out to the fallow fields of Flushing to sit and watch Shea's erection while eating finger sandwiches, like the war-watching gentry at Bull Run. He looked at me as if to say that he'd been ready for Koufax and Drysdale and Gibson and Marichal and Jenkins and Carlton, not to mention Seaver and Koosman and Matlack and Gooden and Darling and Cone and Leiter and Hampton, as if to say that he'd grimly come to work to wipe the seats down the first time Pat Zachry had put on a Mets uniform. He looked at me with those little red eyes set deeply behind the busted capillaries of his nose as if to say that given everything he'd seen and experienced, anticipation and preparation were the last things this particular third starter called for. Then he swiped my seat with his chamois, which looked particularly grotty.

I can't say I disagreed with him.

It didn't augur well when the national anthem was sung by the "Physically Challenged Team" of P.S. 87. One might be forgiven for suggesting that the Mets have more than amply demonstrated their rightful ownership of that title between 2001 and 2004. (When in the pregame video Steve Trachsel was shown announcing that coming onto the field during the game was illegal and could result in one's arrest, I began to think of all those Mets of the past few seasons whom I would like to have seen placed under arrest the moment they set foot on the turf.) The P.S. 87 team swung their wheelchairs onto the dirt path leading from the on-deck circle and after arriving at home plate sung a spirited, discordant version of the anthem. The DiamondVision camera panned across the little faces working hard to generate their dissonances. The entire stadium seemed suspended in a state of mass discomfiture.

But Benson started throwing strikes. It was good to see. As a man who has become helplessly lost within the labyrinth of marriage one, two, three, four times, I worry about Benson. Every time his enormous likeness loomed on the scoreboard I saw the haggard face of a man struggling to keep pace with his mistrust of his wife. Have you noticed she's begun increasingly to brag about their sex life in her tabloid columns? It can't be easy for Benson in the locker room these days. Or maybe the other players actually feel for him, and that sympathy explains the run support. However his teammates handle it, though, there's a banal tragedy in the making between those two. Dana Andrews and Virginia Mayo. Just who is this stranger that I met in a dance hall and married two weeks later?

But he was throwing strikes. He struck out six guys in four and two thirds innings. From where I was sitting it looked as though he was working the corners. The plate umpire gave him a lot of third strikes, but they didn't look egregiously off the mark, despite the somewhat bush posturing of some of the Phillies batters. When they did hit it, he had them popping it up and hitting it on the ground.

Randolph said he'd give him eighty pitches and sure as shit, once he'd thrown them all he wound down like a toy, which was fine, because Heilman came in and then *he* proceeded to pitch like an old reliable member of the staff, adding another five strikeouts to the total and allowing two base runners in three and a third.

Swell news, since Glavine's apparently torn a hole in the enchanted portrait up in the attic and become an old man overnight, while Zambrano . . .

Floyd sat, his hit streak at twenty. Some oohs and ahhs when they announced the lineup and he wasn't in it. I was disappointed, I'll admit, but I imagine Cliff's enchanted portrait might be a little shopworn too, so I think he probably deserves a rest. Cameron came off the DL, hit two doubles. In right field he was a little shaky. On the other hand, the Mink was brilliant in the field, knocked down a certain double up the line and then initiated a 3–6–3 double play to get the existing runner at first. It's something to have a real first baseman for the first time since, what?, Olerud? He also hit a double. They walked him intentionally to face Wright, so what does Wright do? Hits a two-run double. Diaz hits an RBI double. Marlon Anderson comes off the bench again to lead off the eighth with another pinch-hit. Somebody better find out what position this kid plays so he can hit five times a game. And Piazza seemed really comfortable behind the plate for the first time in a while. It was good to see. They weren't fluke hits; he was really whacking them. Four for five, with a three-run home run that proved to be cake as well as icing, since DeJean nearly blew the game in the ninth. The home run was classic Piazza, rising high in the air before disappearing over the fence. Everyone knew it was gone the second he hit it.

Pierrot got all hincty at one point. Some dummy in a Yankees jersey paraded along just below the upper reserved seats and an entire section of fans let him have it, "Yankees suck! Yankees suck! Yankees suck!" The guy tipped his cap and smiled, which enraged Nassau County's best all the more. "YANKEES *SUCK*! YANKEES *SUCK*!" they ranted. Pierrot turned and, addressing nobody in particular, said, "Zey are not ze Yankees we are playing. I do not see ze point in zis." Then he waved his hands dismissively. You've mentioned this hand action to me before but I've never actually seen it: a dispelling motion, as if the entire vulgar phantasm of the United States were being scattered to the wind. He turned and locked eyes with me. "It eez totally uncalled for," he said, "totally!"—as if I were responsible for these mamzers—his hands are fluttering in the air, reacting spasmodically to the puzzling discourtesy of American sports. I told him to relax. Started reciting to him a vague but damning litany of Eurosports-spectation transgressions; a nightmare vision of angry faces pushed up against riot barriers, of overturned Citroens and flaming tyres [*sic!*] in dampened provincial streets. It amused him, the knave.

The security guards took the Yankee-uniform wearer aside and not too quietly told him in their jocular way that he was a fucking moron. It was a lot of fun.

Time Warner Cable, chapter the second: I called them up again, told them that I was calling to see if the "serviceability order" had gone through, or whatever it does. The operator put me through to a rep—Angela, again, as it turned out. She told me that it was necessary to "add my address" to the system in order to actually "enact" a "serviceability order." I wondered aloud if the address wasn't already added since every single apartment in the building receives cable. I mentioned this offhandedly, Mr. Casual, the way you might point out a looming mountain to the preoccupied pilot of a jet aircraft, assuming that for all his craft and skill he had simply fallen victim to an understandable oversight. Angela told me that it was necessary to enter the address to enact the serviceability order to send out the technicians to determine whether to send out another set of technicians to install the cable. I chuckled sympathetically and told her it seemed like there were at least two steps too many to the process. Her response? A psychologist would have jotted: *notable lack of affect.*

Harris, come out, come out, wherever you are.

Ivan

May 8

Ivan,

Last night, under, I'll confess, the mixed influence of Richard D. E. Burton's *Baudelaire in 1859: A Study in the Sources of Poetic Creativity* (Amazon.com sales rank: #3,511,061) and two icy half liters of Kirin (you know the zaftig chrome tankards of which I speak—and distantly imported beer is always my instinctive response to our weekend opponent, the Brewers), I fell asleep before the conclusion of a radio broadcast of an enthralling, Pedro-pitched "New Mets" game, one in which Beltran, very much Pedro's Useful Boy, clouted two home runs—and this merely in Milwaukee's time zone, no worse than an hour out of phase. I must be growing old. In truth, Mike DeJean was ambling to the mound when I nodded off, Beltran's second clout already in the books, the four-game win streak seemingly secure enough. I can't be expected to stay awake through every one of Braden Looper's undistinguished saves. We're winning, Felt. So's every other team in our division, but never mind that.

But before the narcotic embrace of my calico Barca-lounger devoured every last tendril of consciousness I did find myself, under the mixed influence of Burton on Baudelaire, Kirin, and New Mets, in the throes of a "Paradis Artificiel," as Baudelaire used to call his hashish-induced visions. Oddly enough, my reverie was on the subject of loss. The tsunamic tide and survivor-sucking undertow of loss in baseball as in life, that mountain of losing on which each pebble of winning rests, and on which it depends, and by which it is nourished: those scraps and chips of victory which shimmer and tremble atop an uneasy perch, like diamonds sprouted from a hillock of dung, *Les Fleurs du Mal* if ever there was such a thing. I was dreaming of the Yankees, partly, with their cirrhosis of the payroll (cue the Rolling Stones' "Sympathy for the Yankees"), but of course I was mainly thinking of the Essential Condition of Metsdom. Not only do I remember last year, Ivan, I remember last week. I even remember two weeks and six weeks and four months from now. We're due to suffer, my friend. Yet Baudelaire-Kirin led me to wish to savor the wins as much for their use as a lens onto the dark beauty of the losing as for themselves.

Follow me, Ivan: even a Yankees fan, the most over-glutted and power-drunk and American among us, must in the long settling of accounts that is life on this globe of death we inhabit accept loss and failure at least three-quarters of the time. In their absurd and insane greed (depictable, I think, only by a Fellini, George Grosz, or Michael Bay) they've taken merely one-quarter of their sport's championships. They're certainly doomed at the moment, and perhaps for years to come. And that's just the Yankees. Other cases I needn't go into. Forget romanticized ineptitude, insufferable Cubs and the like. Dwell on the Astros, say. The Giants. Or, yes, the Brewers, of whose quite scrappy and hopeful seven-game win streak we New Mets happened this weekend to be the executioners. Tides of failure lap at the bluffs of mountains of failure atop which every once in a while a Pedro Martinez drifts by in a hot-air balloon and cultivates a tiny wind-tossed garden of winning.

So, yes, let's get to Shea when the boys come home, I'm in agreement. The weekend opponent's the Cardinals—a real test of where this season might actually go. But I have this request, perverse though it may be. Pedro's scheduled to pitch

Friday night; let's skip it. I want the day game, Saturday—I want Glavine. My logic: I want to fly into the teeth of loss, one way or the other. If this season's what it sometimes promises to be, Pedro's wins must be taken as a given, and, if so, there's no sport in that. Glavine's our practical problem—if he doesn't turn it around (he's 1–4/7.04 as I write, and about to take the mound to attempt to complete the Milwaukee sweep), we're looking to who as a number-three starter in the playoffs—Zambrano? Ishii? Anyway, in the symbolic realm, Glavine's our primary link to the 2003–04 teams, the last Yankee-like acquisition before this blessed Minaya era. Doesn't Glavine in fact seem, at the moment, like a Yankee—wouldn't he slip into their current rotation like a dream? So let's go on Saturday, to the day game, and try to bring Tom G. into the New Met fold with our rooting. Besides, I've got another motive. Your last letter was so fine, it made me miss Pierrot. So let's sit in our usual section. Where are his kids? Can he no longer afford to drag them along? I'm practically worried. I might even buy him a copy of *Les Fleurs du Mal* so he'll know it's not some anti-Frog thing that nags me about him.

Look at me: we start winning, I start feeling guilty.

Devotedly,
Harris

May 9

Harris,

Glavine's start having been rescheduled (don't let that stop us from going out to Shea anyway, Har), I instead watched him on the tube yesterday while trying to assemble an Ikea coffee table. Let me describe the table to you: it seemed like a good idea at the moment of purchase, it is large and pale, and spending a couple of hours trying to figure it out left me vexed, nervous, and trembling. So far the Glavine parallel holds up.

I'm being unfair to Tommy Glavine. He did not pitch badly yesterday, but seemed to fall victim to an unusual number of bad breaks. It occurred to me while I watched the Brewers reach base on a succession of weakly hit balls that Glavine's style has undergone a peculiar metamorphosis: while his pitches are no longer unhittable, balls hit off him have become uncatchable. They dropped behind backpedaling infielders. They dropped in front of charging outfielders. They rolled slowly on the infield grass. Still and all, we took the series.

Need we worry about anybody in the NL East other than the Florida Marlins? I know I say it every year, but every year the odds against the Braves get longer. This is a statistical fact. The Braves are the cast photo of *The Fall of the Roman Empire*. OK, so it looks good for them now. But I refuse to believe in John Smoltz. Smoltz is Charlton Heston in *El Cid*, strapped upright and dead in the saddle. I refuse to believe in Mike Hampton. Hampton is Arthur Kennedy in *Bend of the River*, a mercenary out for number one. I refuse to believe in Tim Hudson. Hudson is one of the front-running denizens of the little Alaska Territory town who shuttles back and forth between the two competing saloons in *The Far Country*. I haven't figured out yet who Thompson and Ramirez look like. Maybe Tony Perkins in *The Tin Star*: green and untested.

You may be right that the Yankees fall short of ultimate success far more often than they achieve it, but they still win too often, unnaturally often: through boom times and depressions and depleted wartime rosters, through eras of reserve-clause feudalism and free-agent yeomanry. Something must be behind it.

I know you'll never concede this, that it is your belief that as a rational human being and a holder of advanced degrees I should shun such thinking, but I insist that the Yankees' fortunes spike and dip with ownership's willingness to deal directly with Satan. This theory explains the slough of the CBS years: television networks can afford to traffic in degradation, humiliation, and iniquity without ever having to lay the bet off on a bigger bookmaker, and so Satan, not receiving his due, left the Yanks to their own devices between 1965 and 1973. The Joe Pepitone–Tom Tresh–Horace Clark–Ron Bloomberg–Roy White–Bobby Murcer years. Years more notable for the curious partnership of Fritz Peterson and Mike Kekich than for anything that happened on-field.

(Wasn't it a great time to be a Mets fan? They owned the town! Did Oscar Madison wear a Yankees cap? Did the Beatles play at Yankee Stadium? [Nay, Father Conklin—Pope Paul did. Zzzzzzzz.] An inherent lovability, first as losers and then, later, as winners, that I think only expired and disappeared completely with the unfortunate arrival of the Saberhagen-Coleman-Bonilla years.)

This theory also helps to explain the haunted legacy that surrounds the Yanks, the slow doom that being one seems to invite. Wasting diseases. Cancer of the stomach, of the lung, of the colon, of the prostate. Progressive dementia. Drug and alcohol addiction. Plane crashes. Pickup trucks in ditches.

Stolen kidneys. The Yankees are like the history of country music cross-pollinated with the history of jazz. Gehrig dead at thirty-eight. Ruth at fifty-three. Mantle at sixty-four. Maris at fifty-one. Munson at thirty-two. Catfish at fifty-three (of Lou Gehrig's disease!). OK, DiMaggio lived, but as an old recluse, counting his money. Maybe even washing it, nutty old Dago. These superbly conditioned[1] champions should be soaring to Olympus only after attaining a ripe old age. But it's Steinbrenner who's the one getting old. And it's my thinking that as he approaches the bottom of his own personal ninth, down two runs as we all are at that weary moment, he is leery of seeming to be too chummy with the Prince of Darkness. A similar avoidance of even the appearance of impropriety was in evidence after George was banned from baseball in 1990 for dealing with known gamblers (and the Yankees skidded then, too). Ultimately Fay Vincent let George off the hook. He's hoping God will too.

So the Cards on Saturday, then. Just as well. Friday night I have to be in what used to be called Bushwick (it is now "East Williamsburg," I am advised) to meet with Gena. The poor kid. I'm to serve as intermediary between her and her mother. What we've got here is a failure to communicate. This is a by-product of our over-connected age. Constant communications have enhanced life, wholly overdetermining everything, in particular our knowledge of one another's whereabouts. I mean, who cares? I am in the taxi now, corner of 68th and Lex. I have just exited the A train at West 4th Street. Here I am, 40,000 feet above the Great Plains, with

---

[1] *Pace* Ruth.

nothing to say except that I will arrive in San Antonio on schedule. The two of them, she and her mother, leave little messages for each other, terse little darts. And so likewise the third Mrs. Felt telephoned *me* from the rear of a limousine shuttling her from a currency conference to her luxuriously impersonal hotel suite. Precise location unknown. She is presently involved in the design and implementation of new, probably worthless, currencies for small, broken, wartorn nations around the globe—makes a fortune, my eighties bride. According to her, Gena needs to stop getting paid to get coffee for people her own age whom she likes in a milieu in which she's comfortable and instead should serve an internship in which she gets coffee for prematurely old people whom she can't stand in a milieu that makes her stomach lurch. She wants to rent Gena a studio in the East Seventies where she can live shut up like Rapunzel with ten thousand dollars' worth of hair-care products when she's not at Credit Suisse learning at the feet of the masters how to sew her asshole up tight. Anyway, I will make the journey to Hipster Heaven with my hat in my hand and my most adventurous palate. Honestly, Gena's world bewilders me nearly as much as her mother's does, but at least there seems to be something *to* it. I'm inclined to make absolutely minimal demands unless I find chanting hooded figures or an arms cache in her living room.

Ivan

P.S. Today Time Warner called *me*. Angela, actually. It's wonderful the way that I make zero impression on these people. She reminds me of one of my wives; walk right by me on the street. "We have your info and are just calling to set you up with cable!" she perked. I cautiously asked if that meant the "serviceability order" had gone through. She said something to the effect that she'd been unaware of the need for that and hung up.

May 11

My dear Felt,

A brief note. No sooner had I spent a grumbling, pre-caffeinated half hour this morning deciphering the online ticket ordering forms at Mets.com (for our Saturday seats in the accustomed section 101—yes, Felt, I bit like a sturgeon on the wriggly glowworm of your hagiographical evocations of both Pierrot and Mesch), than I flipped the *Times* open to discover what your letter affirms: that Randolph has flipped the starting rotation, for reasons unclear, and that now we were in fact fated to see Pedro Himself hurl on Saturday. Could be worse. Much as I assume the Ikea table remains in its inconclusive form in the center of your living room, Glavine isn't going anywhere anytime soon.

Experienced my first memorable sex dream in several years last night, Ivan. I was thrusting vehemently, and at great duration, into the cavity of an enormous barnacled sea turtle, who writhed before me, whether in pleasure or agony I cannot presume to say. Awoke to find myself not in the least tumescent, which managed to seem both a dreadful omen of coming decrepitude and, given the image, a vast relief.

Conklin

P.S. Gena's in Bushwick? When I recall Gena it's as a keening redhead spitting up a pabulum of carrots over my right shoulder—I jollied her while you and her mother stepped into another room of the West Broadway apartment to carry on a chapter of the epic argument that comprised that marriage. As for Bushwick, I think of that strange, decrepit used bookstore you and I discovered on Montrose Avenue while "waiting for your man" to convey us a dime bag of lousy grass. I found a copy of Northrop Frye's *Anatomy of Criticism* there, inscribed by the author to Harpo Marx. The Jewish gnome running the place (he resembled Sol Yurick's author photo) had bins of old *Playboy* and *Gent* magazines in front of the shop due to the exigencies of his neighborhood, but he also knew the antiquarian trade, and understood I'd fleeced him when I brought the Frye up to the counter and he saw the inscription he'd missed when pricing the book. I still treasure the memory of the look on his face as much as I do the volume in question.

You want me to look in on your daughter? We're sort of neighbors, if I consider the L train as an adjunct to my orbit. Perhaps she needs to hear a voice—or bend an ear—outside the familial matrix (as if I know what I'm talking about).

May 19

Harris,

"Look in on" my daughter? I'm charmed, mainly by the locution. I see a fetching little boarding house, in a cutely seedy brownstone district, like the one where Judy Holliday, working yet again with George Cukor, entertained both the supremely sleazy Peter Lawford and the excitably earnest Jack Lemmon (in his motion-picture debut) in *It Should Happen to You*. Gena is required by her landlady to keep her door open when she has gentlemen callers. The landlady is Thelma Ritter. Charles Ruggles, a retired army colonel, lives upstairs. Mary Wickes, a primly snoopy librarian, lives across the hall, but Eve Arden, in the adjacent room, watches her back. In her closet are a sad mannish hat and coat like the ones Anne Baxter wore when waifishly she haunted the stage door outside Bette Davis's latest hit. Of course. I'm tempted to run through the entire cast of characters of this jolly tale of pluck in mid-century New York.

But suit yourself. Don't look for a redhead—fuchsia comes closest to nailing the hue, though it's still not quite right. Tall girl. None of the prominent-featured, very-image-of-the-classic-anti-Semitic-cartoon stuff of her father's. She's got the small-nosed, delicate looks you probably sometimes see on those little chaste Hasidic babes on the L and the B. That little dish Natalie Portman, e.g. If you see a Natalie Portman walking around "East Williamsburg" with burns on her arms from the espresso machine, you know you've got her. If there's a boy around, coolly take stock. You have my proxy on this: I don't toss them out. I don't chuck the tablets of law at them like a skinny Moses in a pair of chinos and a work shirt. I look these kids up and down like a butcher in a hard hat and a bloody coat standing on Little West 12th Street and scrutinizing a side of beef in much the same manner as I imagine Henry Moore looked at a slab of marble, both of them wondering where to start carving.

Speaking of food, don't bring any. Unless you want a lecture. On the subject of proper nutrition, she's a kvetch. A vague 'un, I tease her. Bring books. *You* can lecture. She'll be charmed by her old uncle Conklin. Then you can start getting your ear bent. Though I have to say I think it'd be better for you than for her, frankly. At the risk of repeating myself again [*sic*], let me urge you to lift your ass out of your Barcalounger, stop waiting for the Emperor of Ice Cream to turn up, and go whip up some concupiscent curds of your own. Just not in my daughter's kitchen.

Ahem. I wanted to apologize, just a little, for my behavior at the game Saturday. I know you get embarrassed even when everything remains convivial. Let me try to explain. Once the Cards got their two runs back in the eighth, via those two shitty little hits Pujols and Edmonds blooped, my heart wasn't in what had been a pretty good game, Pedro having an off day notwithstanding. So when I saw Pierrot's kid, the grungy one, thumbing through that *Peanuts* anthology I thought I'd strike up a conversation with him. Keep everything jolly in the upper deck. The way the kid looked up at me, you'd think I'd interrupted some sort of carnivore tearing into its prey. You'd think I'd interrupted a session with one of the Holy Computer Games. Maybe it was that undisguised petulance, maybe it was something about that fully anthropomorphized Snoopy of the later cartoons, potbellied and strutting, with his annoying little friend Woodstock and his assortment of shticky personas, just got my goat at that moment. Not that I don't think Schulz's achievement was considerable—but sometimes the uses to which an innovator's advances are put by his successors make you question the innovation. Like, for example, we can hold Charles M. Schulz responsible for *Garfield*, I'm afraid. Anyway, I simply wanted to point out to the boy that once upon a time Snoopy was simply a dog capable of human thought; a dog who went about on four legs, with recognizably doglike contours and features, a lack of costumes, and so on. That the true focus of the strip wasn't on some Disneyfied animals, ho hum, but on the strange bloody struggles of these children, articulated so perfectly unsuitably in adult language in a wholly adult-less world. How was I to anticipate that what was simply an attempt to turn the pages of the book back to a good example of an earlier Snoopy would cause that feral child to scream and then throw the book over the parapet? I agree that it was *very* unfortunate that the book hit that elderly woman in the wheelchair. I have a mother. But it wasn't me who tossed that book. When Mesch turned up, it was absolutely unnecessary for him to threaten to "escort" me from the stadium. I feel fully justified in having protested— successfully, I might add. All right, I agree that it was inadvisable of me to loudly state that the old woman would have been "shit out of luck" if she'd been struck in the head by a foul ball hit "by a fucking millionaire." You know that these aren't my true sentiments. Mesch can push your buttons, you know that; the little pig-eyed petty official seems to have stepped out of the pages of Gogol, a "titular councillor" extraordinaire, another Akaky Akakievich. At least Pierrot took it in good part. He seemed happy to allow another adult to chastise his children, European-style.

So forget his kids, his smelly lunches (sardines *and* anchovies, I know, I know; and the Camembert was particularly effective, like something they'd have used at the Somme)—wasn't it nice that he passed us conciliatory paper cups of that excellent muscadet? I love that yeasty taste. Don't mention again that it aggravates your athlete's foot, please. I know this is strictly bullshit; I checked. On the Internet, the effortless font of medical factoids. You may be gratified to learn that muscadet can, "according to studies," cause toxic shock syndrome.

Pierrot's really all right. And we're stuck with the guy, Conk. Make nice.

After taking three straight from the Reds, I'm feeling good for the Yankees. I feel as if we're meeting them head-to-head for the first time. Granted, the Reds are one of the sorriest teams we've managed to see this year, but a sweep is a sweep, and I think after last year's pretty-OK performance against the Yanks we've finally crossed the Rubicon and its sweeping sharks of intimidation and pummeling waves of fear (not bad, Felt!). Can you believe they're coming into Shea with a worse record than we have? Verily, I feel we have the better team. Or are about one season away from it, at any rate. I am not at rest on the subject of Pedro and his sore hip—it can't be that Saturday against the Cards was his last start for a while—but not at all in the I-told-you-so mode of the Yankee fans, or the worried hand-wringing of the posters on alt.sports.baseball.ny-mets and elsewhere. Saturday was just an off day, an off day, an off day. Sunday will be better, better, better. Chant it with me, now!

I.

May 21

I.,

You've put your finger on something about Snoopy, certainly. The Red Baron is to Charlie Brown as Richard Brautigan is to Richard Stern. A pop-art distraction from real pain, is what I mean. Schulz's opus, like all American culture (excepting, I suppose, moon shots and Mets), took a dive through the decade of the sixties. And sure, Pierrot's muscadet took the edge off Pedro's hanging curve to Pujols (if only he'd smuggled in stemware, too). Yet you're edging off base with the curds remark. Or perhaps I should call it a balk move. I hold Gena in an esteem reserved by one who's never had a family to forsake or demolish. I mean that in the best way. I envy your paternity. Nothing else is possible.

H.

May 21

Sir!

This was no gauntlet I flung down. Merely one phrase, a famous poetical-type phrase too, in a missive of some 1,200 words. I thought you'd enjoy the reference, especially coming from a poetry philistine like me. If I'd told you not to roll any cigars in Gena's bedroom, that'd be something else. Accept my apologies, Avuncular One. Though it's my opinion that you need any jostling my sharper elbow can provide. Shut-in.

Standing, waiting, unarmed,
BARRY LYNDON, esq.

P.S. I'll have you know that while I've demolished a family or two, I've never forsaken one.

May 23

Ivan,

It's May, and yet I already fear we'll end this season counting how many of Pedro's starts we've wasted. Like a month's days flapping free of a movie calendar, like rarified beasts glimpsed on a safari, like those evenings where one glances skyward to spot a plummeting meteor's arc at the very moment it flares into gaseous nullity on penetration of earth's atmosphere, one would feel corrupt, cavalier, cruel, and capitalistic to frame his voyages to Shea's mound as commodities, as clicks on a doomsday clock—yet that's what they are, in short supply, and bought and paid for, too. Let's say he climbs the hill thirty times this year, the number of days in September. Is it too crude (in my alliteration I neglected that word, or perhaps I was saving it) to conclude that we're coughing up (sorry, I'll stop) between a third and a half mil for each ascent? So, in this weekend's series we let another one vanish, unconsummated, unconsecrated, unremunerated in the standings.

Other reflections: it has to be admitted that Wright, our Wrunderkind, kicked away both the Friday and Sunday games with his boners in the field. So, in another economy, we've paid the price of callow youth, of potential, of sending overWrought young men in to face down too rich a freight of lore, too dire a thematic, too proximate a bogeyman.

And Beltran, at the close of the weekend, finally admitting he's been playing injured, and inviting Randolph to bench him. Randolph explaining to the press corps that in Beltran he sees a man too smooth, too graceful for his own good: the fans don't glean the effort beneath the glamorous surfaces. Ah, the subtle politics of announcing an invisible injury as retro-justification for a less-than-stirring debut. And so the screws of expectation have begun to tighten on our less breezy, less ridiculous million-dollar man.

And yet: Can I say that though we lost two of the three games, that Saturday's victory (tiny Benson's Brobdingnagian innings, Reyes's frantic triple, reliever Koo's insane double off Randy Johnson, and his subsequent slide into home on the bunt—the Dada Highlight of the Spring, I'll warrant) had enough heart in it for a sweep? That nothing our opponent accomplished in the bookends, Friday or Sunday, struck me as noble or well earned, or in the least possessed of a sense of humor? Is this what it is to be a Met, Ivan? To know that you're the finer franchise, the more sublime, jubilant, endearing, heartfelt, in a world that coarsely validates only the blunt economics of win or lose?

I say it anyway: we're the finer franchise.

And I omit, out of sheerest disrespect, our opponent's name from this capsule report. For, when Laocoön wrestled with the serpent, was it really the serpent with whom he wrestled? Or was it existence itself—life, death, the universe? I say we were not playing a team worth naming this weekend—rather, we wrestled with the void, with ourselves, with the malign cosmos. It only happened to be wearing pinstripes, that's all.

Obstinately,

Harris

May 29

Conk,

It's hard to believe that the Mink was our safety choice for first base, after Delgado, since he seems such a perfectly good fit for the Metropolitans. "Put 'I suck' with a big picture of my face on it." Isn't this just the essence of Krane, of Boswell, of Mike Phillips, of Youngblood, of Theodore, of dozens, perhaps hundreds, of Mets platooners, of utility men on teams for which utility men played every day, of subs and scrubs. "I'm a career .270-plus hitter," the Mink says, adding hastily, "in the big leagues." One can only imagine those four-for-four nights in triple-A. Actually, in going over Mientkiewicz's statistics, I'm a little surprised to see that he's adjusted himself for his Mets service, adding mediocrity to his portfolio of skills with ease. Is this the key to my weakness for the Mink, for the Mets generally—that they take a thoroughly professional approach to underperforming? Is it the ingrained professionalism in such athletes as Foster, Bonilla, Vaughn, and perhaps Mr. Beltran that leads them to their monumental acts of underachievement while in a Mets uniform?

The Mink's gone over and above and beyond the call of

duty, though, with his flaming self-abnegation before the eager recording angels of the press. "I apologize to every Met fan in America right now." The pained comedy stylings of Doug Mientkiewicz don't stop:

"Guy tonight screams, 'Mientkiewicz, you suck.' I turn around and agree with him. I say, 'You're absolutely right, sir. I feel I owe you. I should pay you the admission you paid.' "

Ba-da-bump.

"My wife's carrying a baby. That poor child isn't going to stand a chance if I keep this up."

Ba-da-bump.

"I apologize to every Mets fan in America." Hardly necessary, Doug, to apologize for anything in May. Not necessary to apologize at all, now that I think of it, nor to advise reporters to lambaste you. They don't need reminding. Besides, the noisy implosion of Doug "Eye Chart" Mientkiewicz at Turner Field distracted from the quiet soughing sound the Mets made in their collapse. It's as if the schedulers book the Mets during those Atlanta home stands when they feel that the Braves need a rest, or a boost to their tired egos. Odd how the Mets have remained the Braves' putative rivals in the East even though they've been out of the running for four seasons. Somehow these two franchises are joined in a way unprecedented in Mets history. The rivalry simply doesn't feel good. It's not like the old ones against the Cubs, the Cards, the Reds, and even against the Astros. (Has it ever occurred to you that the Mets are much more of a Central Division team, spiritually, than an East team? All the old resentments and scores were misaligned, left unsettled, when they shifted everything around to create the three divisions.) To lose three in a row against the Braves—the Mink's apology somehow trivializes the brutal violation I feel. The rivalry I never quite feel is the one against the Marlins, and so while I take, happily, the three games we won against them (today's loss being notable mostly for the bad news it brings from the bullpen—an unsettling omen), to win against them somehow never feels as significant as it probably should, particularly since they've been, curiously, the most consistently success-ful team in the majors, after the Yankees, over the past ten years, if one measures World Series victory as the only prize that really counts.

Yours,
Ivan

- -

May 30

My dear Ivan Throat,
    I always knew it was your creepy uncle Mark.

Love, Judge Harris Sirica

- -

May 30

Father Confessor,
    Meet me in the parking garage, and I'll tell you all about it.

—I. Felt Throat

3

Vote for Pedro

June 1

Harris,

Perhaps I'm mistaken but it seems to me that the papers—well, the *Times*, anyway, which may not count—are speaking of Zambrano in the same way that they used to talk about Jose Contreras. "A pitcher with this much talent can't just be a washout." Wanna bet? Though this cynical aside is not justified by Zambrano's effort last night.

I have to say that my reaction to the sight of Rick Peterson's ridiculous haircut popping out of the dugout under his cap is tempered by my feelings toward the pitcher. Usually I've felt that Peterson's hair and Zambrano's efforts have been well matched. In the case of Tom Glavine, I'm usually filled with sympathy that a pitcher of his caliber must stand and deal with that hair. Martinez, of course, rarely has to talk to the hair, and his own do more than adequately responds. And so on. Last night, for the first time, I felt enormous sadness seeing the hair locomote from the Mets' dugout to pull Zambrano from the game, especially when I cast a glance beyond the right-field wall to see Braden Looper entering the game.

Could Braden Looper actually be in the employ of John Schuerholz, or still drawing paychecks from the Marlins? The ninth begins as a three-hit shutout and ends as an eight-hit squeaker? I really thought he was going to throw it away.

If any of my former wives had been pitchers, they would have been Braden Looper.

Believing,

Ivan

P.S. Will you indulge my pinstripe schadenfreude? The Yankees have dropped four in a row. I spotted an interesting statistic, vis-à-vis their pitching staff: they're 0–17 when scoring three or fewer runs. You have to wonder what that figure was during that '98–'00 period of Yankee—ugh—greatness.

June 3

Dear Ivan,

I realize I'm obsessed. Another Pedro start, another game imbued with a sense of certain victory, another Beltran homer. Pedro striking out nine, pitching in the fine mist thrown up by the malfunctioning sprinklers. Pedro genuflecting to Cameron after another beautiful, slightly showboaty catch. Pedro dinging a little roller halfway up the third-base line, where it stops dead in fair territory where three or four Marlins stare uncomprehendingly at the unexpectedly still object. We just need a four-man rotation and we're winning 20 percent more games. Don't do the math, I'll be embarrassed. Of course, Pedro would have had to retire last year under such archaic practices, his arm swollen up to Popeye-size proportions.

Did you see Piazza lumbering around the bases on Floyd's double in the fourth? I suppose not: no cable yet. Well, there's a classic picture in the *Times* this morning of Piazza easing into his slide at the plate. He looks about as enthusiastic as I would.

Gloatingly,
Harris

P.S. Indeed: the Yankees' loss streak's now at five in a row! Swept by the Royals! With a worse record than the Mets, in JUNE! I'll go you one better: I suspect the Yankees won't be winning the division this year. Throw it in my face later on.

June 4

H—

I was walking up Seventh Avenue in Chelsea yesterday and I passed a little boutique (no need to make wisecracks) with a shirt in the window that said "Vote for Pedro." I assumed it was a Chelsea Thing, and you can make of that what you will, but soon enough I saw a young man wearing the same shirt when I was walking down the street in my own neighborhood. It was one of those whatchamacallit

T-shirts, the kind with the band of elasticized fabric around the sleeves and the neck. Looks nice if you happen to have biceps, which has never defined me in the virility department. Some people have big dicks, some people have hairy backs, some people grow extensive beards with east and west wings, some people have washboard stomachs, some people have biceps the size of Clincher softballs, and some people can crack nuts between their toes. I happen to be the pubic-hair king. But that's neither here nor there. We were speaking of a shirt, ah, weren't we?

I'm assuming that the Pedro who's earned the shirt's 100 percent cotton endorsement is none other than PEDRO! as I believe we all should excitedly refer to him. PEDRO! on a hip T-shirt direct from Chelsea. We may have questioned his Jheri curls but clearly he's made an impression where it counts. So I took heart: the hippest of the hip are hip to PEDRO! Nominating him for high office, even.

Now, I doubt that Tom Glavine—as a person, a pitcher, or an entity—would manage to gain much traction in Chelsea. He's more of a Westchester County Rotarian type. Glavine's people would be the type who tuck their dismal patterned sport shirts into their pleated chino shorts. But he's been on the money lately, steadily improving, and playing against a Giants team that is a shadow of its former self he looked terrific. Could it be true that Bonds is to Giants as Jordan was to Bulls? This is supposed to be baseball, you know, with 80 percent more teammates. Actually, this is looking like a Giants team of old. Lots of hitting, a mediocre starting staff, and a disastrous bullpen. The starting lineup must have a combined average of around .290, and that includes the pitcher. But Glavine handled them pretty well, "scattered," as they say, nine hits.

Speaking of Piazza, it looks as if he's breaking out of this week's slump. 3–5, 2 RBI, 1 run. And another chugging jog around the bases.

The Mink and Pedro were seen sitting together in the dugout. They were doing some kind of hand jive together, either an ancient Dominican, Polish, or Red Sox curse. Pedro also grabbed a bat at one point to try to show whoever was up just how to go about it.

Heilman closed it out. No save opportunity, so the Prima Donna, Florida's man in New York, sat it out.

Yrs,

I.

June 5
(postcard)

I.

I'll only add that the Yankees lost another: six in a row. And, that I'd buy VOTE FOR PEDRO shirts any day. VOTE FOR PEDRO socks. VOTE FOR PEDRO underwear. VOTE FOR PEDRO dentures. Sign me up. You better not be kidding about this.

H.

Harris,

You can remember this as the day that the Florida Marlins woke up in first place, went to the ballpark and lost, and then went to bed in last place. In April, maybe. June? At the same time, the *Times* tells me, a Washington team is in first place this late in the season for the first time since 1933 (though we have to discount those intervening thirty-five or so seasons when there was no Washington team). Not even the St. Louis Browns can claim so dismal a heritage (didn't the Pete Gray–era Browns win a pennant?).

(I think I can parenthetically insert here that brown is absolute *death* as a team color. Cf. the checkered history of the San Diego Padres.)

(Did you see the little piece sometime last week about uniform colors? Some psychological study has determined that teams who wear red tend to play more aggressively and tend to win, though there's a big But in here somewhere that I can't quite remember. Something like: *but* a lousy team in a red uniform is still a lousy team.)

(I think golf color teams will have a bad time historically, too. The Teal Menace may have had some winning times but those uniforms will cost them in the end.)

Well, Ishii provided some punch at the bottom of the order, as the beat reporters like to say, but at a certain point he had two of the Mets' three hits (and their only RBI), so that didn't do any good. This was a generally listless game, notable mostly for Ishii's performance at the plate and for the presence in the starting lineup of Marlon Anderson, yet another player who plays second base at least as well as Kaz Matsui. (Time, I think, to take Kaz and send him to live on a nice farm in the country, where he can run around and be happy.) Reyes made a point of swinging at a lot of first-pitch breaking balls. Cameron made a point of looking at a lot of first-pitch fastballs in the zone. Piazza slipped into his alternate-day slump, as day follows night, giving Seaver and whatshisname something to talk about, voodoo advice and invocations of past glory. A lot of fly balls made themselves scarce on their way to the outfield. It looked hot and glary out there. There were about four hundred people in the stands for the makeup game, the first of this doubleheader.

Game number two was another matter. Brown-bag-supper game—a reference from the days when you could still bring brown bags into public spaces. Well, Pierrot manages somehow. I always loved the twi-night doubleheader, the evening cool and the soft illumination of the field, the fluorescent green of that grass, like an ignis fatuus, when the lights first pop on. Though I can kind of see why the players might have hated it, back when they used to play them regularly. All that hoarded heat down on the field must be streaming out of the turf and dirt. Is that a possibility allowed by physics, Bronx Sci boy? Zeenat—you know, the once-and-future Brenda Felt—would have laughed so gaily at me had I dared to ask a question at the dinner table. Hunter College High School bitch! Yet even then I knew that my real future lay at the bloody core of things; amid the shiny cellophane packaging of the snack aisle, amid movie posters and musty stacks of old *TV Guides*.

The Mets apparently decided to win last night. They had that massive and hungry look. It was not accidental. They had two chances in game one, futile mid-nineties-style late-inning rallies that came to naught, and they apparently just decided to leave nothing to chance, to not leave *anybody* on base in game two. Actually, the box says the Mets left four on. Another sturdy post supporting your theory that the more men left on, the more effective the team. It was all Reyes, Floyd, Wright, and Diaz. Sounds like a Central Harlem law firm. Reyes, Wright, & Diaz, PC; Cornelius C. Floyd Jr., Esq., of counsel: let the names of that good firm haunt the roster for ten more years! And Benson. I don't know, man. He's looking good. An odd duck, though. Seven innings, no walks, no strikeouts. How often does that happen? Anna was home. He dashed up the runway and called, several times. Just checking. Uh, how're the kids? Just you and the personal chef, huh? Oh, the masseur, too? Good, right, gotta go. Runs out and punches an RBI double. Better that than the masseur. He looks pretty big.

Yours,

Ivan

March 7

Ivan,

Did you see the photo on the front of Monday's *Times* sports section? Did it mean as much to you as it has to me? The photograph shows Diaz nestling his jaw against Floyd's shoulder, his forearm against Floyd's forearm, his glove against Floyd's glove (and, below the line of the possibly cropped photo, his Mr. Met against Floyd's healthy, generous buttocks), the senior player, the jaded veteran of Expos/Marlins/Mets sufferance grinning despite himself, the junior player with that vibrancy which balances a barely contained glee at even being *in the show* in the first place against the arrogance of youth, the unruined, never-seriously-injured, why-can't-we-just-win-it-all? cojones or mojo or duende (whichever would be the most apposite and least academic-reprimand-provoking usage), that is also so evident in David Wright (David the magnificent, David the sublime, David who we must award a nickname soon; David whose name brings to mind its inevitable opposite and thus bears his own embedded shadow, much like Pete "The Worm in the Bud" Rose, a player I sometimes fear he may too much resemble; David who last week I saw do what no professional baseball player ever does during an at bat—break concentration to turn his head and crane, pop-eyed and eager as any ticket holder, at the sounds of the crowd cheering a fine fan catch of his own foul ball), the two of them, Diaz and Floyd of course celebrating the four-homer rout of the Giants, the game that, perhaps more than any other, proved to me and perhaps to them that *these Mets are different!* What former edition of our team, short of '69, '73, '86, '88, '00, would have neglected, after losing that first game of the doubleheader, the opportunity to follow declining the option on first place (the whole National East reminds me of those damnable chipmunks: "After you, sir." "No, after you, sir." "Why, I couldn't possibly. After you, sir." "I'm sorry, but I must insist—after you, sir") by losing the second game and grabbing a seat in the cellar.

But no, Ivan! Benson's for real! And we may be for real, too.

Yours,
Harris

P.S. I write on Tuesday morning, after another Yankees loss, another Big Eunuch failure. His tormented visage—did I ever tell you that my sister nicknamed him the Turkey Vulture?—is so evocative of everything misaligned (money, age, spirit, imagination, reverence, and, I think, I.Q.) in this current crop of Yankees, that I begin to think he was bestowed on us as a blessing of contrast to the ingenuous sweetness of our team. Or, to put it in your terms, might Randy Johnson in fact be in the employ of Omar Minaya? He's the anti-Pedro, that's for certain. Except he's got competition in Mussina and Brown. Hoo-fucking-ray.

PHONE TRANSCRIPT, June 8, 11:40 PM

HC: *Teal Menace!*

IF: *Conklin?*

HC: *Teal Menace, I say! You called the Marlins the "Teal Menace." You're good, Felt. Bit of poet in you yet. Calliope whispering in your ear. Got me thinking—*

IF: *Listen, Conk—*

HC: *—an epic lyrical diagnostic of the different uniforms and logos, perhaps the team names as well. It's just the sort of highbrow-lowbrow conflation that's making careers these days. Can't you see it?*

IF: *Uh—*

HC: *C'mon, work with me. Like your demolitcshion of the Padres in their mustard brown—schuperb, Ives!*

IF: *You've had a few.*

HC: *I confess freely to being two tankards of Guinness to*

the good. Listen, we'll write it together, I'm not selfish about this. What's the name of your friend who edits the Harper's Readings section? Because this would be a natural for them.

IF: *I think the point of the Readings section is that everything in it was published first elsewhere, Har.*

HC: *Just try a few of these, listen. I began by tackling them alphabetically: "The A's, with the last vestiges of Finleyism to be found in those jerseys; as such they should persist. Ah, but those white shoes, alas! Their secret weapon, shadow mascot, the white elephant—"*

IF: *Harris, I've got a—*

HC: *"Angels, like their namesake, invisible in the city for which they're named—"*

IF: *Are we really going through the whole alphabet?*

HC: *That's the point, Ivan.*

IF: *Fair enough. We'll do the letter A tonight, and pick it up tomorrow.*

HC: *A's, Ivan, Angels—*

IF: *The A's are, of course, Berkeley Green, like People's Park. Greenpeace. The white elephant ought to be a whale, or a clubbed baby seal. The sole redeeming feature of the Angels was that '70s Leslie Charteris "Saint" halo.*

HC: *That's the spirit! Now, Astros—*

IF: *Right, Astros. Their present uniform is negligible. I do have a sneaking fondness for the '70s "color bar" uniform, however. What's an Astro, anyway? They could have called the team the Test Patterns. Which in turn suggests a home-away scheme where the color bars are featured at home and the road uniforms look like gray* static. *Pynchon's "A screaming comes across the sky" at home, with William Gibson's "A sky the color of a television tuned to a dead station" on the road.*

HC: *(clunking sound)*

IF: *Har?*

HC: *—so fucking brilliant, I knew you'd come through on this one! You really have to call your friend at* Harp—

IF: *Okay, are we through the As?*

HC: *Brewers!*

IF: *Yeast. I primarily think of yeast. Their name sounds like the Padres uniform looks. It's not difficult to crush the two together and think of monk-brewed ale. Also, what was that* Happy Days *spin-off?* Laverne and Shirley.

HC: *You're on fire! Diamondbacks, Ivan.*

IF: *Taco Bell. Carl's Jr. They also look like a third-rate villain that Daredevil or Hulk would battle—call him "Venom."*

HC: *Ezzpos.*

IF: *I gotta go. I'm not alone. Her name's not, uh, Calliope. Besides, you've screwed up the alphabet.*

HC: *Espos, c'mon, Espos.*

IF: *Right. Uh, the inexplicable name always seemed to point to the francophone aspect, a nice touch, I thought.*

HC: *What's wrong with my alphabet?*

IF: *Braves. Blue Jays. Devil Rays.*

HC: *Oh, I have a good line about the Devil Rays—wait— (sounds of rustling paper) "the silhouette on their arm recalling the leeches Hepburn pulls off Bogart's legs in* African Queen—"

IF: *(in background) I'll get him off in a minute—it's not that easy—no, I'm not going to just hang up.*

HC: *(singsong) "The Rangers, bearing the phantasmic Senators in their DNA—"*

IF: *Chuck Norris.*

HC: *"—the White Sox, who last won in an era before color photography; and white, with its implicit opposite forever evoking the Chicagoan's stain, their historical crime—"*

IF: *Remember the shorts?*

HC: *Eh?*

IF: *Sox tried wearing shorts, once. A pop-surrealist use of black and white that could be said to anticipate the Coen brothers.*

HC: *You've lost me, Ives . . .*

IF: *(silence)*

HC: *I think—*

IF: *Har?*

HC: *I need to—*

IF: *Har?*

HC: *(silence)*

IF: *Uh, good night, Conk.*

HC: *I'm sorry.*

IF: *It's okay. Good night.*

June 9

Harris,

First, let me get my discreet inquiry—made, of course, out of concern as to your mental health—out of the way: on top of the blotto phone call, which I can more than forgive, I now notice the subject line of your recent message is May 7.

The date in the body of the e-mail is March 7. The date on which I received this was June 7. Are you experiencing ringing in your ears? Blurred vision? Sudden, uncontrollable rages? Major depression? Tremors? Well, me too, pal, but in your case I'd strongly advise that you put one foot in front of the other and get out of the house a little more often. Seriously, I do worry. You sit at home with your sestinas and centos and sonnets and God knows what else and there goes life, sailing by right outside your window, or whatever passes for life in North Corona. Surely there's a nice coffeehouse near you (not coffee *shop*, mind you: coffee*house*, like where Gena works. Actually, that is sort of near you) where you can sit and make overtures to some pierced and tattooed lovely, though bear in mind that the tongue stud is the feminists' revenge for the ribbed condom. And stop with the bristling. The job of a friend—actually, the job of a psychiatric technician, but that's neither here nor there—is to reflect reality back at you. Reality says: a sestina cannot haul your ashes. A cento cannot yank your emergency brake. With a sonnet you cannot make the beast with two backs. Loving lecture over.

How marvelously serendipitous that the Turkey Vulture's (how I love this moniker!) lapse should occur on the eve of Pedro's most beautiful game for the Mets—so far. Perfect, in a way, that Pedro should hang a pitch to the rookie batting, what was it, under .200? That there should be someone named Qualls involved in the game (though it was not so perfect for Rose and Cohen to keep mentioning it on WFAN. I miss Bob Murphy. Hell, I miss Lindsey Nelson). That he simply got back up there and got nine of the next ten out.

About last night, let me tell you a funny story. I saw a young guy on the subway today with his little girl, she was around nine or ten, and he was reading the sports page. She sort of craned her neck to have a look and, apparently spotting the story about Zambrano's loss, asked: "He hit anyone last night, Dad?" So I'm glad I'm not the only one who has this feeling that somewhere under Victor Zambrano's cap all hell is likely to break loose at any time when he's starting. The guy has some of the most brilliant innings, some of the most brilliant at bats, you're going to see. Then he plunks someone on the elbow, walks someone, and throws a wild pitch. He's one you won't hear me suggesting for the bullpen.

Well, we'll see what Tommy Glavine does tonight. Card-carrying believenik that I am, I consider him to be fully in the throes of a comeback.

These Mets are different. Syntax error: Are these Mets different? I actually am holding out hope for a division flag—it seems a more likely possibility than the Wild Card—though in this division, who knows? I may have been wrong about the Nationals, though my father taught me years ago that June is the longest month for teams missing a horse or two. That may well describe the Mets. The fielding percentages for the middle infield are pretty shocking. Still, everyone (that is, "everyone") is hitting—well, everyone who's supposed to, except Piazza and Matsui. Though I suddenly had a rare burst of indignation the other day, watching Beltran trot out a weakly hit ground ball. Indignation mostly at myself, for indulgently thinking, "He'll come around." Come around? At this price, even I become a boo-bird. Piazza—God help me, I was secretly pleased that he was injured last night—may have done very little the last two seasons, but the Mets never would have reached the postseason without him in '99 and '00. That's an impact player.

Oh, listen to me. I suddenly put myself in mind of the guy Holden Caulfield suffered sitting behind at Radio City, the one who kept turning to his wife while the Rockettes were on to exclaim, "That's precision!"

So, nu? What's the story with this guy Graves? The Mets need another middle reliever with an ERA of around 6.00? Shit, Dave Kingman did better than that. You could look it up.

Yankee notes: And now the Yankees, clutching the booby-prize laugher close to their chests, straggle into St. Louis. Hundred and twenty degrees on the field and loud fans with a championship history of their own. Plus the best team in the National League. No indication, as yet, that the Yankees can beat good teams. Not really too much evidence that they can do too well against bad teams. All I can say is I'm glad the Cards are out of the NL East. (If only the Braves would leave too.)

Why did the Yankees draft a shortstop if Jeter is signed through 2010? "I think I'll be ready in two, three years." Why not just hire an engraver to design a suitably filigreed "Fuck You"?

Conk, in October 2000 if you'd told me I'd be getting indignant on Derek Jeter's behalf, I'd have become violent (ly ill).

—I BETTER SIGN OFF

- -

June 11 (yes, I know what month it is)

Dear Ivan,

I can honestly avow I'm glad we took this past week off from visitations to the Blue Temple. (Have you heard we may now host the Olympics? Or was that just an odd dream?) That the Miracles could have gone so thoroughly into the septic just four days after Pedro's Magnum Opus Metsiana (thus far) boggles the mind and, worse, siphons the essence, the life force, the chi. I suppose rather than spiraling into another existential inquiry I should be consoling myself with pragmatics—injuries, that is. The nagging kind in the lineup being perhaps more insidious to the team's fortunes than the overt, on the fifteen-day-list type. One has to believe that Floyd, Beltran, and the Mink, at the very least, are all swinging the bat "gingerly," as they say. Beltran pops up with such regularity it's like he's launching clay pigeons for a shoot.

Yet, hell, Ives—unlike my papa, I'm no orthopedic surgeon (and anyway, where did diagnosing Mets' aching extremities ever get dear old Aloysius Conklin? Tossed out on his ear, that's where). So, I'll turn to matters existential. Which, in my language, is another word for pitching. In Zambrano and Ishii we've got two not-laughing matters I'm paining myself laughing over. And then there's the bullpen. Let me take them in order:

The *Times* commemorated the Wednesday night game with the headline "Once Again, Zambrano Pitches Just Well Enough to Lose"—cutting close enough to the grain of the matter. Yet, since a rookie batting .205 named Todd Self found himself a recipient from Zambrano of our team's signature token of affection, a leadoff walk in the sixth (see: Ishii, Friday night)—a trinket the team palms off as easily as a corporate party planner sends you out into the night with a gift bag full of skin product and an unreadable magazine— and, since young Self in fact scored two runs in the game, as opposed to the single run scored collectively by all twenty-

five men on the Metropolitan roster, I myself would have preferred: "Zambrano Defeated by Self." He sure is an object of
fascination, this Unvictorious Victor of ours, I agree with
you. I still rank him as the second most likely of our corps
(after Martinez, of course) to throw this season's no-hitter
(it's still coming, Ivan, I swear, I feel it). He's got good stuff,
though by now perhaps that sentence has been repeated in
the form of a quote ascribed to others (to "baseball men") so
often that it ought to be rendered: " "He's" " " "got" " " "good" "
" "stuff." " " But what you see as a craziness in his eyes, I must
say strikes me more (and is all truth, like beauty, in the eye
of the Believenik?) as depression. A darkness that readily in-
fects the Mets' batters, thereby ensuring its own cause. Fun-
nily enough, when he played for Tampa Bay he gained a
reputation as a Yankee killer. Perhaps it was only that, when
he was on the mound, teams with NY on their caps tended to
cough up games as if beneficiaries of a Heimlich.

I'll pass over Thursday night, and Glavine's heartache,
since that more falls under the category of Bullpen, and I
swore to leave the worst for last. So, to Friday, and Ishii. Is
Ishii a man or a syndrome, Ivan? (I suppose it depends, ha
ha, on what your definition of "Ishii" is.) He seems a more de-
plorable train wreck than Zambrano to me by far, perhaps
because he came from the Dodgers—stalwart tradition, National League (I've decided facing a pitcher's spot in the
lineup keeps an NL pitcher saner, all other things being
equal—take a look at those poor Yanks and Sox staffs, psych
wards both)—whereas Zambrano suffered the Devil Ray
identity, surely destined to look as gloomy as the Senators or
Browns in the long arc of baseball zeitgeists. I feel Ishii
should know better the simplest thing an athlete has to

know—that greatness, or at least competence, is defined by how you recover from and minimize mistakes, not by never making them in the first place. I don't see a perfectionist when I look in his eyes—and god knows shouldn't a coach have cured him of any perfectionist tendencies by now?— but when Ishii falters in the least he caves like a road paved over a stretch of everglades. Should we nickname him "U-turn"? Or perhaps "Oh, you're hungry? Here's the keys to my dad's supermarket." This morning I've committed a poem in his honor, my first in weeks:

> Ishii you pitch strong
> For as long as a haiku
> Then a door swings wide

Lastly, bullpen. I wonder, Felt, how the rest of the team—the real team, I'm tempted to say—feels about people like *Bell (record 0–3)*, *DeJean (5.09)*, *Aybar (6.04)*, *Koo (5.65)*, *Ring (5.40)*, these strange young men with their strange, minimally syllabic names, their grievously unathletic bodies, who appear intermittently on the mound to surrender run after run? They don't sit with the team and they never last long in the game, and they must seem as disconcerting to the regulars as they do to us. Are they really ballplayers? Really Mets? *Really*, Ivan? Would anyone much notice if we rounded up a new batch of guys—minor leaguers, castoffs from basement teams like the Reds—and started anew?

Oh yeah—that's what we are doing.

If any of those guys besides maybe Koo (he'll live in my heart forever for that double and the headfirst slide to home) is anywhere near an inning that matters in September (god give us those), I'm the next laureate, my friend.

One last thing: Randolph's using Heilman to mop up hopeless games, after the lesser pitchers ruin them? Start him, close with him, anything. He's just *sitting* there. Wasn't this meant to be a youth movement (*Next Year Is Now*)? Get Diaz into games, get Heilman into games, let Pedro hypnotize them in the dugout and send them in, *please*.

Hurtingly,

Har

Alumni notes: Melvin Mora hit a three-run homer to lead the tenacious Orioles to victory last night. He's got twice as many dingers as, er, Beltran.

June 11
(Mets 5, Angels 3)
(Angels 4, Mets 3)
(Bloomberg 1, Mets 1)

Conk,

My first thought this morning, on reading the *New York Times* hype about the Olympics as the solution to Shea Stadium, was, "What's in it for Wilpon?" Is it out of the goodness of his heart that he's not only going to pay for a stadium but vacate it for the entire 2012 season? I am as patriotic a New Yorker as any other, but if—not *when*, Harris, most decidedly *if*—my number ever comes up on the waiting list at Penn South, I would not dream of ceding those three hard-won rooms to, say, the Estonian race-walking team. Come to think of it, any putative plan for West Side "development" could do worse than to countenance a few more Penn Souths.

Since you're a Queens boy, you'll both understand and seethe with resentment in your passive-aggressive way (I suppose you'll choose some rainy day to keep me waiting on an awning-free corner) when I say that the Olympics seem more suited, somehow, to Queens: the Olympic Dream—the modern Olympic dream, the one coincident with strange instances of telegenic human oddity like Mary Lou Retton—is a dream of the Provinces. To bring the Olympics to his city is the sort of dream one might expect from a character out of late Dostoyevsky (which may aptly describe a Mike Bloomberg) or perhaps Flaubert. Would you believe—to quote Agent 86—William Kennedy?

(Who knows, I may even be able to watch the 2012 Olympics on interference-free cable television. There's always that slimmest of possibilities. Angela and I had our weekly conference the other day, or I should say I struggled to remain polite while Angela disavowed the very concept of autonomy. I now have a sinking feeling at the moment that I initiate a call, knowing as I now do that Time Warner has no central record-keeping system that tracks my calls, or the putatively entered "serviceability orders" that will lay the groundwork for the hard work of hooking me up to the communal trough. I realize that although Angela hews closely to a script, it never stops her from dispensing information that contradicts what she told me the last time we spoke. We may refer to this in the future as Felt's Paradox. Anyway, Angela today chirped, "I see your address is not serviceable!" I asked her about the famous serviceability order. It had been canceled, but she will reinstate it at an unspecified time. I'm to call back.)

You speak of middle relievers and uneasy starters (though, re: Ishii, I happened to spot Steve Trachsel suited up and participating in the welcome ceremony at home plate in Saturday's tenth—could he be readying a return? Where will they manage to find room for him in that rotation?), and yet my sharkishly restive thoughts linger over the inimitable work of Braden Looper, whose teeth-baring rictus is beginning to get on my nerves and in whom the strange disconnect of his presence—he doesn't, through his physical demeanor, seem to register the unacceptable level of mediocrity in his work—seems more and more like symptoms of some grandiose type of personality disorder.

Can I just say that I have come to hate the sight of Braden Looper?

Despite it all, despite the years of specialization and refinement and the endless work of the can't-do-teach technicians (Rick Peterson, Dave Wallace, Leo Mazzone), despite above all multiyear contracts for startling sums, the middle reliever remains a strange athletic curiosity: not quite enough talent for one thing, but too much to cast off. A Special Teams player, in another context. The same thing it was when a drunken Hugh Casey began to define the modern reliever.

(There's an interesting old story about Hugh Casey and Ernest Hemingway. Apparently they became drinking buddies and partners in machismo. They'd get shitfaced, then lace on boxing gloves and take turns knocking each other down. It was Casey who killed himself first, incidentally.)

This leads me to the forking of two points. Point number one, as you can probably anticipate, concerns the relatively prestigious position of the closer. Rivera, this guy Rodriguez on the Angels, even ex-starters with twenty or thirty shells left in the cannon every couple of days like Eckersley and, until this year I guess, Smoltz. They came down on the Mink on Saturday for missing that grounder and on Wright on Sunday for booting one, but these "costly errors" exacted their price thanks to Looper himself, who seems uncomfortable with the prospect of working with the bases empty and does his best to fill at least one, preferably on the first at bat. Some have suggested that Saturday's game had the potential to be a pivotal one (a trifle romantic even for me, as baseball analyses go—but it *was* a magnificent game, from Beltran's catch to Marlon Anderson's inside-the-park home run [the first, Conk, I've ever witnessed, believe it or not] to Floyd's epic final at bat, and one that would have set a great tone for an upcoming twelve games on that long road that leads ultimately to the Major Deegan Expwy). If so, then Looper single-handedly reversed the momentum. I know: the statistics don't bear me out. On Saturday and Sunday Looper's line shows no earned runs. Yet David Wright claims that his muscles "tightened up" on the field—coincident with Looper's being on the mound. He's taking one for the team, game little Nails Rose headfirst-sliding jock that he is—but I have to wonder if this spasm of discomfort could have occurred when Pedro was out there, even working around his fading stuff and pitching seven creditable innings (not to mention "furthering his own cause," to use that peculiarly infuriating phrase beloved of announcers, by driving in a run). Would David Wright's tough little back have clenched up like a black power fist if a Mariano Rivera had trotted out from the bullpen? Well, OK, that's not entirely fair. I'm still not convinced that Mariano Rivera is an actual human being, and not just a pitiless android. OK, how about Urbina? If you think about it, he's probably the coldest of them all. How many games could you save if your mother were being held hostage? (Held by someone other than Fortunoff, I mean.) But I digress:

> Shadow-covered field
> three, orange and blue, flank him
> Looper feels lonely

I can't wait to see headlines like "RING, BELL, WRUNG," "HEATH BARRED," "ROLLOVER ROYCE," "EARLY GRAVES." I don't quite understand the Mets' bullpen troubles either; the disintegration is so complete, yet you'd think that assembling a decent bullpen with an annual payroll stretching toward $150,000,000 would not pose an enormous problem. The confidence I felt watching Turk Wendell or even Dennis Cook come into a game was replaced in turn by the mild unease of seeing Scott Strickland or Grant Roberts, the horror of seeing Mike Stanton or David Weathers, and finally by the sense of hopeless futility I feel today.

(And yes, I agree: they don't seem to be part of the team; it's almost as if there's a tacit understanding that a Heath Bell or a Manny Aybar is strictly provisional. Maybe it was Franco's stature that kept the bullpen from being the lonely right-field outpost it might well have been for the past fifteen years—though, to be honest, I would have done well just now to indicate his own steep and steady descent on that line graphing the decline from Wendell to DeJean.)

(Doesn't it just make you laugh to think that Mike De-Jean is the golem we were able to slap together to replace Ricky Bottalico—seriously, I'm missing Bottalico.)

Anyway, when Pedro, Benson, or Glavine are doing well, I pray for a complete game; when they do unevenly I hope to see Heilman. Which, or who, is my second point. You're absolutely right, why is he sitting there? After Looper fucked up Saturday night, and way way late, couldn't Willie have put Heilman in the closer's role on Saturday without risking the wrath of the oh-so-highly-strung Looper? And who gives a shit? Who's running that fucking team?

Speaking of the Devil Rays, d'ja see Piniella's outburst? I think he may be auditioning for the Bronx.

> Drippingly,
> Ivan

June 16

Harris,

Anything to say about these dreary losses in Oakland? Other than that the Mets should have won? Or that what I was saying about June's being the longest month echoes sharply now? Zambrano deserved to win that one. Another bullpen failure. Glavine, being a 4.00 sort of pitcher now, kind of deserved to win his, as well. Well, kind of. Neither guy deserved an average of one run per game. More later.

So you're going to Augusta. Well, have some fun. I'm being slightly subtle here. What I mean to say is,

HAVE SOME F * U * N * !!

Listen, there must be some sort of visiting-poet-coordinator type, just a little lonely; long sandy blond hair, kicks her shoes off when she comes indoors, lives in one of those new condos, you know, on the hill, the nice ones, not the blecchh ones, she has a great deck, with a view of the woods, and some white wine; she tells you about all this while she's driving you in her Camry that has a backseat full of junk; she's the sort of person who when she's writing a letter she'll always have a line in it like, "I'm sitting here listening to *Giant Steps* in my too-drafty workroom and missing that warm delicious laugh of yours," always Coltrane, can't write a letter without pretending that she's listening to Coltrane, maybe Monk, the reference basically excuses the letter's flaws, whatever they are, or so she feels; she's divorced, by the way, long divorced, she and her husband have no contact, he hated poetry was the thing, liked to read *New Yorker*–type nonfiction, a lover of hard-hitting truth, a real puritan, she says, not angrily or sadly and god knows not ironically, just sort of sounding amused; though actually it wasn't that he hated poetry, something she won't reveal right away—what it was is that he was completely absorbed, *seduced*, by racquetball, his feelings toward poetry, toward everything, mostly resembled apathy more than anything else; ate slept and shit racquetball, a regular racquetball juncquie, he let her have the record collection and the little Picasso lithograph and the now-old Camry and the books and all he wanted was the Premier Membership at the Mid-South Health and Racquet Club, that's all; Let me out of here, he panted, I have a seven a.m. court time; that's what he said, yes, and and and there's a woman like that waiting for you, Harris Conklin, and she wants you *baaaaaaaaaaaaad.*

Elvis Presley played racquetball throughout the sweltering night on which he died.

Trivially yours,

Ives

June 19

Dear Ivan,

Well, gee, thanks, Ives, I blush, but it didn't happen for me, not this time. My long-weekend stint at the Okefenokee Writers' Workshop was perhaps too tightly scheduled for your forecasted liaison to manifest itself: a reading on Thursday night and an endless series of one-on-one student conferences Friday and Saturday mornings and afternoons. If I make it sound as though I'm captive to Southern-fried "I was a Prisoner on a Chain Gang" reveries, you must accept that I was in fact driven past Hard Labor Creek State Park on Interstate 20 on my way in from Atlanta. I won't burden you with images of my serial humiliations—okay, just one: one earnest, wide-eyed kid during the reading's Q&A session asked what I thought about Billy Collins, and I somehow thought he said Phil Collins, and so actually began reminiscing aloud about *The Lamb Lies Down on Broadway* at the Nassau Coliseum in 1972 (and I do still maintain that there's some pretty fine, albeit primitive, Imagist poesy smothered beneath those synth crescendos)—instead recommending that you summon an image of Paul Muni, or better yet, Joel McCrea, in ragged stripes and clanking ankle-chains, hustling through a swamp with bloodhounds keening at his buttocks.

My point is, I had to rise at five a.m. on Thursday to get to LaGuardia for a six-thirty flight. Atlanta is a Delta hub, and Delta's LaGuardia terminal's at the airport's right edge, and therefore brackets the marina that divides the airport from Shea. So, as my car-service driver ascended the ramp to the terminal, the Blue Temple hovered into view. Did you know they keep the neon batsman lit even at five-thirty on a Thursday morning, even with the team 3,000 miles away, stranded somewhere between Oakland and Seattle (a condition I'll now declare the new paradigm of human hopelessness generally:

Between rock and hard place
Up creek without paddle
Neither here nor there
Between Oakland and Seattle).

I digress. They keep the neon batsman lit, that's what I meant to say. Like we keep our hearts lit. The dawn mists of the sound's northwestern shore dimmed the scene to a radiant gray, the marina's boats hardly bobbing in the breach between terminal and stadium. Shea was like a bolt-of-blue banner hung in the vast fog. It vibrated like a solitary hero on a stilled battlefield, like a lunar module descended onto an airless sea of tranquility. My driver lifted my bag to the white-painted lip of curb. A sleepy porter waited for me to advantage myself of curbside check-in, but I was otherwise alone, nothing agitating this scene except the frieze of ghostly memories that emblazoned itself on the sky above the marina's swells, the space between Shea and my fresh-woken eyes.

Do you remember that in 1978 we sat one scorching June day in the loge, third-base side, with our two dates—the future second Mrs. Felt and her colleague from Hunter's English department secretarial pool, an intractably (by me, anyway) shy Turkish girl with what you were then in the habit of calling "splendiferous gams"? (You'll tell me I'm inventing, Ives, but I'll never forget how you incanted the phrase, whispering it in my ear even after we'd picked up the girls.) I think her name might have been Ola, or Olega, or Omega, or some such. You and your not-yet-intended squabbled about something, some mix-up about a dinner you'd planned with her brother, with a displaced sexual intensity that could still, at that time, embarrass me even when not in the company of an evident Turkish-father-certified virgin. Just after I'd returned with a first round of beers (a solitary buyer was allowed to purchase four Schlitzes in those days), wondering whether it might be the first loco juice ever to pass those fulsome Turkish lips, Lenny Randle hit a high, twisting foul that came our way. My way, specifically, as the two girls were between us in the seats and your future-betrothed dived into your lap in fear. I juggled the cardboard tray of beers hopelessly, and Olega or Omega leaned into me—I felt her bosom compress against my arm, the only time I would—and made a sterling two-handed grab only inches above the beers, my crotch, and disaster. This was in the days before hideous wolf whistles would have over-whelmed the authentic, good-hearted cheering for her feat, and as she reseated herself, to examine the stitching and the smudge of Randle's black-enameled bat, several sections gave her a standing ovation. Might have been the best catch of the game, for all I recall about the game. And that you went home with your future divorcée, while the Turk went home with the ball, and I went home alone. You and I may be possessors of the longest streak of games attended without retrieving horsehide, Ivan. We've never actually discussed this. If so, and if—follow me here—our streak is analogous to the Mets' inability to throw a no-hitter, then the Turk's grab was the equivalent of Seaver's "Imperfect Game," the very nearest we've ever come. And, perhaps, were ever meant to come.

I have nothing to add on the subject of Shea Stadium or the Olympics, except that obviously, if the benighted event should actually take place, I'm putting all my money on the Turkish women's teams, in any sport. As for Queens, it can take yours and Bloomberg's imputations. It's taken worse, over the years. As a native of the Borough of the Dead, I receive your scorn as Mets fans do while enduring the gloating of the Evil Empire, and let that small guilt trip stand in place of any passive-aggressive gambits on my part. My aggression, and Queens', is too passive today.

Returning to my small exile, on Saturday night, with my duties completed and a flight home within sight, I allowed my students to lure me from the Ramada for a drink on Augusta's main drag, Broad Street. We visited the Soul Bar, a loud, cheery, high-ceilinged place festooned with James

Brown posters and other hipster evidence, and thankfully free of the autographed Greg "The Shark" Norman posters and other golf memorabilia that festooned my hotel and every restaurant I entered for three whole days. My students were not really a bad bunch, full of wonder at the possibility of living one's life as a writer (if only I could make them truly see!), though when they switched to swilling shots of something cough-syrupy I blanched (I like my juice a bit less loco, thanks), and walked back to the hotel. But before I did I noticed something rather uncanny: behind the bar, mounted on a mirror amidst the stickers mentioning names of bands that might as well be fictional so far as I knew, was a decal that read: "Vote for Pedro." This was the first time I'd seen the phrase, which you spotted somewhere in Soho or Chelsea or NoLita if I recall correctly. A meme grows.

> Still open to the wonder of it all,
> Harris

P.S. The Ramada's cable package left much to be desired, and with the U.S. Open—more golf!—all over ESPN, I didn't even get game recaps. So I learned of Thursday's, Friday's, and Saturday's games by reading the gnomic crawl of scores beneath the golf. Speaking of haiku, those crawls can be strangely expressive. Take Thursday's 9–6 win over Oakland, our sole oasis in this latest desert of runs. I exulted at the score, until the crawl followed with: "Graves, 1 IP, 4 ER." Ah. So much for the relief pitcher for the relief pitchers. Remember when they used to call them "firemen"? I suppose it's as true in baseball as in the "real world": that arsonists dwell frequently among their ranks.

P.P.S. We only hit for Benson now? Perhaps there's more to our theory than we'd realized. Perhaps the other guys feel bad about his wife. Or good about her.

June 21

Conk:

O Brother, Where Art Thou? Your Southern experience brings a chill reminiscence. The last time I was there was to attend a conference at the Savannah College of Art and Technology (aka "SCAT"). Golf would have been a welcome theme. It was on the eve of the Gulf War and the members of the 3rd Infantry had been released from Fort Stewart to celebrate what as far as we all could ascertain was their upcoming deaths at the hands of the Revolutionary Guard. What I recall most clearly was the sight of a young woman—a "herald of death," as I believe I drunkenly and repeatedly put it to the very attractive cross-dresser with whom I intended to demonstrate my tolerance and open-mindedness to myself— whose leg had been amputated at the hip, dancing wildly with all the young soldiers.

Of course, that wasn't even the bad part. The conference was entitled "Nearing Noir: Toward a Comprehensive Definition." That would have been the 612th inning of that particular can of worms. I was booed off the dais for suggesting that in its exploration of light and shadow, in its preoccupation with Freudian analytic technique, in its highly symbolic yet wholly unmetaphoric approach to the mystery genre, the work of John Franklin Bardin certainly deserved the retrograde awarding of the title "noir" more than that of the gaudy Chandler or the rankly incompetent Woolrich—if, that is, one was even willing to extend the designation outside the realm of cinema. With that, violence seemed to swell in the crowd of young scholars. A guy who'd just made a big splash with a monograph on the philosophy of Bazooka Joe— maybe you remember it, it was called "The One-Eyed Man Is King"—told me I was out of order and made a threatening gesture with the light saber he was carrying. That was all it took. I can't remember their faces, the leaders who whipped the crowd into its frenzy, but I remember their bona fides: editors from *Eye Scream*, a movie zine; the author of *The Golden Echo: The Films of Douglas Sirk*; a professor of Commemorative Stamps and Cereal Boxes; and especially the publisher of *Brasher Doubloon: The Chandler Gazette*. Opportunistically taking advantage of the emotional outpouring were my long-term nemeses and fellow commodity aestheticians, the editorial board members of *BURN DOWN THE MALL!*, if you remember that desperate rag. They called loudly for me to be strung up—this is the South we're talking about, mind.

Enough reminiscing.

It's always seemed to me that a ballpark with nobody in it is one of the most tragically unrealized of structures. Null in a way that an empty office building, or even an empty theater, is not. It's sort of like a big prosthesis waiting for its host. It's missing everything it needs without the crowds, the smells, the sound effects, the transubstantiative change that the utterly predictable patch of real estate undergoes when the players take the field—magic!, and the astonishing knowledge that it's the population of a small city concentrated there, in the most un-citylike of spaces, communing amid the tiers.

(Do you have the same habit I do, of instantly translating military and wartime deaths into ballpark attendance figures? I think of Vietnam and I picture Shea Stadium packed to the rafters with ghostly servicemen. World War II, 500 Sheas, SRO.)

Empty, there's enough essence remaining, like the clothes a lover leaves behind, to leave the place charged with spooky meaning, to point out its skeletal inadequacy in its emptiness. So I think I know what you mean—but isn't a batsman something out of cricket?

Ah, Ozlem—the name means *yearning*. I had quite a thing for her myself, you know. The second Mrs. Felt certainly knew. We had some fun discussions about that—perhaps that was the sublimated issue that lay beneath the brother-dinner quarrel you recall, though her brother was a fucking prick named Frank, thought he was the king of Court Street or something, one of those small-time Mafiosi who collect on a couple of cigarette machines. He had this crew of morons from the local orphanage doing his bidding. Sick stuff. Anyway, to avoid spending time with him I would have shot myself in the foot, and so the intensity of which you speak may simply have been my frantic attempt to avoid inflicting grievous injury upon myself. My second marriage started sustaining such body blows long before it even occurred.

Ozlem later went to grad school. It may torture you to learn that her major field of interest was pornography. She caused quite a sensation when she included her entire catalog of hands-on fieldwork in the bibliography of her dissertation. The only title that comes to mind is "Vacuum Hoes."

She did catch that ball, though. I remember holding it, caressing the smooth horsehide and those impossibly large red stitches, reading the lettering designating it an "Official National League Baseball" when the designation—National League hitters, pitchers, umpires, parks, and even equipment were different!—still meant anything. I remember thinking how easy it would be to overpower her, to just withhold the baseball from her. But I knew that I was merely an impoverished TA and she—whatever you happen to think may or may not have passed her lips—possessed both the ear and at least one other part of the anatomy of the department chair. Anyway, maybe it's not meant to be—but at least you didn't get doused with four piss-water beers, and anytime we spring to sit below upper reserved I'm going to bring my glove. You know as well as I that sitting all the way up there we might as well be watching from a midtown saloon for all the foul balls that are going to come our way.

Let me preface this by saying that I'm convinced the phrase has been co-opted by Mets fans for our own purposes. But I spoke to my daughter, enthusing about Pedro— indulgently, she pretends to share my interest in the Mets—and I mentioned the "Vote for Pedro" shirt. She shook her head and mentioned a movie that she said I "had to see" called—oh shit, what was it called? *TNT Bonaparte*, or something? *Napoleon TNT*? Something explosive, jarring, and discordant, a name like a Baskin-Robbins flavor. Apparently the phrase is, like so much nowadays, a catchphrase, a quote.

So it goes.

I have felt frozen and mortified since the Mets fell into the rabbit hole after the Saturday night triumph against the Angels. This is too much, I was thinking. The whole team should lie on the couch and discuss its fear of success, talking it out to the stained acoustical tiles in the drop ceiling of the clubhouse. Of course the Mets would lose five of six against the two worst teams in the AL West! And can we please cancel the interleague experiment? Bring back the Mayor's Trophy Game!

Time Warner update. My call was passed down amongst various customer service reps, each of whom offered a variation on that old hit "Your Address Is Unserviceable," until on the last transfer I landed in the sensuous hands of Angela, who as usual pretended that we'd never spoken. I could marry this woman, Conk, I really could, the dynamic of the relationship is increasingly familiar: *I'm going to repeat myself while not listening to a word you say.* My unattainable object becomes to make my point, and yet language—always my principal device for controlling reality—continues to fail me. That's at least one wife right there. Talking to Angela is what it must be like to take a bride from Japan or Russia who speaks not a single phoneme of English—though that scenario calls up cozy images of a loving couple snuggled together with a Japanese-English dictionary, pointing at objects and giggling. *Toaster. Cat. Jackrabbit vibrator.*

Angela told me that technicians "couldn't gain access" to my address. They'd showed up, then left. She explained, for the first time in our customer serviceship, that I would have to remain home to provide access to "surveyors" who would need to check pads, splitters, carburetors—I didn't concern myself with the technical details. So I was very frank with Angela. I want our relationship to improve. I told her that I felt she wasn't responding in a creative, productive, or helpful way to my repeated queries. That I was very close to drawing the conclusion that even the diligent application of my efforts would yield nothing. I told her that I felt tremendous sympathy for her; that she had been deprived of the information she needed to speak knowledgeably, articulately, and consistently; that her job was not to provide assistance but to thwart the complaints of baffled customers. She advised me that she would reinstate the order, that it would probably be done "by Saturday." That's June 25.

By hook or by crook, willy-nilly, I'll have cable by the All-Star game!

Ivan

P.S. Speaking of the Mets' run production for Benson, you saw the stat in the *Times* today?

GAMES	RUNS
2	12
2	9
1	8
2	7

Still, my old pal Braden Looper just had to hit the first man and allow the second to reach on an infield hit. In *Times*-speak, this somehow translates into "pitchers Royce Ring, Roberto Hernandez, and Looper logged three scoreless innings to preserve the victory for starting pitcher Kris Benson." Looper is always hovering over the jaws of victory, daring himself to stick his hand in.

June 23

Ivan,

Ozlem, Ozlem, how could even a sensibility as decrepit as mine have forgotten your name? That she descended (or ascended?) into the field of porn studies is hardly a non sequitur, for that catch of hers was a kind of erotic scene—gratuitous, heartbeat-skipping, and absolutely devastating to the narrative ostensibly meant to contain it. Who did we play that day? Did we win or lose? Who cared, even instants after we'd witnessed her climactic moment, attained without male assistance?

May I someday feel the same about last night's botch against the Phils, Heilman betraying our confidence, our we-know-better-than-the-manager assumptions that he should either start or close, by divulging five runs to the Phillies in the space described by a single out. Where's my new Ozlem—little as I got out of the Turk, she's still etched in sensual memory, a Proust-cookie—to divert me from this latest of our declined opportunities? This was a game that wasn't close, though Zambrano even pitched well, in his daredevil, load-up-the-bases fashion. Piazza hit a homer, albeit quite hopeless, after we were six down. I even graded a batch of late term papers, submitted after granted extensions. These three phenomena have something in common:

they characterize a universe running frantically just to keep in place, like Lewis Carroll's Red Queen.

Speaking of which, I'm not one of your students, so put away your red pencil. Sure, I can't remember what month it is, and I called Shea's neon figure a "batsman." But don't scorers and announcers routinely tabulate a pitcher's or staff's accumulation of "hit batsmen"? Therefore, thanks to my psychic slip, we finally understand what's being portrayed by the stadium's mighty neon figure: he's twisting his body in the act of getting plunked.

Love,
Harris

- -

June 24

Conk:

Just a quick one; re: the "batsman"—I think we both knew he sure as hell wasn't getting a hit!

Ives

4

[*July*]

TIME WARNER CABLE
"The Power of You™"
120 East 23rd St.
New York, NY 10010

LEGAL DEPARTMENT

M E M O R A N D U M

JULY 3, 2005

To: Mr. Howard Szarfarc
     President
Fr: Adam Riggler, Esq.
     Associate Corporate Counsel
Re: Felt Incident

Attached is a relevant excerpt from the complete transcript of the conversation between Mr. Ivan Felt and our employee Angela Marciano.

As you can see, Mr. Felt appears to be a somewhat ex-citable individual whose preexisting mind-set determined his regrettable course of action more than any potential "incitement" on the part of TWC's Customer Service Repre-sentative. His mishap on the roof of his domicile, while un-fortunate, is wholly of his own making. In my opinion, TWC's legal exposure in this matter is minimal.

In my opinion it would be inadvisable at this time to pur-sue legal action against Mr. Felt for vandalism of TWC prop-erty and/or attempted theft of services, though I agree with you in principle that an example must be made of each of those individuals who commit such acts.

FOR INTERNAL USE ONLY

PARTIAL OFFICIAL TRANSCRIPT
TELEPHONE CONVERSATION BETWEEN
REPRESENTATIVE 143C AND CUSTOMER FELT, IVAN
ORDER NUMBER 05—XC12798IN
1100 HOURS
1 JULY 2005

FELT: *Systemic problems like these need to be addressed, wouldn't you agree, Angela? Can you imagine, hello, can you imagine Verizon or Con Ed declining to pro-vide service on this basis? Refusing to expedite the cus-tomer's diligent good-faith efforts to obtain, hello, service, and unable to, to, to offer a coherent and un-derstandable explanation for the denial of service?*

143C: *Sir I understand your frustration but*

FELT: *No I don't think you do Angela I have now made by my records, just a second, let me [unintelligible] here we are according to my records this is call number um eight   eight calls and this is New York City in the 21st century the last time I checked am I correct.*

143C: *You are correct sir.*

FELT: *About the eight calls or the 21st oh never mind   I am telling you that apartments 2R and 4R and 4F and um 3F are currently receiving service and that 3R had been until fairly recently I guess   I asked her myself and my apartment might have been somehow left out? You bill 2R and the rest do you not? You collect money? From these, um, accounts?*

143C: *It is our policy that we have to do a serviceability check before we can install*

FELT: *Angela, you've [unintelligible] very very clear but what I'm getting at is that you are arguing on [unintelligible] inefficiency, sheer inefficiency, why not just   listen, just send an installation guy, I'll be here, if it doesn't doesn't work I'll pay, I'll pay for the privilege of not having cable installed isn't that an offer you can't refuse?*

143C: *We can't sir sir one moment we can't*

FELT: *[unintelligible] in touch with a corrupt tech, there's got to be at least one crooked guy hanging around the motor pool, you know who I'm talking about, the type, my dad used to be a union man, you know what a union is you poor kid, a corrupt guy who breaks all the rules, just tell him that I'll pay him to come over, come on, I*

143C: *We do not have anybody like that working here sir*

FELT: *Yeah tell me another one Angela, let me explain.*

There are cables on the roof going into one of those lit-
tle whatchamacallits, those things the cables go into,
you know? Angela?

143C: *Sir*

FELT: *I plug a cable into the back of my TV and run it*
through my window and plug it into the thing and I bet
I just bet I get programming

143C: *Sir I would advise against that*

FELT: *Why? It's illegal? Piracy? But wouldn't it prove the*
apartment is serviceable? I make a quick call and say,
hey it works and you run out, not you you but you
know, and you install it. [unintelligible]

143C: *Sir first we have to*

FELT: *Come arrest me if it's piracy, I have the perfect de-*
fense, which is your own statements that I can't possi-
bly get cable, here, in Manhattan, in the early stages of
the 21st century. Angela this is wrong, just [unintelli-
gible] wrong

Felt pushed hard against the steel door that opened onto
the roof of his apartment building. It swung open, revealing
the roof's defamiliarizing view of the neighborhood. He
strode out onto the lumpy surface, blemished with splotches
of tar, and stood there, arms akimbo, surveying the scene.
Here was a barbecue grill. Here was a coleus plant. Here was
a folding plastic chaise longue. Surrounding roofs had hot
tubs, elaborate lighting systems, gas-fired outdoor ranges.
His was a humble renters' roof. But we all share our connec-
tion to the great humming feed of news and entertainment
programming, do we not? And now Felt was about to become
Of the Body! Here were the lengths of black-sheathed cable

snaking across the surface of the roof to drop down the side of the building, where each disappeared through its own tiny hole drilled next to one of the windows facing the air shaft. Up top they ran together, conjoining at a little bejacked device that then fed a single cable into an official-looking gray metal box attached to the side of the building. If Felt could run a cable from his own TV set to the roof and then plug it into one of the electronic udders of the little device that gave suck to the other four cables, he'd be in business. He studied the device, feigning expertise, then backtracked to the edge of the roof, the low parapet that looked down upon the street. It would be easier, he guessed, just to run the cable straight up the front of the building rather than via the air shaft. He could carry it up the fire escape. None of his yuppied co-renters would notice; they'd be out turning the crank at whatever money-printing factory they worked at. He bent over and peered down. The fire escape leading from the top-floor apartment was a good ten feet below the surface of the roof, and there was no ladder leading to it from up here. He'd have to carry the cable up, then toss it like a lariat onto the roof. Could he manage? He leaned out a little farther. His reading glasses slipped out of his pocket and he reached—

---

july 6

conk,

i am writing this in lc like ee cummings or in any case like joel oppenheimer (a fellow believenik) to stress that it even hurts to hit the shift key. a herniated disk. like jake barnes's friend i have gone bankrupt two ways, gradually at first and then suddenly. dr. sandhipal says the 'three rs' will guide my treatment. that is, rest, relaxation, renunciation. he found his little joke to be very funny. 'the patient must not scale the rooftop of his apartment. he will cause his physician to feel inadequate and out of condition.' who's the kid fooling. he has the body of a marathon runner. but the loneliness of the long distance runner is mine. tom courtenay. billy liar. julie christie. shampoo. warren beatty. parallax view. hume cronyn. shadow of a doubt. alfred hitchcock. family plot. bruce dern. long distance runner. i still got it, conk. percodan notwithstanding. i'm not withstanding much either though. ouch, ouch, ouch. here's something you could do for me. i practically laughed out loud at you when you offered to look in on i believe was your phrase gena. i am sorry. i know it was a good-hearted gesture and a generous one. may i please redeem the rain check i took then and ask you to visit the girl. the problems remain the same, the difficulties with the child's biological mother. would that she had a sunny and nurturing adoptive mother. in fact she'd be better off if she had a comfy orthopedic pillow like the one st. vincent's sent me home with. nicest thing in my bed in six months.

time for another percodan.

conk let me know if you can manage this.

i.f. /no truer inits were ever penned/

ps/ can't believe we lose to gnats 3–2, wasting that fine pedro start.

Dear Ivan,

I send you well wishes on death row, the death row we all inhabit (even cummings eventually couldn't evade CAPITAL punishment) with news that may be relevant: with our team's help, I've discovered that limbo and satori are the true states. Nothing lives, but then again, at least nothing dies. Zero-sum karma is universal law. Flux, monotony, stasis—you'll get better, you'll get worse, it'll all even out in the end. The proof? For the twentieth time this season the Mets' record is becalmed. We landed at .500 four days ago, two days ago, and again last night. The vice president may have to be called in to break the senatorial deadlock. Schrodinger opened his box and someone had made off with the cat. The voice of the team is heard, producing a deep utterance— "maybe." And heads are turning, the world is beginning to prick up their ears at the sound, the great nullity issuing from Shea, from the Team That Might As Well Never Have Played—we're threatening to become some kind of paradigm of five-hundredness, of pure diffidence in a baseball uniform. Few teams have ever been so five-hundred as us. We're the world's tallest midget, the world's shortest giant, the world's fattest thin man, the world's hungriest—well, you get the point.

Here's my vow to you in your ruined state: for every day from here on that the Mets settle again—from either direction—into their characteristic state of indeterminacy, I'll offer them a poem. Not only that, but I'll vary them amongst trad forms. To begin, a pantoum.

Pantoum of the Five-Hundred Team

Equilibrium's no crime in May or June
Come July it seems a sodden doom.
Aaron Heilman's languishing, entombed.
Braden Looper's grimace, a cartoon.

Come July, it seems, a sodden doom
Pervades a team whose bullpen's wholly porous.
Braden Looper's grimace, a cartoon
Of stoicism enduring boo-birds' chorus.

Pervades a team whose bullpen's wholly porous:
A ragged resentment in the starter's precincts.
Of stoicism enduring, boo-birds' chorus;
Exists both grains in Met-fan instincts.

A ragged resentment in the starter's precincts,
Though Pedro chortles as if sipping nitrous.
Exists a grain in Met-fan instincts,
Believing baseball gods may yearn to smite us.

Though Pedro chortles as if sipping nitrous,
He weaves his pitches with a sober loom.
Believe, though baseball gods may yearn to smite us,
Equilibrium's no crime. In May or June.

There's the first poem. May it be the last (but I doubt it).
All flippancy aside, terribly sorry for you in your pain. You
sounded horrific on the telephone. I mean that in the most
sympathetic possible way. Empathetic too. What ages you,

ages me. And needless to say, I'm more than willing to look in on Gena. Advise, listen, spy, anything. Glad you felt you could ask, after that hiccup of misunderstanding those weeks ago. Stay off rooves (roofs?), pal.

Avuncular, elephantine, staunch,

Harris

- -

July 11

    He ordinarily avoided the L train. There was something bitter, something corrosive, something toxic to Harris Conklin's native outerborough heart in that subway line's literal manifestation of gentrification's plunge into the deepening reaches of north Brooklyn—Williamsburg, Bushwick (now renamed East Williamsburg), Bedford-Stuyvesant, beyond. The L train, like a hollow spear carrying poison, this was the image Conklin found himself reaching for. A hollow spear carrying poison, one thrust deep into Brooklyn's heart. Or a cartoonishly huge doctor's hypodermic, injecting the essence of the "East Village"—white suburban youths bedecked in false-proletarian costume, or in black Goth disguise, or in red patent-leather or vinyl breeches (there must be a more recent word, but Conklin couldn't dredge it up), toting pebbled black portfolios and sketchbooks, tinkering on open laptops even as the train rumbled beneath the East River, oblivious to the city's fading aura of vigilance and fear, kissing and flirting on the station platforms, disembarking to nightclubs, coffee shops, boutiques—deep and then deeper into the heart of the old immigrant preserves.

Yes: the subway train a hollowed spear filled with gentrification's venomous essence. Or hypodermic. He'd have to choose. Brooklyn a heart in either instance. No doubt on that one. Then burnish the image in mind's ear until it screamed "poem." Draft the poem. Revise the poem. Submit to The New Yorker *first, as ever, an act less of faith than of enduring misery given voice (he'd collected more than three hundred of their superciliously genteel rejections), a sort of keening in postal form. Send one copy to Philip Levine, a sentimental flourish. Expect nothing there. Selfish bastard. Then, collecting* The New Yorker's *slip, submit to* Kenyon, *submit to* Antioch, *submit to* Triquarterly, *all the old names. Then the newer names:* ZYZZYVA, Backwards City, Fence, N+1, Empty Bowl, Versegasm. *Children (or so he judged, from their scrawl or syntax) were often kinder to him than his peers, truth be told. More patient. He kept a file card inked with fountain pen, one for each poem, in a small gray-painted steel box, some poems requiring the stapling of a second file card to a first. Then a third. Keep them in the post, out of the house, that was the game.* Glimmer Train, Lullaby Hearse, Orphan Leaf, Fourth Coast. *Submit, submit, submit. Submit. Brakes screaming, the L shuddered into the Montrose Avenue station. Conklin nearly missed the doors, stood on the platform jolted from the depths of his reverie, heart pounding.*

On the street he felt far from home, disconcerted, lost. In part it was the burp in midsummer's flow—no Mets tonight, nor last night, nor tomorrow night. The All-Star break, which felt like one this year. Felt, spine nearly broken, groaning in his recovery room. Conklin just plain broken up, and far too easily. He found himself weeping lately at the sight of his old '69 pennant, an orange felt triangle proclaiming WORLD CHAMPIONS. Just a deep chestal sob, a moistening of the eyeballs, a pruning of the chin. Nothing worse. Still, he'd had to put the pennant in a drawer. The Mets sustained and drained him, that vernal ebb and flow. He loathed the break. At least tomorrow he could watch the contest itself, Piazza and Beltran in the starting lineup. Two ambivalent cases there. But the sacred uniform, represented amidst the league's others, in motion on a field of emerald—he knew well enough it could stir him.

Tonight, nada. The home-run derby, the stupidest single night in baseball's year.

So, his errand instead. Keep one's eye on the chance of doing service to helpless, injured Felt, small enough return on so many years' good faith, dragging Conklin out of the house, to games, to book parties, to Chinese restaurants where they'd sometimes cross the room on Ivan's steam and chance a proposition across a booth table full of moo goo gai pai, dare some pair of ladies to join them. That Felt's own pitching seemed slightly to thrive on proximity to Conklin's hung curves, bounced sinkers, passed balls, balks—Conklin told himself again and again never to think this way.

Number 249, Ten Eyck Street, apartment 4L, this was it. A tenement, the only word. Somehow, despite the mocking tone, Ivan's earlier letter had implanted the image of a boarding house on a shady block—think Sophie's Choice. Nope. This was pure Daniel Fuchs out here. Except the

Hasids had given way to Dominicans long ago. Conklin buzzed.

"Czzxxxxhghhr?" That's how he'd have rendered the sound emitted from the speaker.

"Gena?" he replied. "It's me, Harris Conklin."

"Czzzxxxxhghhr."

He waited, expecting the door to be unbolted. Instead, nothing. Then, peering through the chicken-wired glass, Harris saw besneakered feet leading upward to bejeaned legs, moving down the stairs. He straightened himself and backed away, not wishing to seem impatient or peepish. So, she wouldn't invite him upstairs. Was something being kept occult there? A "works" for preparing baggies or vials of some illegal stash? (Would he even recognize such a thing?) Or, more likely, a fellow, a roustabout, addict, laggard, pirate, or pimp? Had Conklin already failed Felt in his capacity as mole—if that was, indeed, what he was meant to be doing here—by not insisting on penetrating Gena's domicile? She opened the building's outer door.

The hair was hardly so grotesque as "fuchsia." Either Felt had been blinded by a progenitor's morbid disapproval, or she'd altered the shade. Henna, Conklin was certain that from his teaching he could name the hue—and, come to think of it, the faintly yeasty smell. Anyway, if it had been fuchsia, so what? Gena was "put together," that was the only poetry Harris could make of his first impression. Every lineament of her mother's beauty, yet uninflected by Felicia Felt's acrimony. The night was hot, the sidewalks and pavements still shouting heat back at the sun which had cooked them and then departed. Gena had no sleeves, nor any covering nearer than two inches from her navel in either direction. There were no burns, none at all, on her golden Cleopatrian arms. Her tattoo read, opaquely, "Donnie Darko."

"When we spoke on the phone I wasn't certain if you remembered me," he said. "Does the face ring a bell? Or a buzzer, ha ha?"

She grinned and touched his shoulder. "Harris, you must be crazy. I grew up with you."

No, he wanted to cry, that was someone else. Two someone elses. A child, and a father's friend. He failed to speak.

"You look just the same except all this is so white." Now it was his temple she touched. And ear. "And that beard is awfully sincere. You look kind of emo."

"I promised your father—he's laid up—you know of course—"

"Right, you said. Promised him what?" Her gaze was sweet, exact, and a hairbreadth from mockery.

It was as though father and daughter had conspired in satirizing Conklin's kindest impulses. He'd be damned if the phrase "look in on you" would blurt from his mouth, though. "About your mother. I mean, Ivan said she'd been giving you a hard time."

"My father does a lot of projecting. Felicia's voice mails bother him, not me. I usually delete before she's done talking."

"Ah."

"But it's nice of you to come all the way out here."

He didn't know how to tell her that he'd come from even farther "out"—since he knew the mileage from Washington Square Park would certainly be her standard. Just one of so many things he didn't know how to tell her. This extraordi-

nary woman. If only she would stop acting so familiar, as if she were truly a self continuous with the wailing, grubby child he largely recollected. Or the acned, elbowy, quite bucktoothed thirteen-year-old he was fairly certain he'd last glimpsed, seated miserably in the second row (behind a vacant first) at the St. Mark's Poetry Project, back when her father was still capable of dragging her to one of Harris's readings.

He mentally shredded the unwritten poem of half an hour before. Yes, the L train had borne Gena here, an injection straight from Greenwich Village, from the walk-up where she'd come of age steeped in Ivan and Felicia's terroristic rages. Yet that hollowed spear—hollowed flaming spear, he thought now—had embedded not in Brooklyn's heart but in his own.

"Well," he said. "We could—is there a local place you like—we could have tea—iced tea, I mean—"

"Why don't we catch a flick, as my dad would say?"

---

july 13

hareris, i have languished my message unanswered. cold comfort that i can watch the so-called all-stars on good ol broadcast television. for the dh and for harboring the yankees and for foisting the milwaukee brewers upon us the american league deserves little but censure dammit. you watch it, question mark, or did you say fuck it. you turned against the whole affair long ago memory suddenly served up. hard to blame you   that ghost town of detroit, enjoy the party suckers. i could use a party sucker around now. ha ha ha   you know it doesn't hurt when i laugh just two home row fingers   thank god for typing the key to computer literacy   thank god for ms. schultz and her gleaming row of olivettis in i.s.70   i'd like to thank ms. schultz and her patience and her glossy and protuberant permanent surely a genetic precursor of rick peterson   i am wondering conk   serious again here did you talk to gena   phone rings and i think deliver me and my daughter sweet god of my christian friends   from felicia   the third missus felt   i should leave her off like the 13th floor of a postwar high-rise   just missus one two and four   three a disastrous nonstart like apollo one   or french connection two   felt three

perk o'dan,
ivan fell

- -

July 14

Ivan,

The first game of the second half. Watching on the tube, I was able to lip-read Kris Benson, standing in the dugout in the seventh, when Jose Offerman, pinch-hitting, singled to tie the game: "Yeah, motherfucker, yeah!" Perhaps the fellow has depths we've overlooked?

Piazza won it with a three-run homer in the ninth. I sensed shades of 2000, of a younger Mike stirring inside his crotchety carapace, aroused by the fervor of the "New Mets." Perhaps this present agglomeration of men bearing the sacred brand name has depths we've—well, not overlooked, but persuaded ourselves we'd only persuaded ourselves of?

This one felt wild and fine, my friend. I may not need to write so many poems after all. Not to shirk my muse, but I'd rather be at Benson's metaphorical shoulder, bellowing obscenities.

> Glistening with Believenik perspiration,
> H.

P.S. Oh, almost forgot. I wandered 'round Gena's place. Nothing wrong there. She's fine. She's great. No worries. None at all.

> July 15, back to .500
> (postcard)

The Carol of the Five-Hundred Team

Wright, MVP of some future season.
Reyes, lunging at what's in the dirt.
Piazza, still playing, for no reason.
Floyd, behind his eyes, eternal hurt.
These Mets are awfully young.
Their song yet hardly sung.

Up the middle, consider Cairo,
Bulwark of sturdy sufficiencies.

Or Matsui, bicontinental rookie,
Tableau of callow deficiencies.
These Mets are awfully old.
Their fortune long since told.

To contend would be stretching, yet
Rebuilding's no Gothamite's pleasure.
So, alert to fannish kvetching, Met
Officials seek free-agent treasure.
These Mets are awfully young.
Their song yet hardly sung.

Which points to that idol of bafflement:
Beltran, not young nor old, but between.
His only stellar numbers in October.
A month in which the Mets may not be seen.
These Mets are awfully old.
Their fortune long since told.

July 17, back to .500
(postcard)

The Double-Dactyl of the Five-Hundred Team

Sacrifice-hackrifice
William L. Randolph
Grumbles intensely but not
To the press,

Assigns fundamental drills
Extracurricular
Hoping to bunt his way
Out of this mess.

July 19

Ivan,

Here, under a fatalistic shroud of humidity and talk of
Supreme Court justices, is where a season deepens into the
murk, teams grow thorns, tusks, and tumors, lineups curdle,
a player somewhere is "released" while another decides to
live with his injuries without informing his manager, and we
brace ourselves against the chance of a panicky trade—
farewell, we hardly knew ye, to Diaz? To Heilman? The tale
grows old, blurs into memories of other seasons (the Yankees overtook the Red Sox for first place last night—snore—
and the Braves are tugging on the Nationals' collar),
wondering whether next year is in fact this year or whether
it might actually, um, be next year. All of this is to say that
the San Diego Padres have made their annual visit to Shea
Stadium, a guarantee that the earth's eyes are elsewhere. But
a Believenik's eyes are faithful, and thanks to the magic of
satellite television, I was aboard. The season is old now, Ives,
but somehow our team is still a newborn, a tabula rasa. We
discover ourselves anew each night—we're the Mets! We can
pitch! Hit? Just a little! Our relievers will walk you!

Ah, the Padres, whose mustard-brown souls cannot be
concealed by their generically awful new uniforms (they

look exactly like the Blue Jays now—and have you seen the Blue Jays lately? They're not looking like themselves, but rather, like the Padres). How far can you go with a monk with a tonsure—a double image of enfeebled manhood—emblazoned on your shoulder? This team is loaded with so many journeymen (they just picked up our old friend Pedro Astacio, by the way) that I began to speculate whether such a thing as a journeyman opponent existed—a journeyman franchise, perhaps. (Though I suppose you'd reserve that for a team that really had wandered from place to place—the Braves?) Does it even seem possible that this franchise has gone to the Series twice? They never seemed in any danger of winning it. And yet how many more decades would have to go by before anyone spoke of a "curse"? They're merely the Padres. Someday Tony Gwynn will be elected to the Hall. Or did that happen already? Could a team like this, Ives, sustain fans like ourselves? The mysteries of bad taste are fathomless. I suppose even David Hasselhoff must have some four-starred, rave reviews on the Amazon page for his musical recordings, yes?

Let's now hoist a glass to Mike Piazza, so recently an attendee, like Huckleberry Finn, at his own funeral (or was it only me who found his elder-statesman's farewell tour of the All-Star game too much akin to a wake?), and who tonight gracefully accepted a demotion to sixth in the batting order, an indignity he'd not suffered, we've been informed several times during the broadcast, since his rookie year. Piazza swapped places, of course, with David Wright, a move I and every caller to WFAN has been advocating for months, and yet it does jostle at the heart a little to see it done—a spadeful of dirt chucked onto the pine coffin. An impact player, as you've said. Cliff Floyd's defiant half season aside, we're not in the company of another such, not yet (ahem, Beltran?), not unless of course you count Pedro, every fifth day. So how does Piazza handle his relegation? Raps two singles and—gadzooks!—throws out Brian Roberts attempting to steal second base.

Benson was the recipient not of the usual barrage of runs but rather of a more typical Met starter's support, and left in the seventh with the game tied one–one. Koo—oh, Koo!—walked two of the lefties he was specially brought in to face, and let another lefty smack a hit off him; his inning was only salvaged thanks to Piazza's uncanny throw to prevent the steal. Following Koo, Old Man Hernandez was glorious as ever. We stranded men on second in each of the last five innings, a deep enunciation of our refusal to budge above the five-hundred mark—could we just keep this game tied, please? No? Oh well, extra innings, then (and our record in extra innings, if you wondered, is 3 and 3). Let's have a look at Braden Looper!

Enough of my play-by-play. You'll have read the newspaper. Piazza slugged another single in the eleventh and Chris Woodward hit a "walk-off" (I'm unsure I can live with that neologism, yet every time I complain in my poetry workshop classes that some item of slang seems too green, too "hip-hop," some wag appears in the subsequent gathering of said class with evidence that said vernacular dates back to the eighteenth century, to newspaper accounts of pirates or roving balladeers or players of the game of "rounders"), driving Piazza and himself home. You'll have read the newspaper, but if you missed this one you'll never know the vast pensiveness—the boredom, truthfully—and the enormity of the relief. Yes, we're a team that won't budge from five hundred, but as Vanessa Redgrave explained to Winona Ryder in *Girl, Interrupted*, the state of *ambivalence* does not consist of a wish to remain inert, but rather of strong twin impulses pulling in opposite directions (ambi: forked; valent: intense). Can these human players bear, as individuals, this course they're on as a team—the infinite vacillation, the straining uncertainty, of being a 2005 Met? From the way they danced in a circle around Woodward as he touched home plate, they might have won the World Series. Had they a wicker man available, they'd have climbed into it and lit the pyre. Had I been on the field, I'd have joined them.

How long since we swept a team? I want us to sweep these guys, Ivan.

Intensely Forked,
Harris

July 20

Harris,

I feel I've arrived at some sort of medical milestone; I can reach for my shift key again. Goodbye, e. e. cummings, back to somewhere I have never traveled. Hello, normative punctuation and capitalization. Now my brain just has to follow my fingers.

Speaking of poems, I've been enjoying yours—not that your poetically illiterate correspondent can make head or tail of them. They seem to me to be beautiful things though, shiny and complete (not like my own work). Inspired, even: I can tell when you're in a cheery mood, Conklin, I really can after all these years. Do explain how it is that when your insistent buddy is laid up for a few weeks your imagination takes flight!

The Padres. How relieved I am about having missed their annual visit, whatever the color of their uniforms this time. I am certain that I've said this before, and no doubt I'll say it again sometime, but certain franchises are terminally self-impugning. No matter how hard they try, and no matter how often they change their uniforms, the Padres always will look to me like nine men whose mothers have dressed them for Halloween as buttered baked potatoes. They can go to the series ten times and their success will still seem the result of a technicality perched atop a series of unlikely events, much like the presidency of Gerald R. Ford. Into this dismal category of illegitimacy I would cast the Texas Rangers, the Colorado Rockies, and any team, like the Tampa Bay Devil Rays, to which over-the-hill players desire to go to enjoy warm weather and proximity to lap dancers. I would count the Milwaukee Brewers, a team that's somehow grown less legitimate over the years, as a recent addition to the list. Possibly it's that horrible ballpark of theirs, which seems to be shaped like a twelve-pack.

Does my heart good to hear of Piazza throwing out a man stealing. Never so bad a catcher as is claimed. Besides, since base stealing is a largely undeveloped skill nowadays, why shouldn't throwing out base stealers be? But we win, we win, ugly coinages (no fan of "walk-off" myself, it makes little sense to me, like the voguish substitution of "walking on eggshells," so confusing to my ear [crunch, crunch, crunch], for the crystal-clear and thoroughly evocative "walking on eggs").

I'm ready, I think, to "do" things. Walk, talk, fart on elevators, and so on. Interested in checking out one of these upcoming games, if not against the Buttered Spuds, then against L.A. (the National League L.A., that is)? You can tell me about your muse, if it's even worth my hoping that's what you've got.

Reporting for Duty,
Ivan

P.S. One final note: Is there not—oh, how would you know this, I only remember it from its presence in one wife or another's arsenal of hair products—a shampoo or some such called "Ambi"? Forked? As in split ends? Hmmmm.

P.P.S. I may be wrong, but I believe Magwich speaks of going to visit someone's "crib" in *Great Expectations*.

- -

July 25

Dear Ivan,

Buzzed by the week of winning at home; high, I will admit it, on feasting and lust and lust's occult partner, shame at feasting (more specifically, I dialed something called 1-800-HOT BIRD and consumed a takeout rotisserie chicken all by myself, doused with some fiery sauce)—in this condition I made a terrible error, Ives. I stayed awake to watch the first game of the road trip, deceiving myself that this could be a good thing, a right choice. Yet our bout of winning was at home in Flushing, on eastern time, against more-or-less "natural" teams—Dodgers, Padres—while this road game was in an unnatural zone, mountain time, against that least natural of teams, the Colorado Rockies. Has it ever struck you that just as Colorado is a kind of imaginary site, an El Dorado or Ocladoro or Odlaroco of white-capped peaks, the Rockies are an imaginary team, saddled with an idiotic dilemma, a weakness-in-strength that makes them like a band of barrel-chested bullies in a kung fu film, the type who, having spent too much time in the weight room, makes an easy target for a more lithe and crafty opponent? They're literally drunk all the time on too little oxygen, like a fish who can't handle shallow water, are too near the roof of their biosphere. Their strivings ought to receive coverage in the Science Times, not Sports. Worse, they're overcompensatingly bland, white, and generically decorated. Have we ever noted that one would merely have to complete the curve of the "C" of their uniform letters (easily done by squinting one's eyes) to behold a team bearing the word "Rookies" on their chests? The Rockies should be exiled to the movies, where they could play the losing team in a saga about the Indians or the Cubs finally attaining glory.

We arrived in town on a drizzly night, just in time for a promotion called Petco Dog Night, in which the Rockies have specified a section in the park where you can bring dogs to watch the game. God help us if the Mets ever sink this low. The Rockies' broadcast crew interviewed a man with a 160-pound Great Dane that had waited with him through the hour-and-forty-five-minute rain delay. Grand fun for the dog,

I'm sure. Early on, Glavine, an older gentleman who'd been on an airplane, then shifted two time zones, then waited through the rain delay for his warm-ups, struggled in the thin air. Reyes, jubilant youth, oblivious to these hardships, hit another triple (he really is looking better and better at the plate). Things degenerated rapidly, however. With the nearly two-hour delay this was the last game being played in all of baseball, and our first night West, and by the fifth inning the batters looked tired and ready to quit. My reward for staying up past one a.m.? That with the Rockies leading 5–3 in the seventh, Mike DeJean, a zombie from the netherworld of our own bullpen, now paradoxically revived by having his lungs denied full breath, mowed down the side, one-two-three.

At times in the eighth inning you could hear, echoing at the edges of the broadcast, dog barks resounding in the vacated stadium. The team was up past its bedtime, as was the Great Dane, as was

Yours truly,

H.

- -

July 28

Harr,

The papers are full of chatter about Floyd and Oswalt: Will Oswalt hit him? Will Floyd charge the mound? Considering that Oswalt isn't supposed to pitch until Sunday, you'd think the series would present more interesting possibilities. For instance, Beltran's return: booing at each sighting of him; you'd think the Astros actually had fans. But more importantly, these Astros are tough, and angry, and are our real competition for the Wild Card. And the rivalry is real; this team's our fraternal twin, the NL's other '62 expansion franchise, neither as well loved, or as well named (they were, after all, the Colt .45s to begin with, and now that "Astros" seems as quaint as those trolleys the Brooklyn team used to Dodge), or even as well housed, mirabile dictu. And their ball field's named after Enron.

I am feeling a little weary. Perhaps it's just our waste of Pedro's start. He gives up two runs, but at 100-plus pitches he's starting to labor, and we pull him. In the ninth, Hernandez leaves one up in the zone with one away, and Ausmus singles in a runner. Oh well.

No, really weary: not even a trek to a bar tonight to watch the game, which was broadcast on WPIX. I just might have been a bit ambitious. As the Mets edge toward .500 I'm feeling something like a .500 person myself.

Sleepily,
Ivan

July 28

I,

Trade talk: apparently we want Manny Ramirez. That's the big buzz. The little buzz, detectable in the chat rooms, says we're talking to Texas about Soriano. I could get excited about either of them, but I have a weird soft spot for Soriano. He's a fellow I always liked despite myself—when he first came up with the Yankees his breakneck, elbows-out grace

reminded me of the cartoon character Felix the Cat, induc-
ing stomach cartwheels of involuntary nostalgia. At the same
moment, the Yankees, desperate to plug in some starting
pitching, have been heard talking about a soon-to-be-released
Hideo Nomo. With this possibility, and thinking of your remarks about Leiter, I made a quick count (okay, not so quick)
(okay, I overheard it on WFAN): Miguel Cairo turns out to be
the 90th player to play for both the Mets and the Yankees. Soriano would be the 91st, Nomo the 92nd. This suddenly began
looking to me like a countdown to—whom? Herewith, a spec-
ulation:

93. Kenny Rogers, 2005. The Yanks, still desperate to plug
    in some starting pitching, on the trading deadline reach
    for the obvious temperamental sequel to the Big
    Eunuch and Kevin Brown.
94. Ricky Ledee, 2006. Acquired from Giants straight-up for
    Victor Diaz, in the off-season. Killed by enraged fan
    who smuggles plastic pistol into Shea, 2008.
95. Mike Piazza, 2006. Designated hitter. Finally gets his
    ring hitting game-winning home run off Mark Mulder in
    game seven of the '06 Series. Retires with 501 home
    runs, goes into the Hall in a Dodger cap.
96. Kaz Ishii, 2006. Hurls a perfect game against the Mets in
    interleague play. In an interview his translator credits
    Pedro Martinez for teaching Ishii, through hand
    gestures, how to retain his focus and thrive in the New
    York environment.
97. Homer Bush, 2007. Fan-favorite backup to oft-injured
    Soriano, hits a career best .312 in 108 plate appearances.
98. Jeff Kent, 2007. Designated hitter. Finally gets his ring

and an ALCS MVP award with a .465 postseason,
including three-homer game off AL Cy Young winner
Scott Kazmir.

99. Bernie Williams, 2008. .238, 5 HR, 32 RBI in two
seasons on Mets bench.

100. Victor Diaz, 2009. After three All-Star seasons the Giants
sell him to New York for prospects and cash at the trading deadline. Goes into the Hall in a Yankee cap, 2023.

H.

July 29

Harris,

Much as I'd like to see Manny come here, it's too perfect
in its way: hometown boy/Red Sox DNA/fierce and perennial
desire to be traded—does this not sound like a recipe for the
Past, Revisited? Cf. Vaughn, Bonilla, Everett. Where's our
Kirby Puckett? Where's our Tony Gwynn?

Speaking of Kirby Puckett, another reason not to ven-
ture too deeply into trade talks with Epstein is the Milledge
kid. Going to be a great one (so great he'll no doubt be the
101st on that Yankees/Mets crossover roster)! But, Harris,
please! Record, shmeckord. That kid was guilty only of having an underage girlfriend. Who can pay attention to such
things? He's eighteen, she's fifteen: I know you can't refer to
personal experience, but no doubt you'll remember how frequently boys who'd reached their legal majority would dally
with girls whose physical flair transcended questions of le-
gality. Try to have an open mind about these things.

I am still tired, but devoted: to my friends (how are ya?), to my family (checked in on the kid lately?), and to my team (I'm reminded of the story of the late great Bob Murphy, who checked into a hotel once after a late and long flight and gave his name as "Robert G. Mets." Lovably addled. Amazing how much more I like Murphy now that he's dead).

Around in Right,
Ivan Metz

July 30

Ivan,

At the end of a lost week in lost places—Colorado and Houston—we've sunk to five hundred, thus I owe you a poem. Tonight Glavine steeled himself to a pitcher's duel with Andy Pettitte, but blinked first. The team's just not hitting, Ives. I think the Good Men of Flushing may be paralyzed by these trade rumors—apparently Minaya's in a parley with the Red Sox front office on the subject of exiling Cameron and our "untouchable" criminal-record-bearing minor-league slugger-prospect Lastings Milledge to Boston, for Manny "Right on the Verge of Recording a Rap LP" Ramirez. I'm enjoying a turmoil of mixed feelings: it's a pleasure to see how Minaya likes to play with real money, and possible to imagine that Manny might benefit from being embraced into Los Latin Mets, yet I'm hardly willing to part with Milledge—that name, if nothing else, is precious. And are we meant to believe this team is ready to make its big run, after such a faltering week? Yet I confess I want Manny, I can't help myself.

I don't want to speak as though I believe or even pretend to believe the New York Mets, either the players individually or the gestalt team-entity, actually know that I, Harris Conklin, exist, but it feels like they're torturing me now with this five-hundred nonsense. Okay, here, I'm certain you're on the edge of your seat:

Theodore Roethke Homage of the Five-Hundred Team

Here in the cellar, dank as a ditch, we still root,
Our tendrils clutching for nurturance in envy.
San Diego's team, inferior to ours, leads its division.
Lolling obscenely from mildewed pates,
Our hopes won't wither here in the manure of
    unreason;
Rather, pulpy, sunk in recall's greenage,
Where Sid Fernandez forever tops the hill,
Ripe, wincing, rotting in the sixth inning,
Tapping leaf-mold from his spikes he hands the ball
To Jesse Orosco or some other capable man.
Loam of yearning, moist with sabermetric fear,
Our dew-dreams feature Reyes stealing home,
And Wright, his uniform immaculately soiled.
Clutching soggy dogs from a seller who rooted too,
The stadium a bog of hope by the time we sang,
Yet in this root cellar, rays shone through chinks.
Nothing would give up life:
Even the sauerkraut kept breathing a small breath.

Yours truly,
Harris "Mossy" Conklin

July 31

Dear Ivan,

I settled in, full of dread, for what couldn't help but feel like an imperative day of DIRECTV, a decisive one for any Believenik's threadbare conviction: the trade deadline was at four, with Manny Ramirez for Cameron-plus-the-future ESPNEWS's most ballyhooed story—a nonstory, the kind they love best—and the team staring down .500 again. We were destined to step into August through the basement entrance either way, but sinking below the sacrosanct threshold, after last week's inklings of glory, seemed too grievous. I hate it when our wards are out of town, Ivan. In Texas. We can do nothing but watch them twist in the wind of rumor—Cameron, of course, but Floyd too looks positively awful, and Randolph is obviously feeling the boys' pain. And by some deviltry our hopes of redirecting fortune and skirting a four-game sweep fell into the hands of none other than Ishii, facing Roy Oswalt (14–8, 2.33) (and by the way, these scrappy, Red Soxian 'Stros, with their three ace starters [two of them Steinbrenner refugees, never forget], look this week like likely repeat Wild Card Titlists to me, much more than any Phils, Fish, Nats, Rats, Cats, Gnats, or Mets).

I set the "PREV" button on my remote to ESPN, which provided a counter reading "MLB Trade Deadline: 2:03 remaining" just as Oswalt served up the first pitch—flipping channels seemed to hold out promise of a mild outlet for my Ishii-itchiness, my sorrow and apprehension. You doubtless recall, Ivan, that I try to take the Sunday *Times* in small doses—Sports first, with my bran and germ and apricots, then the Book Review on the shitter, where as a very young man I learned it belongs ("I am reading your article in the smallest room in my house. Now it is before me, soon it will be behind me . . ." etc.), there to consider the latest pinup novelist (*must* they print their glamour shots?) pillaging my counterculture, and yours, for their "sweeping" "historical" "panoramas" of "homegrown" "American" "terrorism"— really, why can't these smart young men find some subject to call their own? I keep the rest of the paper folded as when I purchased it, to decant in properly homeopathic doses throughout the day. So, it was only during the second inning (down a run, already, Ishii having coughed up a home run to some player I'd never heard of who's got more dingers this year than Carlos "top the ball to second" Beltran—sore point, sure) that I fished out the *Magazine*, to be greeted by the grinning visage of Pedro—speaking of glamour shots— illustrating a lead article (mostly about Minaya and his Dominican minor-league empire, as it turned out, and quite grindingly informative, in a *Times-Magazinian* fashion), entitled "Viva Los Mets."

Wrong Sunday. Wrong year?

Apologies, but I woke up gloomy, friend. "Woe Is Mets" felt more like it.

By the sixth inning the ghost of the Ramirez trade had departed the premises, and soon enough the MLB Trade Deadline ticker was down to 0:00 with no result worth speaking of, for Mets or anyone else. Soriano's still a Ranger, the moon yet orbits the earth, my mother reliably phones on Wednesdays. So, to the game. Floyd, swinging angry, hit a two-run shot to tie it. Sandy Alomar got thrown out arguing a bizarre botched call by a plainly chagrined umpire: our infielders caught Lance Berkman (my favorite Astro, for no reason I can discover, unless it's that he looks like Andy Kaufman pretending) in a rundown and apparently registered an out, only to discover Berkman had meandered from first base because he'd heard the home plate umpire shout "Ball four!"—yet the pitch from Ishii was only a third ball. The ump, unwilling to penalize Berkman for his own flub, absolved the Astros of the out and returned Berkman to first base—so, Alomar was rightly incensed. I couldn't keep from wondering if the umpire had simply tired of waiting for Ishii's inevitable walks and decided to hurry things along.

This led to a fugue: What about an NBA-type change of rules, in which three balls made a walk? Heck, if it were the NBA, they'd award a batter first base for any pitch not in the zone—the One-Pitch Walk! Now, listen: forget the DH, this would be a vibrant alteration to the game! Scads of offense, sure, base runners everywhere, but follow me, Ivan: think of the effect on the art of pitching. Actually, on the art of scouting and signing and developing pitchers. There would be no more Ishiis or Zambranos on this earth—they'd simply vanish. For that matter, no team would have borne a Nolan Ryan or Randy Johnson through his wild years, no matter how good the "stuff." No, every pitcher would aspire to be Pedro Martinez or Greg Maddux, and the typical staff, instead of being loaded with strapping men who threw hard but had no clue, would be jammed with craftsmen, junkballers, surgeons, men like Terry Leach. Terry Leach! Terry Leach, I tell you. Have you ever read Leach's autobiography, *Things Happen for a Reason*? It may be my favorite on my entire Mets Bookshelf.

But I'm unfair, at least today. Ishii shrugged off the

ump's injustice. He walked a few, but survived, and we scrapped our way out of several holes to tie the game, then to go ahead in the eighth, looking as good as we ever could. (Is it true, or just my inkling, that teams receiving a blatant unfairness from the umpire, and who have a coach ejected as a result, usually thrive thereupon?) Floyd, swinging angry again, drove in another angry run. Cameron, swinging angry, boomed two doubles. Beltran, swinging in misery (he'd been booed lustily all week, even for catching flies), lashed a double into the corner of what I shall petulantly call Enron Field. Beltran stole third. I know these things don't need listing, but they were succor in the starved land of my heart. Wright singled Beltran home, the insurance run. Cameron, swinging angry, on the day he was spared exile to Boston, added another. And so on. So, to August a game above .500! Viva los Mets!

Sturdier than I sound,
Harris

P.S. Yankee update: Giambi hit two solo shots, finishing with fourteen homers for the best month of his career. He's the first Yankee to hit fourteen in a month since Mickey Mantle.

P.P.S. This just in at the trading deadline! The Red Sox trade all the black and Latino players on their team straight-up to the Mets for Wright, Benson, Mientkewitz, Piazza, and Glavine! Really, though, what were those Bill Jamesians thinking? I know I've mocked them for underrating Pedro, and for their Millers, Muellers, and Millars, but does this franchise's difficulty with minority players really cloud understanding that Manny Ramirez is one of the league's finest sluggers, and the linchpin of their first-place team's lineup? Perhaps they were misled as to Cameron's skin tone—maybe they thought his *first* name was Cameron, the better to fit with their tradition of Teds, Theos, and Wades. Which raises a question: Why, with those names, were Todd Van Poppel and Andy Van Slyke not Red Sox?

P.P.P.S. Let's welcome them home. They need us. Tuesday, for Zambrano? I feel bad about the guy, he's been trying hard, and come trading-deadline time everyone's always waving the name Kazmir around.

5

The Apple Is Dormant

[*August*]

August 3

Ivan, my Ivan,

Sorry you're still feeling poorly. I held off offering your ticket around as long as I could, thinking you'd rally. So ended up going to the series opener against Milwaukee alone last night, having—well, I did offer the ticket to one—but never mind, never mind. I went to the game, and our section, alone. Which leads to the incredible report I'm here to make this morning. To do with Filthy Pierrot.

If you're capable of bending to retrieve your doorstep's *Times* you'll know this was the night Zambrano finally went wholly off the rails, capitulating four home runs among the first eight Brewers, and plunking one too, for good measure. The trouble with Zambrano is that he doesn't seem to enjoy hitting the, ah, batsman, takes no pleasure in it. Which would, from my perspective, be at least something. The evening's crowd was barely settled in their seats before Randolph had yanked Zambrano for Heilman (who looked superb, of course). Our section seemed particularly sketchy, with no regulars, or so I thought. In Pierrot's seat huddled a skinny fellow wearing a bizarre headset, a device resembling a sort of crash helmet with several antennas and what appeared to be a miniature satellite dish on the crest—a sort of high-tech propeller beanie, that's what it looked to be. I ignored him, figuring another victim of TMRPCS (Technologically Mediated Retreat from the Public Commons Syndrome, pronounced "trumpucks") was hardly my problem, and merely grateful Pierrot was nowhere to be seen. Then, startlingly, I smelled what could only be fresh crepe. The TMRPCS sufferer bore in his lap a tiny circular crepe pan, every bit as high-tech as the helmet, with blinking red, yellow, and green flashing cursor lights to indicate the pancake's degree of doneness, and a neat built-in spout for ejecting the contents of tiny, premeasured, astronaut-sealed packets of batter onto the heated surface. At that moment the satellite dish, and the antennae, and the whole helmet rotated in my direction. The goggles flipped up, revealing the wearer's features. It was Pierrot, Ivan. He scattered shredded Gruyère and crab into the first of the crepes and proffered it, wordlessly. Delicious.

"What's that on your head?" I asked, after I'd rinsed down his offering with a paper cup of Portets Muscadelle. (Still wish he'd bring glass.)

"Achh, mon frere," said Pierrot, shrugging. At first I mistakenly parsed it as one of his endearments. "He sends me zees merde."

"Your brother?"

"He is warking for Gonogo Concept Sarl. You have heared of zees?"

"No."

"Electronics firm, zee vairy best in all of France. Sends me zees, what you call, epitome? Ah, prototype."

"The hat, you mean? Or the cooker?"

"Both. However, with zee hat I won't again bothair."

"What's playing?"

"Behold."

Before I could duck he'd plopped it on my head. It featured the Mets broadcast. Fran Healy and Ted Robinson doing play-by-play, with some color remarks from Keith Hernandez, in Quadraphonic, or Googlephonics, or Surround Sound, whatever the latest name for that atrocity (give me Mono, Ivan, Mono every time). Then Pierrot flipped down the lenses, and I saw the field in triplicate, as HAL or Robby or Gort or NOMAD might have viewed it: highlighted and cropped, with statistical readouts lurking in the corners where there ought to have been a pleasant blur of foul territory and lower seating areas.

Ted Robinson was droning on in his dutiful way about Rudolph's patience with the younger players, his reluctance to hurry Heilman into the rotation—the problem with Robinson is that he's the one-eyed man in the kingdom of the blind, which forces him to play the role of bargainer, apologist, appeaser. Like Kofi Annan, he'll crack one of these days. In the sporting event before me, now rendered as a neon-glazed cartoon, our team was actually creeping back into contention, much thanks to Reyes, a one-man attack this night, with two hits, a run, and an RBI—a young player Randolph wasn't holding back, I'd say.

"No thanks." I thrust the thing off and into Pierrot's hands. It was already reeking of crab-saturated butter. "I get enough of that at home."

"Oui." He reclaimed the greasy science-fiction device, and we began to ignore each other again. The game evolved despairingly, Randolph removing the stellar Heilman for a pinch-hitter, the Brewers tacking on a few more runs. I wished you were with me—I can't handle these kinds of games without you anymore. At some point Pierrot removed the helmet again and placed it on the seat between us.

"Harry, may I ask—you view zee broadcasts in your house?"

"Yes."

"What you tink about zees—Fran Healy?" He pronounced the name *Frown Heedly*—shades of Inspector Clouseau.

"Hopeless," I said. "A total homer. Maybe your brother can invent a chip which edits him out."

"Homer?"

"He roots."

"Ah, oui. He roots maircilessly. Zees is bettair left to zee fans, no?"

"I couldn't agree more," I said heartily, before I could catch myself.

"The fairst inning, he say a ting that perplex-ed me. The Brewairs hit four homer runs—" (He always calls them homer runs, Ivan.)

"Yes, I saw."

"Frown Heedly said, 'Zee apple remains dormant.'"

"Sorry?"

"He said, 'Unless it eez a Met homer run, zee apple remains dormant.'"

"He means the apple, the gigantic papier-mâché apple in the top hat, beyond the outfield." I pointed. "He's just saying that the apple doesn't rise from the hat for a home run by our opponents."

Pierrot offered his most exasperated frown. "But zis is obvious, no? Zees Frown Heedly must be a vairy insecure man."

"Well, I might rather say frustrated, but yes."

"Oui, but zees word, 'dormant'—it is ze same in English?"

"Dormant? Sure, you're right—a French root, dormir."

"Frown zays more than he knows, eh?"

"Sorry?"

"An apple such as zees, a pomme in a chapeau haut de forme, a pomme zat ees dormant . . . zees speaks of faible désir, no?"

"Sorry?"

"Sleeping, yes, but also ze pomme is . . . weak in desire." He spoke knowingly, perhaps a tad leeringly. "Zees is what we say is dormant."

I stared. Pierrot and I were peering together, from opposite banks, into the abyss of translation, where poetry goes to die.

"He didn't mean that," I said, irritated to be in the position of defending Healy, that scrub Yankee, that lifetime .250 hitter. "Sometimes an apple may only simply be sleeping. Not lacking desire in any respect. Merely in abeyance. Resting. Ready at any given time to awaken."

Pierrot closed his eyes and shrugged. "Soit. Tres bien."

It was at that moment, in the seventh, that Wright, the mighty child, hit an enormous solo home run, while Pierrot and I were both distracted by our transatlantic muddle. I won't prettify the situation: we briefly tussled for the privilege of donning his brother's prototype satellite helmet (such things aren't on the market yet, Ivan, are they? Am I hopelessly behind the times?) for the privilege of seeing Wright's shot replayed. I won't brag: I won the tussle. The miraculous helmet broke the home run down by several angles of view, traced its arc in bluish fire, calculated its distance, and showed footage from a pitcher's-mound POV as Wright trotted the bases (really, how do they do all that?).

Mere television, not to mention reality, is doomed. For this night, though, I surrendered the helmet to its owner, and watch au naturel as we staged a bizarro, multistage comeback, the kind of comeback that I believe could be a season's watershed, truly. First, the Mink doubled. Castro doubled. Marlon Anderson singled—tie game! Then Hernandez came in and gave up a home run, and we faced Derrick Turnbow, the Brewers' hot-shit closer (why does every lousy team seem to have one?). Cameron, miraculously, took him deep, tying the game. So, extra innings. In the tenth Cairo led off with a walk. This brought up Beltran, the only Met without a hit tonight. He topped it to the first baseman for a double play. He was 0 for 6, tonight. What a concavity in the lineup.

But: bottom eleventh, Wright singles! Cameron hits a line drive and it goes through! First and third, no out! The Brewers walk the Mink! Bases loaded! Piazza, the last man on Randolph's bench, pinch-hits. Piazza walks!

Mets win on a Piazza walk-off walk!

In the cheering and high-fiving among the sparse attendees, I saw Pierrot, already fitting together his accoutrement (surely he'd use the same word), his head lowered, not in sadness but perhaps with a kind of modesty-in-satisfaction with which I'd never before credited him. (Strangely enough,

the crepe cooker seemed to actually fit inside the helmet—
could these be modular components of some sort of vast
Gallic system of fixtures and implements we'll all be using in
a few years, like Lego for adults?) In a kind of passionate fit,
I seized him by the arm, and at last, at last, Ivan, I popped the
question:

"Pierrot?"

"Harry?"

"Why are you a Mets fan?"

"Ah, Harry—please." Pierrot frowned, shook his head,
gestured mildly at the field, alluding to events preceding, the
absurd hairbreadth escape, the sweetness and fragility of the
hopes embodied thusly, the stadium and sky, jet engines just
at that moment screaming overhead (I wondered for a moment whether, as he glanced trepidatiously down from a 747
coach window, a Shea night game had been Pierrot's first
glimpse of his adopted nation), the blue and orange, the scoreboard Mets logo twisting and contorting in some scoreboard-
animator's notion of an inanimate logo's jubilation.

"Zees is simply a mattair of taste. One could nevair explain."

Wonderingly,

Harris

August 4

Harris,

So: as I always maintained, Pierrot truly is one of us. *De
gustibus non est disputandum*, in oh so many ways—how

very well a Frenchman could understand that. The Mets are like a faintly puerile cuisine, for those who enjoy strong flavors that waver at the edge of inedibility. 1986 is not quite itself without 1983 and 1992. The one hones the appetite, the other keeps the aftertaste from becoming saccharine. I don't think I have enough room in this apartment for this metaphor anymore.

Happily, my convalescence proceeds apace. I braved a schlep to the Strand yesterday to sell off some books. Geoff (it may be Jeff, but as far as I'm concerned he behaves like a "Geoff"), the buyer, was his usual overparticular self: when, in response to his sneering inquiry about the whereabouts of the missing volume of a two-volume survey of German philosophy, I deadpanned, "Germany," he knocked ten dollars off his offer for the whole lot. Sick man that I am, I accepted and got the hell out of there.

After my afternoon nap, I headed to a bar, to sit at a table nursing a beer and watch Pedro, hoping that all would be well in the world at least for a little while. Of course the Brewers were all over him early, my bad luck, or his, but Cliff socked one over left center that woke that apple up; he actually touched it.

The man who owns Gold's horseradish was interviewed. He sponsored the Martinez bobble-head night coming up Sunday. Turns out he started the first Mets fan club back in Year One, 1962. I'd say there's a little something anticlimactic about going on to run a horseradish company. At the very least he should now be executive director of the International Fraternal Order of Mets Fans, or something. But I guess there's a lot of money in the horseracket, 50,000 Pedro bobble heads' worth.

Piazza evened it up in the fourth with a homer, and then in the fifth Beltran doubled, attaining slight convexity, and the Brewers, who apparently didn't get the book on Wright, walked Floyd to face him, and Wright promptly singled in two runs. But Pedro just didn't have it; he gives up another dinger, and then Hernandez does too, and so, with the score tied, do I even need to tell you which Cheshire cat strolled in from the bullpen to blow the game?

This pretty much scotched my resolve to get out to Shea for the rubber game today. Too fucking hot anyway. I listened on the radio, hopeless, hopeful, Benson gives these bushers three runs, then we come back to tie. Piazza drives in five, but our bullpen looks awful, just awful—we don't even need Looper today. Hernandez, who seems over the last few days to have suddenly become a fifty-year-old arm attached to a forty-eight-year-old body, surrenders five in the ninth. Beltran lets a ball get past him and it's 12–9. Disaster, squared.

Is this Waterloo? The Brewers?

The longest nine-inning game in Mets history. A lot like watching cricket. I take three naps in the course of it.

Thinking, a bit, about Rafael Palmeiro and his troubles. At last they've found their man, I guess. You saw that Vecsey wrote one of those great self-impugning *Times* columns the other day. Regarding Palmeiro and his chances for the Hall of Fame, he said, "He was already facing skepticism as a hitter with excellent career totals who had never dominated his sport." Neither, I suppose, did Aaron, until the hype blizzard overcame the quiet steady output of the small-market star. Palmeiro's is just a different kind of hype, I guess. Vecsey, outdoing himself, then makes fun of Palmeiro's Viagra ads. Nice.

This is something we've barely talked about, Conk. May I now confess that it's probably partly because I, for one, don't give a shit, at least from a punitive standpoint? Horrors. I suppose part of my indifference—not ambivalence—has to do with that famed hobbyhorse of the Level Playing Field, not merely the one which says that if everyone's doing it then the harm's merely inflicted by the players upon themselves (though there's a point in there, somewhere), but also the one we hear about (in this connection, anyway) less frequently, the one that wonders why it's OK for a brontosteroidal team like the New York Yankees and their two hundred million to lay in an excess supply of power-hitting outfielders as obsessively as Molloy with his sucking stones, but it's the end of baseball as we know it when we turn on the lights in the dim little sweatshop in which a hardworking immigrant like Sammy Sosa manufactures nearly 300 home runs over the course of *five* seasons. And, now that I'm ranting, try telling me, just try, that it was the *players* who invented long ball, who brought about the starters with the 6.00 ERAs, the QuesTec strike zone, the little-league ballpark dimensions, the golf-ball-like physical composition of the ball. When one team beats another on the bases today, announcers and sportswriters alike act as if they've just borne witness to some quaint exercise in old-style baseball. Hitters swing now like they're taking a whack at a piñata. You just thank god all this started too late to ruin some wonderful hitter like Keith Hernandez. You can see how much damage it's done to a guy like Piazza, who could be enjoying a second life as a contact hitter but swings for the fences every time like the dumbest lunk never to make it out of double-A ball.

Now, you know what, or rather who, all of this got me thinking about? Dave Kingman. Kingman the dead pull hitter, the man who regularly used one hand to knock low and out-side pitches over the left-field fence, the Great and Terrible Kong, he of the Dead Rat, traded to San Diego (for Bobby Valentine, yet) the same day Seaver left for the Reds in the Great Vituperative M. Donald Grant Purge of '77 (and, I have to admit, it hurt, it really did, it was like trading Clint East-wood for Roy Scheider), Kingman! Imagine Kingman now. Fuck steroids. Imagine him in some Tinkertoy ball park, you know, TriMeriCorp Short Left Porch Field in beautiful Metro City; imagine him sitting on that low fastball each time out, whipping that bat up like a sleepy man trying to destroy a beeping smoke detector, spending his life as a DH, *the* DH, *pace* Big Papi Ortiz. The guy would hit 870 home runs. They'd all be with no one on and his team ahead or behind by a min-imum of five runs, but still. 870 home runs and 5,000 strike-outs and a batting average of .206. He'd be the guy to prove definitively that whatever steroids do they can't make you lay off a high fastball. It occurs to me that Dave Kingman's opposite number, his psychic counterpart, is Nolan Ryan— yet another with Met DNA. Same single-minded devotion to one thing and one thing only, the home run and the strikeout as fetish. Nolan Ryan, who pitched some no-hitters in which he allowed more base runners than most pitchers do in rou-tine outings. And Dave Kingman, who could never quite get it that a solo home run still was worth only one run even if you did hit it nine hundred feet.

So who'd you offer that ticket to? Didn't think I'd pick up on that, did you? A little spring in your pen, there. If you're *seeing* someone, Harris, don't you think I ought to receive some notice? Your love life has been the trench campaign of my existence since adolescence. Every now and then I vault over the top and advance slowly, and in full view, toward a blazing machine gun, trying to get you laid. The names, the dates, the fiascoes. It's a great novel in the making. Dick Lit. And you're the one who trips off into the clear, while I spend however much time it takes straightening things out with the offended, or just plain bewildered, party. So: cough up, to your walking wounded friend.

> With malice aforethought,
> Ivan

August 5

Sir Felt,

O! Valiant Wounded Progenitor of Miracles! I hail you across moats of twin castles. See your lamps burning. Have lit mine in reply. Tonight we batter Cubs, '69 victims, wretched of baseball's earth. Von Sacher-Masoch's team. Or was Von Masoch a Phillie? First inning, Glavine sharp. Reyes bloops, steals second, Beltran hits him home. The preseason blueprint, assembled, now open for viewing. Then Beltran overruns second on a Floyd single. Tagged out to boos. Carlos B. has death wish with Met fans. Always follows coming through with screwing up. Yet that necessarily entails the reverse too, no? Tonight I identify with everyone. Consider Nomar Garciaparra. Weird guy, Mr. Curse. As if Cubs traded

Ernie Banks mid-season to Red Sox, then won title. Yet good things I insist may come to even Garciaparra, if patient. A Cub goes deep on Glavine: I suffer psychic downshift, worlds crumbling, towers tottering. Belief Doomed. Yet no! We spring back. A six-run second. Whatever's needed, we nowadays find. Reyes at the center of it all. Glavine, sturdy on the back end. The young and the old, partnered. Commingled. Pardon a fragmentary missive. My mind's reeling. Sonnets, cascades of sonnets. Admit this note written under the influence of—well, what's the true Red Juice if not that which hearts urge through excitable tissue?

Honorably,
Sir Conk

August 6

Harris,

You're in some good mood. I'm glad, even if you have evaded my query. Fine, fine—whenever you're ready to spill, I'm the Bounty paper towel of the soul. Feeling stronger every day, ready to soak it all up and then balance two coffee cups on top. Just bear in mind, while the urging of the Red Juice is always a good sign, it's best to avoid, er, hypertrophy.

From experience,
I.

August 7

(postcard)

I,

Forgive unseemly exuberance. You misunderstood, un-
derstandably. I'm only elated at your mending, the reinstated
beacon flashing from your turret. And the games, lately.
Smashed on them.

H.

August 8

Harris:

Sometimes it seems as if the Mets are not the Mets, will
never be the Mets, never possibly could have been the Mets,
without Jae Seo returning from the minor leagues, more or
less triumphantly, at some point during each season. That
Korean American neighborhood in the reserved section of
the mezzanine hauls its thundersticks out of the closet, in-
flates them, and then carries them to the park for some
serious Enhanced Rooting. When only one section of the
stands is rooting in a certain way—trying the wave, or pa-
thetically Let's-Go-Metsing, or whacking those thundersticks
together—you realize just how peculiar rooting, as an organized activity, really is. When you think about it, it makes perfect sense that one-ninth of the crowd at Shea should be
there specifically to cheer for Jae Seo, for one player. They're
just sensible enough to sit together.

Jae Seo: another member of the Disordered Dozen on
the Mets' staff, each member of which, I'm now reflexively

accustomed to thinking, wills himself into victory, defeat, or—in the case of Braden Looper—a two-on, one-out situation with a left-handed power hitter coming to the plate. For instance: today I pick up a newspaper in my somewhat-still-addled state (I'm just on ibuprofen now, Conk, I swear) and see a headline reading "Battle of Zambranos," and rather than associate it with the duel between Carlos of Chicago and our own mixed-up Victor (misnomer if ever there was one), I immediately assume that everyone has seen what I, and perhaps you, have: the innate instability of the Mets' number-four starter.

I know my recovery has reached its end because the process has been drawn out enough to attract those who, for having shared my name, my bed, my life, are least likely to want to wish me well. Yet, in a little spate, I have begun to receive mail from each wife:

The first Mrs. Felt sent a letter (smelling of patchouli and filled with Mylar stardust) explaining to me that my chakras were fucked up. Just in case I was considering being touched, I noticed that the outside of the envelope indicated the letter had come as presorted bulk mail.

The second Mrs. Felt has added me to her People's Park Party e-mail list. Every day I get a take on the upcoming mayoral election from the slightly conspiratorially minded point of view of New York City's number-one "Parkist," explaining why her nominee for mayor is being shut out of the debates: it's an unusual effort being exerted by the Department of Parks and Recreation which, to quote newsletter #76, "orchestrates and manages the vast majority of political appointments and activities around the five burros [*sic*]." The first such e-mail contained some hand-typed (how sweetly ingratiating!) well-wishing from her, plus the dark intimation that since my injury was "leisure-derived" I might be well advised to pay attention to the newsletters. I suppose it should make perfect sense that Francesca would shift so easily from a peripheral involvement with organized crime to an equally marginal spot in municipal politics. A lateral career move, you might say.

The fourth Mrs. Felt has turned up, according to my colleague (and our mutual friend) Ozlem, on a little-known but provocatively essential reference to contemporary performative sexuality, www.exhibitionistsrus/facefuckers/amateurs/2005/July. Also, apparently, June, May, April, March, February, and January. The view isn't too good, but the technique is super-familiar. Her collaborator looks suspiciously like "Bubbles" Buckingham, a perennial grad student and sometime book reviewer for *The Hoboken Weekly*. He is, as always, a stern critic.

What about number three, you ask? What about the third Mrs. Felt, Harris wants to know! The third Mrs. Felt is bearing down on me about our love child, Gena. She calls her "the most overeducated serving wench in history," and indicates that she is exploring whether my disinclination to aid in delivering her up to the altar of Wall Street is actionable. It seems to me, Conk, that there's something more behind her anger than simple (and chronic, to tell the truth) annoyance with me. In fact, her response to my unwillingness to play along with her fantasy of transforming our daughter into Alexis Carrington Colby is disproportionate. I'll quote in part from her own special sort of get-well card: "Once again, you've led our daughter onto a path that puts her in harm's way, both emotionally and very definitely financially (though

I know you don't give a fig about the latter, Professor High-and-Mighty in his 14th Street–John's Bargain Store irregulars!). You may find it funny to jeopardize the future of your own flesh and blood but I do not and I happen to find your cavalier attitude to be irresponsible, unethical, and morally repulsive. Rest assured that I will be exploring all my options up to and including legal action." This from a woman, Conk, whose job it is to tie the survival of hungry millions to the possession of brightly colored slips of paper!

NO MORE MRS. FELTSES!!!

I return to action to find former Great White Hope Lee Mazzilli given the bum's rush by Peter Angelos.

To find the season ordered much closer to the way I might have expected, though I did not expect the Mets to reside at the bottom of the division. Cold comfort that they currently maintain a winning record.

Return also to see that Ring and Bell both have been struck. Ishii becomes yet another shadow fading from the rotation. One thinks of Hart Crane: . . . *not for long to hold each desperate choice.*

But to the battle of the Zambranos. Do we say this is the measure of a surging second-half Mets team (the rhetorical division of the season into first and second halves has become acute lately, like the epidemic of those "walk-off" home runs you mentioned) or of a crippled Cubs team? Do you think crammed division records like those of the NL East would have been possible, statistically, in the days before interleague play ate up fifteen games per year? Do you think the enervated fans in "cities" like Denver and Arlington and Phoenix will end up screaming bloody murder if teams there endure a succession of last-place/winning-record finishes?

I doubt, actually, that it would be a problem in those pallid baseball outposts. Yet, would it not be particularly Metsian for us to reach the playoffs—with a last-place finish? Best of five against . . . who might it be? San Diego? They seem to be the perfect Division Series opponent, tailor-made for this MLB Marketing extravaganza that nobody seems to watch or care about. The Division Series was invented for teams like the Padres and their non-sequiturial uniforms to lose in four games, and to be the David eternally thwarting the Atlanta Goliaths. I actually think all of this is worth rooting for.

Impossibly Yours,
Ivan

August 9

Ivan,

Regard this missive as the equivalent of an old-time-movie slap applied by one friend to another who's been gibbering with fear or stress, bringing said friend mumbling gratefully back to his senses: you speak of reaching the playoffs as a last-place team, but you can't possibly really need me to point out that three other East Division teams are cued ahead of us for that spot. You suffered a temporary and forgivable hallucination, I suppose, that the Phillies, Nationals, and Marlins *simply don't exist*. I can't blame you, I've indulged that one myself. Our NL East Division for the last decade-plus being simply a matter of the Braves in first place and us in last. This self-pitying cartoon omits, of course, the

Marlins' two idiot-savant championships—and by the way, Ivan, don't the Marlins remind you of the career of Tom Wolfe (I mean, Tom Wolfe the best-selling novelist)? One minute there is no such thing, merely a slick, exasperating magazine writer, and the next he's America's greatest novelist, to the horror of the ostensible titans Updike, Mailer, Irving, et al. (think: Yankees, Cardinals, Dodgers), with their air of holding the keys to the kingdom of the Prestigious Bestseller. Let alone to the cursed who'd labored for decades; Gilbert Sorrentino, say, or Richard Stern, the Chicago White Sox of American fictioneers. That the Marlins whupped the Indians head-to-head in the series is as if Wolfe had penned *Bonfire of the Vanities* in Jerome Charyn's blood.

But no, my friend, we can't storm the gates from last place. And, even when three or four games over .500, we are a last-place team. WE ARE A LAST-PLACE TEAM. Have been for weeks now. In this M. C. Escher season we're better—on paper, in the standings, and head-to-head—than all four of the Western Division clubs, and, yes, we're "contending" "for" "a" "Wild" "Card" "spot," but we are also cellar-dwellers, wearing the whole of the division on our back like Igor's hump. We must stomach this gall—cold equations inform us that not only the Marlins and the Nationals but even the horrendous, misshapen Phillies are our superiors. And yet, if you turn this tale on its head, the other four teams in the NL East are losing the race for a distinction vastly rarer than winning a division or a Wild Card berth, let alone coming in third or fourth.

What am I on about, you rightly ask?

I don't believe it's Metscentric to say that we've spent our lives rooting for the most famous last-place team in the history of baseball, Ivan.

But if this year culminates thusly, the 2005 edition could be the *best* last-place team in the history of baseball.

Toughly loving,

Harris

P.S. You call yourself a "poetry philistine," I recall. ee cummings routines I can accept from a philistine, but now you're dropping lines from Crane's "The Broken Tower"? I know when I'm being patronized—humored, slummed, worked.

August 10

Felt withdrew from the manila envelope the short stack of papers. "PROOF OF SERVICE BY MAIL," the top sheet read. That couldn't possibly be good news. He stood momentarily in the mean light of the vestibule, reading papers, cradling the other envelopes, his arm bent behind him to absently knead his back, the empty aluminum box gaping before him.

Nice and slow on the stairs. In the apartment he tossed the junk on the kitchen table and, carrying the manila envelope, made for the phone. The old rotary, at his bedside: a defiant gesture—he wanted to see if his former wife was still reachable by ordinary means, or if he was going to get stuck dealing with the digital version forever. He could use a digital version of himself, he thought, save a little on the wear and tear (the right hand reaching compulsively to massage the small of his back). He had his leatherette address book. His reading glasses. A pad and paper. All the paraphernalia of an old man. His digitized self would laugh like a crow at him. Palm Pilot? Sounded good and dirty, like something you'd buy in a store off Times Square. The old Times Square. Don't get him started. He went into the kitchen, for a fortifying glass of ice water. His back hurt. He'd lied to Conklin about ibuprofen only. The little pink Percodans sat brightly on the kitchen table, a chemical link to the present day, even if technologically he might as well have been squatting in a cave. When he returned, the papers were still there, on his chenille spread, but already seemed less difficult to deal with.

The connection was achieved slowly, in stages of discernibly different pitch; a succession of whirs, clicks, and buzzing sounds. Ghostly flurries of other conversations, conducted in unfamiliar tongues, occasionally became audible. For once the phone betrayed the vast distances it bridged. As it drew him nearer to a woman he'd once shared his life with, the room he sat in became lonelier.

When she answered he received the impression of a body being carried forward through space at great speed. Maybe it was his.

"Where are you?" he asked.

"I'm on the corporate jet. I'm headed to Niger. We're talking about introducing edible banknotes."

"That sounds wholesome."

"Not necessarily. Banknotes of greater value would have a higher nutritional content, of course. But there are the usual snags, hitches, and hurdles."

"I can only imagine."

"Don't be sarcastic. It's one elegantly simple solution for those economies for which the only remaining commod-

ity is survival." She paused for a second. *"Tactically, I shouldn't even be talking to you."*

"How about strategically?"

"Probably not that either."

"How about statistically?"

"Ivan, are you all right? You sound a little funny."

"Just a summer cold." Felt rolled over slightly, to stuff a pillow beneath the small of his back.

"OK then. What do you want?"

"The King Crab legs at Ray's, on Puget Sound. But that's my question for you."

"If you're referring to the complaint, it's not what I 'want.' It's what the situation warrants."

"False imprisonment? Racketeering?"

"They're civil causes of action. If you're worried about being clapped in irons, don't. Though you'd be in much better shape exposure-wise if you'd incorporated, as I suggested many years ago if memory serves. But, really, all I want is to strip you of whatever rights and privileges you have concerning our daughter and to exact certain harshly punitive measures at the discretion of the court."

"Is that all? Hey, she's of age. This is strictly harassment."

"It'll cost you to prove it."

"I know my rights. I don't have to prove a thing."

"Like hell."

The connection severed, Felt lay back on the bed. His only consolation this evening would be Pedro, going for number thirteen against the cursed Padres in their new pitcher's park. Felt turned on the set, linked to TV's bounty only by a pair of rabbit ears, and gazed into the static. The idea of marshaling the energy he'd require to confront Angela at Time Warner made him think he might never have energy again. This must be what major depression feels like. A rivet right next to the spine, dull and hot and unavoidable. He was disinclined, frankly, to pursue the matter. Frustration had led him into danger. Getting old, Ivan. No more rooftop adventures for you. Felt v. Cable, and cable had won.

To tell the truth, Felt had always been jittery about having cable installed. In his last four years of solitude, television had become terra incognita to him. He understood that he'd been missing quite a bit. People always told you that. He nodded and smiled whenever someone, some colleague who'd published a musty dissertation on Leslie Fiedler, who pronounced the words "Alice Tully Hall" with the same rapture that he, as a thirteen-year-old in 1966, had uttered "Raquel Welch," would explain to him that HBO's prime-time programs were superior to anything the contemporary novel had to offer. Even if Felt's knowledge of the novel, these days, hadn't been limited to what he read about in the Times Book Review *(which, come to think of it, had until recently been edited by the man who'd voiced one of the loudest claims for television's primacy), he knew that the conversation had been brought to an abrupt halt by this faux–insurgent revelation. Yet hidden somewhere in there was his fundamental agreement with an argument for withdrawal, for disengagement, for navel-gazing solipsism.*

It was Gena who'd urged him out of his burrow. All the time he spent bugging Harassed Conklin, teasing him, and Felt was actually the introverted misanthrope recataloging his books and dusting off his old syllabi and course notes. He visited her and she took him out—"blew the stink off him," she'd put it. Her recommendations. Films, records, exhibitions. Food, wine, beer. Stores, neighborhoods, entire countries. His envoy. When had she formed these sophisticated opinions? Beer alone was a whole universe of connoisseurship. If she knew this much about beer, he didn't want to go anywhere near sex. It seemed a tacit agreement between them. In return for her counsel he offered up reading lists he was shocked that an expensive liberal-arts education hadn't made redundant. He began to bring her the books themselves, fat little Penguins, Gargantua and Pantagruel, Stories of Maupassant, Gulliver's Travels. *Start her off easy. He was pleased to find that some of them looked as if they'd been read. These weeks at home he'd relapsed somewhat, at least as far as she was concerned. Good of Conk to try to help out, though from his terse reports Felt could see that Conklin didn't know how to get through to her. That eternal awkwardness around women, a sort of sex-specific autism, Ivan'd always felt.*

It only took one batter for Felt's nightly dream of a no-hitter to fizzle, or whatever pipe dreams did. Triple to right. The line score was brutal. Even with his fucked-up back, Felt sat hunched throughout in the agonized position in which he'd been listening to the Mets losing for nearly forty years. The only bright spot was a supposedly phenomenal catch by Wright. Here was the moment when any nostalgia he might have had for the good old days of radio went out

the window. Gary Cohen sounded almost dementedly ec-
static. It was like walking, straight, into an acid party and
listening to the guests describe their impressions of the
parquet floor. Fuck you, Angela, he thought. Fuck you, Time
Warner.

August 11

Ivan,

I was watching live—I mean, of course, watching the San
Diego game on satellite—when the gruesome outfield collision between Cameron and Beltran occurred. FSN only replayed it twice, and then Ted Robinson realized just what we
were seeing, and said "enough of that," and his crew in the
truck switched solely to live coverage as the medics cradled
Cameron's neck and taped his limbs into place on the
stretcher. I wish I was kidding when I tell you Ralph Kiner
began ingenuously reminiscing about being in the game
when Pete Reiser slammed into a wall and they were so un-
certain he'd live that they gave him last rites on the grass of
the outfield. I wish I was kidding when I tell you it seemed a
perfectly appropriate story to tell. The way Beltran's and
Cameron's heads and necks intersected, with utterly un-
braked force, was as if they were trying to occupy the same
inches of space, as if conducting some sort of misguided
physics experiment. Never seen anything like it, Ives. I wept,
thinking I'd just seen a death or at the very least the end of a
man's life as an athlete and perhaps as a walking person.
Cameron, with those high Indian cheekbones, Cameron the
painstakingly recovered, Cameron the near traded, Cameron

the multiply dissed. He once hit four home runs in a game, breathing air so rarified—ah, it's too fatuous, I'll stop. To make any sort of thematic hay of a moment like this is putrid—though saying that, I must add that the Mets' broadcaster's on-the-spot responses were pure and fine. Yet I can't keep from thinking (and thus, mentioning to you) that this disaster was lurking in our displacement of a Gold glove center fielder, a man prouder of his glove than bat, to make room for a star player, a heralded fielder too, yet perhaps just a micron less superb. What we saw in that twin plunge for a quailing line drive was of course two natural center fielders asserting instinctive dominance—the ball, horribly, belonged to both of them.

Harris

August 12

Conk,

I thought instantly of George Carlin's old routine, riffing on baseball's marketing of itself as a sort of charmingly pastoral pursuit. Then I considered the self-protective armament that's popped up in our lifetimes. Ear protectors on the helmets. Elbow guards. Shin guards, leg guards. Chest protectors, throat protectors, shoulder protectors; stuff made of high-impact polycarbonate and dual-density foam: nothing can deny the physical evidence of that ball, thrown at speed by a specialist into the immediate neighborhood of three crowded human beings. Yet the fielders are still remarkably unencumbered—and exposed. Every terrible injury I've ever seen has happened to a man in the field, slamming into a wall or tearing himself up on the base paths or getting drilled by a comebacker. Carlin aside, it's a serious game played under potentially deadly circumstances—that ball is a sewn rock—and an event, a tragic (a word I nearly never use) event like this maybe helps to disclose why so many phenoms never make it out of the high minors, helps to reveal the unquantifiable that makes the sabermetric bottom line just another on-paper assessment: superb is a perfect word, Conk. Hemingway would have appreciated that collision—not in the bloodthirsty way his detractors would accuse him of but as the only apt demonstration of the consequences of magnificence—particularly the sad obvious fact that they each had the exact same read on that ball, as you observed.

They say—it's a cliché to say—of winning, "You have to want it." But I think you have to want it. At the very least I hope we don't hear shit for the rest of the year about Carlos Beltran's $119 million. Juries have awarded more for less harrowing encounters than what happened in right center in San Diego.

Ivan

August 12

Ivan,

Not to make this all about me, or my patrimony, but I realized that another reason the Beltran-Cameron Episode shook me so deeply was the spellbindingly long on-field medical intervention, the rushing onto the grass of the ballplayers' caretakers, their unself-conscious, camera-oblivious effectiveness and concern, and the feelings that witnessing this aroused in me about old Aloysius Conklin, M.D., Original-Mets-Team-Doctor-in-Exile—that was meant to be my dad out there, Felt. Okay, sure, he's eighty-two now, and though he does continue to keep hours, two days a week, at his Sunnyside office, tending patients as old as he, as though unwilling to break their spirits by acknowledging his own creeping ailments, his own crumbling powers, he likely wouldn't *still* be the team's doctor. Fair enough. But with his talent and his love of the team, who knew? He might have still been tending the Mets through the seventies, maybe even have made it to the '86 championship before retiring. He could have been the Ralph Kiner of team doctors, a treasured fossil, propped up in his responsibilities by younger men, yet linking us historically to '62, to the team's inception. That's the irony of his dispute with Ed Kranepool, "the original Met." Kranepool became the living link with the past, but his playing career could never have stretched as far as my dad's team doctoring might have. Are these idiotic reveries, Ivan? I'm sorry. But you know, I think it broke his heart that failing to diagnose Kranepool's bone spur cost him his stewardship of the entire team before it could even begin. You may even recall that before his exile, my dad once got to throw batting practice to "Marvelous" Marv Throneberry and John "Thumper" De-Merit.

I've spoken to you often of my father, Ivan, and you know him well—he adores you, always has—yet I doubt you know the following tale. It concludes before you and I became friends in high school, by which time I'd settled out of any yearning to play ball myself, indeed, had retired from any physical discipline more strenuous than self-pleasuring (which activity did, in my thirteenth year, so overdevelop my right dorsal that I became worried the disproportion would be visible to others, and so quit ever wearing sleeveless T-shirts). Therefore, you'd never have known that the years of my childhood following my father's tribulations with Kranepool and the team, I was a fairly good peewee ballplayer myself, dedicated to the "hot corner," in emulation, I regret to admit, of Brooks Robinson. I wanted to make diving, stabbing plays for balls, that was my aspiration, more even than to clout a ball over the fence. Yet I was hounded out of sports entirely by my father's compensatory over-dedication to protecting me and my teammates from injury. He'd show up at practices at the local field—I'd never know when he might appear. If any of us tripped, slipped, or stumbled, or fouled a ball off our shins, or got a mote in our eyes, out he'd come charging, onto the field, no matter whether the play in question was resolved or not, and ignoring any protest that the child in question was fine and didn't need his help. He'd insist on attending to the injury, rolling down socks or up sleeves, asking us to flex or blink or grip for him, forbidding those he judged truly injured to continue at their position, regardless of our eye-rolling demurrals. Soon enough, the coaches began to bench me to discourage him. And when that didn't work, they asked me to stay home.

I'm getting maudlin, so here's an aside, to stem tears: Have you ever observed how integral the letter "k" seems to be to the team's deep identity? Kranepool, Koosman, Kiner, Kingman, Keith, Knight, MatlacK, Dr. K? (I realize that to add

Cal Koonce to this list might be pushing things.) I don't know what it means, but, due to my fondness for Franz Kafka, and yes, to my patrimony, I like it.

Yours,
KonKlin

August 13

Harris,

Idiotic, no. Fathers break your heart. Or maybe it's your helpless remembrance of your own obnoxious reaction to their best efforts that breaks the heart. Can't win for losing, as the old expression goes. It wasn't when everything *really* went kablooey for my dad—his whistle-blowing about the irregularities in the union's books, the subsequent smear campaign, his ending his days working as a tax preparer at one of those seasonal H&R Block storefronts on 14th Street—that I was concerned. By then of course everything my father did was idiotic; I was the young Saracen, wielding my sword to save academia from itself, and he was simply an old grind in a bad suit. The problems of the Old Leftist whose naïve illusions had predictably—at least as far as I was concerned— been dispelled didn't interest me in the least. He'd thought the union was interested only in protecting and defending the rights of its members? How primitive. If, I was inclined to opine, he was interested in serving the People, then he should try to adapt his outmoded Communist Party of America attitudes to *today*! Think *now*, Daddy-O! Think Weather Underground! Think Symbionese Liberation Army!

No, what humiliated me happened earlier, when he and my mother put out their sad little folkie single, "Two-Cent Plain." It was a sincere enough song. Perhaps you recall the lyrics?

Ain't no jerk
there at the fountain,
mixing white and mixing black.
It's good work
to climb that mountain—
mix 'em up, and don't look back.

Come hand in hand,
don't be afraid now.
Hand in hand, don't be afraid.
Through all the land,
here's what we said now.
All the land, hears what we said:

Two-cent plain
two-cent plain
two-cent plain
is what we're like.
Mix us up, and don't look back now:
two-cent plain
is what we're like.

This should have been mortifying all by itself, but at ten I had somehow managed to convince myself that between the pure (and oh so righteous!) talent of "Albert and Sophie," as they called themselves, and the mighty marketing apparatus of Apple Seed Records, which resided entirely within the confines of a P.O. box at Village Station, this song would become the anthem of the entire right-thinking nation! When it sank without a ripple, and fourteen cases of unsold 45 rpm records arrived to share with us our living room on Waverly Place—you remember the size of that cracker box—I was so disappointed. My father seemed to shrink in stature, physically, right before my eyes, although maybe he just looked tiny next to all that unwanted merchandise. I never felt the same way about him. And he knew it too.

Talk about maudlin, let me push on to the game.

Is this what's known as the bright side? Diaz, called up from the minors, swinging three times, with a strange and beautiful abandon, at the same pitches, a little low and a little inside, connecting—twice for home runs and a third time for a single. I think he's trying to say, I'm ready. Of course Randolph was right to send him down to keep him playing. Could he have come off the bench to do that?

The more I watch Wright, and Diaz, and even Reyes (although more than any of them I think he could have used another year in the minors), the more I'm thinking this is where things will cohere. Beltran has not shown us as much—but I think a man who's spent his career in the boondocks is entitled to an adjustment year: the Dodgers' triple-A team (Vegas, baby) conceivably draws more attention than the Kansas City Royals. The three kids coming into their own, Beltran entering his prime, and veterans like Floyd and the Mink keeping things together. Well, maybe someone like the Mink, but who hits around .260. Now all we need for 2006 is a bullpen, and a starting catcher to stop the stuff they throw in his direction. Catcher: could be the key, Conk. If you think about it, the only time Mets teams have really gelled has been when they had a great catcher. Grote. Carter. Even Piazza, who I'll admit is mostly a great hitter but who has never been as bad a catcher as people say. I point to all those misplayed balls in the outfield in 2004, when Piazza wasn't behind the plate to position the players.

This was a fuck of a game to watch until two-thirty in the morning. I was sorry to see Zambrano and Heilman throw a perfectly good 6–3 lead away, but we kept coming back; Hernandez pitched himself into and out of a jam as if he were following the directions in some middle reliever's recipe book, and the much-maligned Offerman saved the game with his spearing of a line drive, and generally the Mets looked as if they were completely unwilling to concede the game even as it neared four hours and the umpires started widening the strike zone and gesturing impatiently at any pitcher who even hinted at indulging OCD-like tics. It was around the time when the first of the drunks outside on the street started staggering homeward that the chill thought first frosted my mind: Looper's going to end up with the ball. Looper's going to come grinning his deathly grin from the bullpen and then toss the game aside and I'll have been sitting here for hours to watch the anti-Mariano throw it away. Well . . . Rookie . . . Catcher . . . Navarro . . . Looper threw him outside; even *he* could tell this little brick of a man was dying to pull an inside pitch over the right-field wall. And then it just floated in, the very mirror image of the pitches Diaz had tagged. We all knew it was gone: whoever was left watching WPIX in Gotham. The forty-eight people who hadn't left Dodger Stadium, as per tradition, after the seventh. The blonde with the incredibly expensive hair who was sitting directly behind home plate knew it. Navarro certainly knew it, and that grinning bastard Looper knew it too. Wonder what he had to say? "I just didn't get the job done," I'll bet. Let me check.

Per Mets.com: " 'One bad pitch. I didn't get the job done,' said Looper."

Who needs coffee,
Ivan

P.S.

(1) If it ever made either of you feel any better—and, not for nothing, no rap against Kranepool; Krane was always one of my particular favorites—I don't think discovery and prompt treatment of the bone spur ever would have made a whole hell of a lot of difference in Steady Eddie's career. Took him twelve years to find his stroke. Maybe he would have stolen seventeen bases overall, instead of fifteen. Legged out another couple of triples.

(2) Could DeMerit hit him?

(3) Hey, you missed Karter and BacKman and DyKstra and Kevin Mitchell. OrosKo. MooKie. David Kone. And the late great Hot Rod Kanehl.

August 16

Ivan,

We've limped home to Shea after the nightmare. The team had Cameron's jersey hanging prominently in the dugout tonight, as Benson pitched against Pittsburgh, his old embittered compatriots. Word tonight was Beltran has elected against surgery. The team physicians are presently trying to rig up some kind of mask to protect his cheekbone and orbital. As a result of the calamity, Wright's batting third. A glimpse of the future, I suppose—the prodigal child just pushed into the league's top ten in average. Trachsel sat in the dugout, mulishly chewing seeds, another specter of pain and recovery.

We got to the Pirates' godawful pitcher in the second. Benson drove in a couple himself, making certain Pittsburgh felt his exile's poison kiss. Floyd provided insurance runs on a titanic homer in the eighth, Looper was adequate, and we won. Yes, even in this listing schooner, we can keelhaul the Pirates. Tonight was the anniversary of the 1965 Beatles concert at Shea. And the anniversary—though our announcers left it unmentioned—of Elvis Presley's 1977 passage to another world, while "straining at stool." The Mop Tops at the Stadium, the King on the Bowl.

> We're caught in a trap, I can't walk out,
> Harris

- -

August 18

Dear Harris,

I see Beltran is back, no mask. These good tidings tempered somewhat by news that Piazza is showing another crack in the chassis, a slight fracture of the left wrist. Carlos scored last night in the first inning, all the way from first on C. Cornelius Floyd's single. Then he scores again, from second this time, in the fourth, after the Pirates commit the fatal error of walking Floyd to face Wright, who then whacks a single, making Pittsburgh pay, in his customary manner, for insulting him. (When will word get around?) Beltran responds well to the cheers. Who knows? He may never hear a boo at Shea again, after the other day, but give the upper deck a couple of weeks of 4–3 groundouts and they'll probably be happy to make him wish he were the one out of the lineup for the rest of the season.

Speaking of which, I didn't notice Cameron's jersey in the dugout tonight. Good thing, too. There's a kind of voodoo hanging over this sort of tribute, as if it were honoring a player who'd died. Cross yourself and avert your eyes.

Glavine pitching well, in his second-half manner, finding his spots, scattering hits (the Pirates actually outhit us), making them hit it on the ground or pop it up. A small masterpiece of quotidian craftsmanship. Let Pedro paint the masterpieces, Glavine will build the frames. From my lips to God's ears.

Beltran flies out in the sixth, OK, better than grounding out, but Cairo had led off with a double and guess what the Pirates do, again? Base-on balls for Mr. Floyd, leaving David Wright to work a hostile walk. Then Offerman slaps a two-RBI single—our sterling bench! We could have gone .500 starting this bench last year!

(What would a Yankee fan have to say about so modest a goal, so humbly proud an observation? On them all I wish the Hell of the prideful invented by Stanley Elkin!)

Heilman comes on in the eighth with two on and no out, manages to strike out two and pop-up the last guy—these Pirates have no names. Heilman's stranded eighteen of twenty-three inherited runners this year. Yet Closer, thy Name is Looper. Wherefore?

Here I go again, asking where you've been,

Ivan inkling

August 19

I.

Okay, I'm feeling it again, something's happening here, what it is ain't exactly clear, but it seems to involve—Jae Seo? I'll admit at first I didn't believe you. But tonight I'm sold. Seo looks absolutely stellar. So where was he all season, Mister Minaya?

For six innings a zip–zip duel. Then Diaz singled home a run in the seventh. Then almost gives the run back flubbing a catchable Nats flare in the top of the eighth, but Seo pitches out of it, beautifully, and a charge goes through the thundersticks. Seo pumps his fist. We like this. We feel this guy. He's no Ishii, no Zambrano, no cipher. He's pitching his ass off.

Oy. Come the ninth and a one-run lead, Looper gave up the leadoff hit, just as Looper would. But Reyes turned a sparkling double play (I decline to credit Looper with throwing a double-play pitch). The camera found Seo in the dugout, exhaling. Meanwhile, on another channel, the Phillies are down eleven runs to the Pirates. It's a race!

Ted Robinson mentions we've got the best record playing within the division of any team in the East, excepting the Braves. Holy hell. That means we're presently losing this

Wild Card race to the Pirates and Diamondbacks and Reds and Giants, just as it feels we are. Teams that couldn't tie their shoes two days in a row. Oh yeah, and to the A's, Mariners—and Yankees. That creeping interleague hangover could still spoil our late-summer's rush.

I'm full of good feelings, though—including the ones I can't tell you about, yet. Like Prospero, slapping together his thundersticks.

H.

August 20

Puerto Rican flag or Cuban? The middle in a group of five young men walking abreast carried it aloft. The quintet swerved and swayed in formation, a flying wedge of precipitately inebriated patriots. The banner hung limp in the windless air. Felt, watching from where he leaned against one of the chipped concrete barricades protecting America and the Game Day Ticket Sales booths from mad terrorists, couldn't remember for which of the two republics it stood; the two nations' designs were identical, though with the colors effectively reversed. Could it possibly be Communist Night at Ché Stadium? It was already Hispanic Night, and PetCo Dog Night, and a concert, sponsored by Budweiser, would follow the final out. Beer, dogs, a celebration of ethnicity, and song: didn't seem like the wisest of combos, if you asked Felt. Certainly didn't seem like the right admixture of ingredients from which one might reasonably expect an arm-in-arm rendition of the "Internationale." The Horst

Wessel song, perhaps. "Es schau'n auf's Hackenkreuz voll Hoffung schon Millionen." *Felt wondered what that might sound like translated into Human.*

He looked once again at the Timex on his wrist. 6:55 PM. *He and Conklin had agreed to meet right here at 6:30, though Harris had seemed unusually equivocal, something beyond his typical kvetchy hesitance. As evasive as a teenager, he was, with only a slightly better complexion. What "things" couldn't Conklin tell him about? After forty years Felt believed he'd earned residuals on his investment in the man's personal life.*

The contingency plan, only rarely enacted, was long-standing: the on-time party would enter the stadium before game time; the tardy one had to buy a general admission ticket at his own expense and then meet the other at the usual spot in section 101. Despite the simplicity of the plan, the departure from custom irritated Felt. It didn't help that Harris neglected, make that refused, to carry a cell phone. He supposed he could leave a few cathartic messages on his friend's answering machine. He pulled out his phone, noting the time on the display, 6:58, composing:

... Schmuck, where are you? I'm surrounded by the Sharks with nary a Jet in sight ...

... Harris, Spuds McKenzie just showed up in a 1921 Pierce-Arrow with Anne Waldman as his date—just thought you'd want to know ...

... Conk, the ghost of M. Donald Grant was just spotted walking the ramparts, doomed for a certain term to walk the night until the foul crimes done in his days of nature are burned and purged away! ...

After two rings the phone was jerked off the hook.

"Hello?" said a familiar voice, unfamiliarly breathless.

"Conk, what are you doing there? I'm waiting for you."

"Uh, sorry . . . wrong number." The phone clattered back into its cradle.

That *was funny*. He'd dialed the number right out of his phone's memory—though he'd heard about wrong numbers just sort of happening with cell phones, signals colliding in midair and transmuting electrons or whatever they did. But it wasn't a wrong number. He gazed at the device expectantly. All it told him was the time: 7:01. Time to go in.

Felt strolled around the circumference of the stadium to gate C, the huge central portal leading to the cheaper seats. Something odd about it here tonight; then it dawned on him that all around him in the usual pregame crowd were people with leashed dogs. It was an unusual promotion, as if people had been invited to show up at Shea with grocery carts or laundry baskets. It involved maneuvering and physical avoidance. There were barks, growls, whimpers, fecund deposits of doggie ordure. He nimbly sidestepped it all. That's what growing up three blocks from Washington Square Park had taught him. He couldn't have felt more at home if the Mets had summoned folk singers, drunken undergrads, and pot dealers to Shea.

Inside, the harried ushers and ticket-takers were trying to herd the dog people into whatever special dog-person place had been set aside for them. The dogs were barking for the love of barking—the sound, multiplied, bounced around the concrete-and-steel interior. People had these looks on their faces that were like the living expression of Second Thoughts. Ushers made sweeping gestures with *their hands, their arms, their upper bodies. One was using his jacket as a muleta, executing sweeping veronicas against the dogs. Felt strode meaningfully up the ramp, leaving the dogs behind.*

In 101, Felt found Pierrot, alone, spreading a gingham napkin on one of the seats that his children ordinarily occupied.

"Zis 'Hispanic Night'? Qu'est-ce que c'est?" He opened a container of olives.

"It's like if Quebecois and Haitians and Vietnamese were tossed into a room and told to get along," offered Felt.

"Zank God zere is not Fransh Night."

"Franco-American Night. That's next week."

"Quoi?"

"The actual name should be Hebo-Italian. It better describes the food and its partakers."

"Je ne comprends pas."

"Canned spaghetti. Have you tried it? It's really quite good." Felt affected the voice of George Sanders. Ten dollars to the first man to identify George Sanders. James Mason. Clifton Webb. Shiny can of SpaghettiOs to the first man to correctly identify the members of Hollywood's supercilious auxiliary! Felt was in a funny mood.

"Whatcha got there?" Pierrot had just uncovered a large Tupperware container that held what appeared to be a rich stew.

"Ah, Ivan—zis you will enjoy. Smell."

"Yes, yes."

"It's good, hah? Maybe you are full already from this smell?"

"Definitely fix me a small plate."

"You would like a dish of this? You are certain?"

"Does a fat baby fart?"

"No Polish saucisses?"

"Fuck the kielbasa, Pierrot."

"None of the puces de nacheaux?"

"Wrong number, baby. Hit me."

Pierrot clapped his hands excitedly. *"Ah, ha ha ha. You would like maybe to know what this dish is called?"* He ladled a dollop of stew onto a Chinet plate and tore a hunk off a baguette, setting it next to the stew.

"Sure, what's it called?"

Pierrot handed over the plate. *"Eat. It is bourguignon de poulain. A fine old Parisian dish."*

"Like beef bourguignon."

"Exactement. But with a different main ingredient."

"Tastes like beef."

With his fingertips, Pierrot set to drumming on the seatback in front of him, a loping syncopated rhythm. Involuntarily, Felt's head filled with the opening trumpet call of the "William Tell Overture." He followed this free association to its logical conclusion.

"No, you're kidding."

"Foal stew."

Felt chewed thoughtfully, nodding. *"Foal stew,"* he repeated, between bites. Pierrot seemed immensely pleased, and slapped him on the back. *"My friend, you have not left me toward the bottom. Bourguignon de poulain! Very good!"*

"Very good," said Felt. Hippophagy, now. Was there no limit to his perversity? And where was Harris, who would

have been the first to ask him this, the arc of whose physical recoil from the delicacy Felt could trace in his head as easily as if he'd witnessed it. Pedro was cruising along, leaving the field at the end of the top of the second. If he had it tonight, the Mets might be setting up yet another turning point in a season of turning points. Really, these pesky Nationals. They really weren't being good fellows at all (the voice of George Sanders echoed in Ivan's head). Hadn't they realized they were supposed to sit down and stop making noise during the fourth week of June? And where was Conklin?

Ivan sneaked a look at his watch, but Pierrot caught him. 7:25.

"Your friend Harry, where is he?"

Felt shrugged. "Running late." He mopped up gravy with the bread and took a bite.

"Cherchez la femme."

Felt nearly choked on his mouthful. "Conklin?" He offered a dismissive wave. He noticed that Pierrot was studying him, an amused look on his face.

"Maybe, my friend, he keeps a secret from you? Non? Non possible?" Pierrot pared an apple, then spread soft blue cheese on the pieces. He held out a hunk to Felt. "The young lady, you do not know her?"

Ivan just shook his head.

"At the commencement of spying the duet, I think it is a different man. Because of the joy and laughter, the corporal language, the friendly hands here, and here, and—"

"Cut it out," said Felt.

Ramon Castro hit a dinger, driving in Wright and Marlon Anderson on the way. Mets up three–zip. Felt was relieved to rise from his seat, applauding. He sensed something more primal than ordinary in his howl of appreciation.

After the sixth inning, the seat next to Felt remained unoccupied. Pedro came out then. With the Mets safely ahead 8–0, Willie was saving the arm for one of those meaningful games that had been anticipated around Shea for two or three seasons. Ivan felt a hand touch his shoulder. He turned to stare into Mesch's inscrutable red eyes.

"Your friend's having trouble," Mesch said.

"My friend's having trouble."

"He told me come get you. So I got you."

"What friend?"

"What do I, look like Dear Abby? The usual friend."

"So where is he?"

"The concession stand right down the ramp. They rejected his credit card." Mesch said this as loudly as possible without actually shouting.

"Harris never pays with a credit card."

"Maybe this is why. What do I, look like his financial adviser? He needs dough. He told me come get you. So I got you."

"Thanks."

"I don't work for tips, this is not something I can claim with a clear consciousness, but I remember when people tipped."

"Do you take credit cards?" Felt asked.

Mesch moved away with a sneer of disgust. Felt ran down the ramp, where he found Conklin leaning against the counter, whistling and tapping his feet.

"I thought I'd find you washing dishes."

"Oh, no," he said mildly. "They're just holding onto the food 'til I pay." He'd been whistling something that sounded suspiciously like "I've Got You Under My Skin." Felt went to the counter and paid, then took possession of the cardboard tray that held Harris's food. Conklin seemed to have worked up an unusually large appetite.

"Is some of this for me?"

"Well. If you want some. We can get some more."

"Just asking."

Now he was humming "Lay, Lady, Lay."

"Harris. You're very late."

"Unavoidable, my dear Felt."

"I tried calling earlier."

"Did you?"

"Even Pierrot was asking about you."

"Oh, is he here tonight? That's great."

"Did you get hit in the face with the spores, or something?"

Harris squeezed his upper arm. Star Trek was a weak spot.

They arrived at their seats and Felt was astonished to see Pierrot and Conklin hug each other. Before releasing him, Pierrot winked at Harris. Harris took his seat.

"This is marvelous," he enthused, gesturing at the scoreboard. "Do you feel as if we're finally gelling?"

Felt was used to a somewhat more taciturn companion. "Maybe, maybe," he offered.

"Seems to me there are two reasons. Are you listening, Pierrot?"

"Way, way, mon ami."

"One is the collision, strangely enough. It restored Bel-

tran's adamancy, brought him into the team, into the Shea-fan's heart." Conklin gestured expansively. "Two is replac-ing Ishii with Seo. Ishii had to be eroding the team's spirit with that mystery act every five days. Ishii is a riddle wrapped in an enigma surrounding a chewy center of pure honey-toasted sixth-inning walks!"

"You're shouting, Harris," said Ivan, quietly.

"So? We're at a baseball stadium, not a museum! Everybody's shouting! That's the whole marvelous point!" They were quiet for a minute. Then Conklin asked, "What's with all the dogs?"

Two-and-two-thirds innings later, Harris Conklin's euphoria had dissipated in the warm evening air. Braden Looper, the Mets' fourth pitcher of the game, had entered with the score 8–6 (don't ask), gotten two outs, and then given up a pair of singles. Bryan Schneider thereupon smacked a double to the wall, scoring Ryan Church and Preston Wilson, and Looper had fulfilled his dismal psychic mandate to extend the game by any means possible. Felt turned and was perversely happy to see Harris sitting hunched forward with his elbows buried in his crotch, and his fingertips between his lightly clenched teeth, rocking to and fro, a familiar and wholly more characteristic posture. Beyond him, Pierrot sat glassy-eyed, drinking from a tiny bottle of digestive beverage.

"How can Looper look Pedro in the face after the things he's inflicted on him this year? How can they coexist?" Conklin asked.

"Pedro was off the hook right away," answered Felt.

"Doesn't matter. This should be a win, Ivan."

"OK. They don't coexist. It's a rent in the fabric of space

and time. Through it, the balls from some parallel universe in which Jose Lima is always pitching enter our universe and sail fatly in to the batters Looper is facing. How else to explain him?"

The huge stadium was very quiet, except for the periodic barking of dogs.

"Whose idea was that?" asked Conklin. In the distance you could see dogs running between rows of empty seats in the far reaches of the field-level seats. Ushers took flight after them.

Pierrot grumbled something about bourguignon de chien.

Some Puerto Rican drunks behind them began heckling some Dominican drunks a little up the first-base line.

The game had deteriorated so rapidly that Felt hadn't really had the opportunity to grill his friend about his lateness, his elation, and his strange response to Felt's telephone call earlier. Now he just didn't feel like it as he watched the Mets' listless half of the ninth and the Nationals' too-exciting half of the tenth. He'd take care of it on the long ride in.

But Harris was on his feet and heading down the ramp even before the ovation faded once Chris Woodward had driven in the winning run in the Mets' tenth with an RBI single. "I've seen losses I liked better," he said, waving.

"Wait," Felt said helplessly, "we'll leave together."

"Ives, I've got to run," said Harris.

Pierrot put a hand on Ivan's sleeve. "Cherchez la femme."

August 21

Dear Ivan,

I write to you today, I'll come right out and say it, under the mingled influences of stale pheromones, fresh embarrassment, reheated Folger's, and a sobering effort by the Miracles. (Have I ever mentioned to you that I have the same birthday as Smokey Robinson, Ivan? Bob Dylan once called him America's greatest living poet, and you know, if you get your hands on a lyric sheet for "The Hunter Gets Captured by the Game," "If You Can Want, You Can Love," or "When the Words from Your Heart Get Caught Up in Your Throat," you may find yourself fairly convinced that Dylan was up to more than just baiting a newspaperman when he made the remark.)

Let me offer apologies, for appearing late and scurrying off last night, as well as putting the pinch on you for the vittles (that's what Mesch called them, endearingly)—it must be the fact that we're so near September, the autumnal dying toward which Freud has instructed us to understand we in fact yearn, and yet are still playing meaningful games—truthfully, we've only just begun to play meaningful games! And it feels good, Ivan, it feels justified! Yet we're not accustomed to such games, or to their unexpected wealth of meaning, and so we become giddy, slipshod, inebriated—

But no, I swore not to rave, only to ask your forbearance. I'll reel it in. You requested of me a report. A report, yes. A difficult thing for a poet (unless he's Wallace Stevens, that insurance adjuster of the soul), but I'll try. Your message on my machine this morning requested that I tell you what's going on. And so here, I'm giving you a report. (I assume you meant, of course, that your cable is out again and you needed me to keep an eye on today's potentially vital game.) Dutifully, I settled in at the satellite dish to watch this one, pen in hand. Benson on the mound (which sounds better every time I say it) as we went for the sweep against the Nationals (words which could never be improved). Yet I'll admit I was rattled, goofy with unnameable angst, weirded by the world and by my team's and my own place in it. I don't recognize myself or my franchise. We're winning too much. Why do I feel strangely guilty toward you?

Therefore, in a perverse attempt to soothe my global jitters, I half shirked these duties, alternating innings of today's game with Fox Movie Channel's showing of *The Pride of St. Louis*—the Dizzy Dean biopic, starring Dan Dailey. In the first scene I stumbled upon, Dean had blundered into the Cardinals' general manager's office, there to smartly address the team secretary, who is plainly destined to be his sweetheart, then wife: "Aren't you kinda pretty to be a receptionist?" Looking at Dan Dailey, she ought to reply, "Aren't you rather forty years old to be a rookie?"

Benson, perhaps looking to make things easier for me, gets both the no-hitter and the shutout out of the way, quickly by surrendering a leadoff double to Ryan Church, who the Nats then efficiently sacrifice home for a one-run lead. After Preston Wilson slips rounding first, prickly old Frank Robinson, looking ever more like Louie the garbageman in *Chico and the Man*, comes out to complain that the field's too wet, and we get a weird delay while the ground crew pours "redi-dri" or some such shit onto the base paths.

Benson gives up a lot of first-inning runs. He gives up six

today—the latter five on a string of seven consecutive two-out hits. Someone with a stouter heart than mine should research to discover whether this is in fact a record.

In the interval after Randolph walks out to pull Benson (six runs, two outs, two men left on base) I switch back to *The Pride of St. Louis*. The Mets are down six runs, and Dizzy Dean still hasn't been called up from Buffalo.

Juan Padilla, relieving in the first inning.

Listen, Ivan, the team went in the toilet today. I'll relate the rest of the debacle, but let me spare you the suspense. This weekend series raises the question we recently framed on the telephone: Why do we Mets begin things so well, and end them so badly? I've done some looking into this: in home series this year we've won the first game 80 percent of the time. Great, a world-beater's record. Then we're about five hundred in second games. This itself wouldn't matter if it weren't for the last part of the equation: we're lousy in third games. We never finish a sweep. In fact, to take this observation to a level of intricacy, in the second game, we were good in the first half, and bad in the second half—wilting precisely in the middle of the three-game set. Further, we've got good starters (okay, not today) and a bad bullpen. David Mamet, in the film version of *Glengarry Glen Ross* (I never could afford to see it on Broadway), coined a phrase: "Coffee is for closers." Alec Baldwin, playing the manager of an office of underperforming salesmen, denied coffee to all but Al Pacino, because none of them can close a sale. Well, Ivan, no coffee for these boys.

Back to the Fox movie. Paul and Dizzy have reportedly already combined, at mid-season, for twenty-five wins. But we don't actually see any baseball in this movie, just telephone conversations, backseat taxicab conversations, hotel lobby conversations, and receptionists-turned-baseball-wives sitting at home alone, knitting. It's a wholly baseball-free baseball movie. I can hear the cigar-chomping movie mogul barking commands at the script girl: "Nobody wants to go to a movie theater and watch a baseball game! If people want to see a baseball game they can go to a baseball game!"

In the third inning, Marlon Anderson breaks up Esteban Loiza's no-hitter, but we can't rally.

Back to St. Louis, and we've finally got a baseball game in this movie—the All-Star game, where Dizzy Dean breaks his toe but goes on pitching, which I faintly recall is how he ruined his career. I guess the producers felt forced to show at least this one in-game event. Someone in the stands says admiringly, "He's indestructible!" Ah, but isn't this what happens to all the indestructible men? Give me the destructible man, every time.

Oh, the Mets? Well, Juan Padilla's handling the Nationals, of course, making junk of our "bad bullpen" theory. Padilla looks like a starter to me.

Dizzy Dean's been demoted, somehow, to a team with the word "Tulsa" across the chest of the uniforms.

Willie keeps Padilla in the game and so he gets the first at bat of his career, always a nice moment. Strikes out on three pitches, but hey, he fouled one off. Better than I'd do.

Dizzy Dean has bombed out of his opportunity with the Tulsa club, has begun drinking, and is accused of cheating at a backroom poker game. His wife is leaving him. Dark days. I had no idea, Ivan: this sure isn't the Lou Gehrig story. And, come to think of it, Dan Dailey is no Dan Duryea. He's not even Danny DeVito.

Now that would be a fun movie to make: Danny DeVito in a straight-up baseball biopic. Cast him as Bob Feller, say. Or Cal Ripken Jr. Like the Gehrig story, but with no Lou Gehrig's disease. No explanations for DeVito playing the part. Just deadpan it all the way, cast it straight in every other role, and direct it with the same sober professional studio-era mediocrity on view here in *The Pride of St. Louis*. Could be the funniest movie ever made. Ah, if I ran the world.

Dizzy Dean's wife just called him a "sweet, kind generous child." She then added: "But it just isn't in the cards for anyone to remain a child all his life."

Padilla's now given up one hit in three-and-a-third innings.

Dizzy Dean, who's now attempting a career as a broadcaster, but has been accused of being too "colorful": "A person can't be someone else and be himself too. I'm Dizzy Dean, I don't know any other way."

Diaz (and it occurs to me now to nickname him "Dizzy") flubs his second ball in the outfield, and the Nats have the bases loaded with nobody out. I may have to turn away from this one completely. But hey, we get a play at the plate and a pop-up and we're suddenly on the verge of getting out of it. Then Padilla walks in a run, and the score is seven–zip.

In the fifth inning, after two Met singles, a fresh-faced boy called Mike Jacobs comes up and casually slugs a three-run home run in his first major-league at bat. Go figure. Inexplicable, wonderful, enchanting. But we're not quite back in the game. Still, it's enough to keep me from Dizzy Dean for a while.

In the seventh, after Diaz singles, the Shea boos tell you

who's coming up to pinch-hit: Matsui. Kaz is the present magnet for Metsian self-loathing, much as Roger Cedeno was two seasons ago. I mean, it's not that Matsui isn't bad, Ivan, but the booing has certainly overrun the bounds of anything he's negatively accomplished for the team. We're booing ourselves when we boo like this. We're booing hope itself. Matsui, needless to say, strikes out swinging, bringing a further rain of censure. And that's pretty much the end of today's story—a couple of late rallies die with our big guns, Floyd and Wright, at the plate, striking out swinging. The Pride of Flushing is nowhere on the premises.

And by the time I flip back to the Fox movie, we're fifteen minutes into Robert Aldrich's *The Flight of the Phoenix*. Jimmy Stewart barking at a bunch of ragtag flyboys as they pour out of a plane that's crashed in the desert. Quite remarkable compositionally, I must say, Aldrich making beautiful use of the crumpled fuselage half sunk in sand. It nearly has the quality of a set for a Beckett play.

That, Ivan, is what's going on. By the way, have I told you lately that I love you?

> Responsibly, Soberly, Rinsing a Sinkful of Dishes,
> Harris

August 26

Conk,

Thanks for the recap. You can stop auditioning for Dick Young's old job, though you do it a lot better than he did. But when I asked for a report I had something entirely different in mind. Actually, two entirely different things. (One) What's Going On With You? The lateness, the hanging up (I know it was you, Harris), the suddenly overextended credit card that you've never, as long as I've known you, pulled out of your wallet, the friendliness, the verbosity, the giddiness, the hollering. All new to me. To you, too. I suspect that the only person to whom it doesn't seem uncharacteristic is the person to whom every inch of you is new. Spill, pal. (Two) I thought perhaps you might have a better sense of my daughter's well-being than I do, seeing as you've seen and possibly spoken with her more recently. I've tried calling, but her machine seems to pick up on the first ring these days. Probably hiding from her mother, though I can tell her from experience that it won't work for long. I may take a trip out to her place to see her, but I abruptly realized that the fall semester is nearly upon us, plus I'm currently dealing—daily, it seems—with a young attorney with the perfect name of Andrew Piety, who is helping me through my legal woes with Gena's mom. Whenever I call, he seems to be "in court." Here's an interesting tidbit, though: on one of the few occasions I've managed to fool him into talking with me, he told me that he'd talked to Felicia's lawyer—or, rather, to one of the eighty-five identically dressed functionaries who are billing hours on her case—and got the distinct impression that her grievances arise from the completely false idea she has that somehow I've facilitated Gena's involvement with a young man whom she finds unsuitable! Do you know anything about this? I'm happy if you've become her confidant, but surely if *she* doesn't realize that I'm not inclined—not much, anyway—to pass judgment on such matters, *you* must know I don't place too much stock in that patriarchal business.

Well hey. *Pride of St. Louis.* Sometimes the fact that they don't make 'em like that anymore doesn't matter, because you realize that they made enough of 'em to last the next twenty thousand years. But what have we got instead? I hear Tulsa's submitted a franchise proposal to Selig's office touting a billion-dollar Oklahoma state bond issue floated to finance the building of a state-of-the-art ballpark and an eminent domain plan to raze fifty acres adjacent to downtown. Diz may not be pitching there anytime soon, but Denny Neagle might.

My Maury Allen to your Dick Young: I hobbled to the only bar that happily tolerates my nursing two beers for hours on end to watch the Diamondbacks series with glee, though not without moments of trepidation—predictable moments that didn't pan out as badly as I might have feared, I might add. A four-game sweep! And right after your damning analysis, too! We look great, though the appearance is aided by the gaunt and moribund demeanor of the Diamondbacks. Something about the decimated team; the specter of triumphs past that still linger. Well, it's like the Mets of '02–'04. Hard to believe this nominally is the team that knocked the wind out of the Yankees over seven games in 2001. Great series, that. I remember really enjoying how much I was rooting against the Yanks even as the national media were reporting on how psychically invigorating it would be for "New Yorkers" to win the World Series in the "aftermath" of September 11. Fuck that. Even if they drop a nuke right on St. Patrick's I'll still root against the Yankees in the Series, even if they're playing the Kabul Nine.

I like this Mike Jacobs kid. Surely he's the answer belonging in the questionnaire blank that the Mink has been trying, unsuccessfully, to fill—though he can catch, too, yes he can. Piazza's on the disabled list, dress rehearsal for Piazza being the DH somewhere else. Don't even suggest that the Yankees'll sign him. First game, Glavine, passing Marichal on the strikeout list—not among the loftiest totals in the sport's history, but a hell of a lot for a finesse pitcher. Braden Looper "gets the job done," though he does get lonely, as usual, and walks one.

Game two, Jacobs, homering again. I haven't been this excited about a Mets rookie since Mike Vail! 14–1, and with Zambrano on the mound. The Diamondbacks look especially desperate, as desperate as I've ever seen a second-place team look, lunging at first pitches like they just want to go home. God, it must hurt to be part of this division.

14–1. With the bench doing much of the heavy lifting.

Motif: Is our bench better than our team? Our bench IS our team.

Game three, guess who hits another homer, his third in nine major league at bats? Mike Jacobs, Chef D'Oeuvre of the Future. Or until he goes around the league a couple of times, anyway. Russ Ortiz pitches like a man throwing a log into a buzz-saw factory. Chuck it and duck. Up seven–zip in the third after Jae Seo doubles in a run. Can I even summarize the next six innings? It looks like a highlight reel. Jacobs double. Reyes triple. Reyes home run. Jacobs single. Reyes single. Two Wright home runs. The broadcast begins to confuse. It's 18–4. Thirteen extra base hits for the Mets, a club record. How did the Diamondbacks sneak in those four runs? How are the Diamondbacks not in the basement of this division?

Game four. Can we do it? Pedro has a no-hitter into the sixth, then gives up two hits. He's gone by the seventh, Willie being prudent. Heilman shaky, doesn't get out either of the batters he faces, so Randolph yanks him for Hernandez, who works his way out of the inning.

We've still only scored two runs. Thirty-two runs in two days, that's more than a week's worth for the Mets, so even the two begin to taste like manna. In the eighth, Hernandez gives up a solo homer. This is taking on the shape of bullpen-blowing-a-Pedro-start. Conk, I hadn't realized how much I'd enjoyed the luxury of not having to hate and fear Braden Looper.

But we get the insurance run in the ninth—Diaz sacrifice fly—and Looper "gets the job done." Four-game sweep. Our run is real.

Yours,
Ivan

August 28

Dear Ivan,

Trachsel's back! Hence the slowness of my replies, as well as the progress of peace in the Middle East and the sun's rising in the sky this morning. He's taffy being chewed, he's ketchup coursing down the neck of a bottle, he's Dick Gregory's "Ever been to Mississippi? I spent a month there last week" joke, he's Bob and Ray's "Slow Talkers of America" routine, he's all things slow and funny wrapped in one morose and deliberate package. He's Steve Trachsel—and he almost threw our no-hitter on Friday night, his first day back in the rotation!

Come the fourth inning I was still scoreboard-watching, not yet bearing down on the no-no prospect. The Braves lost—but maybe the Braves aren't really the issue anymore, sadly. Nats and Fish won, alas. Wright hit a genuinely impressive solo home run—the longest, the Giants' broadcasters said, they've seen to left field. And here, still stranded in San Francisco, was Edgardo Alfonzo, once upon a time my avowed "favorite Met." Is it only me, or does he seem a somnambulist, a zombie? Oh, and listen, did you hear me complaining about the Arizona Diamondbacks' broadcasters? I take it all back. The San Francisco camera unit visited the Gilroy garlic fries booth three times in one inning.

It was in the sixth, just as I began to really fixate on the no-hitter, that Trachsel gave up a single. Still looking superb, though, and locked in a true duel. As if destined, Floyd-Wright-Jacobs went easily in the ninth, so, Wright's home run still the only digit on the board, we handed the one–zip lead to none other than B. Looper.

Almost needless to say, Omar Vizquel led off with a double. We were in for another harrowing episode of "I Loathe Loopy." Like you, I'm nostalgic already for Tuesday and Wednesday, all those runs, no need to suffer this man, no need for this man to suffer (for he must be suffering, Ivan, behind that rictus). But Looper "gets the job done," gets it done with ground-outs and a pop-up, around a massive, fearsome, upper-deck foul from Alou. We win. Like we—dare I say it?—have been doing, mostly, for weeks.

> In the grip of a youth movement,
> Harris

August 30

Harris,

(FOUR PM) The *Times* has a little chart today breaking down the Wild Card. We're presently tied with the Astros— my predicted winner. The Phillies are in the lead. If we take two from them, we're tied, with them anyway. With whomever. The *Times*' chart shows that we're number two (behind the Braves) in the division in intradivisional play. Sort of a lame accomplishment, I suppose, but not nearly so lame as that of the Phillies, those would-be champions, who are fifth, or that of the Marlins (aka "Delgado's Choice"), who are third, and with a losing intradivisional record to boot.

"Meaningful games" are on the horizon. How exciting to say it, and only, what?, two years after Wilpon's much mocked comment? "Meaningful games," and against our natural enemies, too, Philly, Florida, Atlanta, Washington, and, OK, St. Louis, who with Chicago have joined the Central Division but are our traditional nemeses. Time again for me to unpack my feelings about interleague play; the way it dilutes the tensions of a season, enfeebles the historical and regional rivalries between teams. We played the Angels just as many times as we played the Dodgers this year, Conk. Seemed that way, anyway. Sorry, I know I'm supposed to be excited about the spunky Los Angeles Angels of Anaheim, but I'm much happier watching the Brooklyn Dodgers of Los Angeles. I'm even unmoved by the so-called Subway Series. Do we really need to play the Yankees six times a year to know that we hate them, and they us? We experienced the mysterious kismet of a real Subway Series, a World Series, in 2000, something I never thought I'd see again in my natural lifetime between the endless playoff rounds and the one's up–the other's down rhythm of New York teams—and it somehow seemed anticlimactic. OK, the Yankees' near sweep contributed, but even those seminally dramatic moments— Doc Gooden, returning to Shea in a Yankees uniform to pitch against the Mets in the Series—fizzled. Didn't we sort of see that already? Yeah, and it wasn't so cold and wet. This is great, the schedule makers should be toasted in cold Rhein-gold: Phillies, Nationals, Mets, Marlins, and Braves, each playing the others for a total of around twenty games.

Quote of the day: "The Mets have fallen in love with Zam-brano, but they may want to consider substituting Trachsel before it becomes a fatal attraction."

I tried calling you today to see if you wanted, maybe, to try to get tickets. Ring, ring, ad infinitum. OK, so you were out. Try to remember to turn on your machine next time, so a person could leave a message if he wanted to. You know, I'm perfectly happy to attend one of these games with your new friend, too. I'll be good. I promise I won't dwell on the old days; nothing exclusionary, no talk about even so much as an old Mets team. Just 100 percent contemporary New York Mets baseball, all the time. Plus Harris Conklin, America's Foremost Neglected Poet, in real time. An incredibly lifelike simulacrum. OK, I'm giving you an example of the sort of crack she *won't* hear. OK? Just old inoffensive pal Ivan, humbly saying, "Care for a hot dog? A cup of beer? I'll be leav-ing you two alone for a few judicious moments to go to the concession stand and stretch my legs." I won't wriggle be-tween the two of you or anything. I'll take the train out sepa-

rately from you so you can get all your (charming) handhold-
ing and (endearing) giggling done. Or I'll just cart us out in the
Town Car, with you in the back, Limo Style, doing whatever.

(ELEVEN PM) May I begin by saying that Keith Hernandez
completely agrees with me about the value of intradivisional
play? Seo didn't seem to have it tonight, but then, he's been
doing so well that even though he gave up four runs in five
innings this still only brings his ERA up to 1.86. He gave up a
home run in the first inning, potential bad tidings, but to
Kenny Lofton, at least. But then a single to Abreu (a two-out
single) and then another homer to Pat Burrell and suddenly
I wasn't feeling quite so charitable there at the Dark and
Noisy Bar for Pierced People. 3–0. Beltran hit one out in the
bottom of the inning, the rally pretty much stops there but
there was a sense we could climb out of a two-run hole. The
Phils added another: good baserunning; a hit, Tejada bunts
him over, then another hit.

Hernandez was voluble tonight, in that particularly intelligent way that makes you remember the days before Tim
McCarver decided that he knew everything and that there
wasn't a single pitch, swing, play, or strategy in baseball that
wasn't worth questioning or otherwise picking apart. Just
solid knowledge, sparingly applied: Keith says that Beltran is
"sweeping," overemphasizing the top-hand part of his swing
and pulling everything on the ground—all those 4–3 ground-
outs and 4–6–3 double plays, concisely explained. "He's in a
rut and it just may be too late to work it out this year," says
Keith.

In the fifth inning, Lofton doubled, and then Utley singled, but Beltran, not sweeping when he throws, cut Lofton

down at the plate—Charley Manuel got chucked out arguing the call; he was wrong, it was a beautiful throw.

In the stands they're wearing "Vote for Pedro" T-shirts. The idiom transformed. *Napoleon Dynamite* my ass. Now let's hear some fucking thundersticks.

In our half of the fifth, another run. Beltran drives in Reyes. Opposite field hit—maybe he's listening to MSG. 4–2, a regulation game, and it was cloudy tonight, too. Seventh: Castro, the human fireplug, doubled; Madison, pitching for the Phillies, hits Cairo; and then Beltran comes up and walks on four straight pitches. Bases loaded, Madison wild pitches Floyd, bringing home a run. Then Floyd strikes out. 4–3, we're running out of time. Or so it felt.

1–2–3 inning for Padilla in the eighth. I could feel the tension in Flushing, sitting there on my little toadstool. Wright walks. Wright steals. Diaz fights off about a hundred pitches on the hands—they know what he likes to hit—then walks. Then, enter the fireplug. Castro hit one, shit, straight up, which then dropped into the Pepsi Picnic Area, nice as you please. Whap! 6–4.

OK, you know what's next. Braden Looper—a two-run lead isn't nearly enough. But Looper does it. No runs, no hits, no errors, and no men left on. And at the end of eight-and-one-half innings of play, it's the New York Mets 6, the Philadelphia Phillies 4, and the Wild Card race that much narrower.

Look, I'll just climb aboard my hobbyhorse briefly to re-iterate: there's enough fun for three, here. Tomorrow?

Your Lonely Scribe,
Ivan

August 31

The forecast was rain. The excuse he'd used with Felt for not wanting to go out to the ballpark. It occurred to Harris Conklin only after he'd ordered the Chinese takeout and rearranged his apartment to bring the television to the foot of the bed—he had no "media cart," so this meant prying the set from where, apparently, it had become glued with spilled diet cola to the chest of drawers opposite his couch, and wrestling it to a spot atop his wicker hamper, which sagged at the weight, the cable, barely long enough, now stretched at threatening knee-level across his bedroom's doorway—that he was helplessly replaying in mind's eye a key scene from Woody Allen's Manhattan. *Mariel Hemingway transfixed in the glow of the tube, chopsticks poised over a white takeout box as she gushed over a black-and-white film, some favorite of Woody's, no doubt. Well, last night of August, September's doorstep, with the Mets on the brink of the Wild Card—if they won tonight, and the Cardinals beat the Marlins, a reasonable bet, they'd be in first place, and they had Pedro Martinez pitching, too—Conklin knew he'd need to keep an eye on the game. More than that, it would soothe him, make the night possible to get through at all. This would be the first time he and Felt's daughter had rendezvoused with not only foreknowledge but mutual acknowledgment of their intention to spend a night together. Denial, Conklin's succor, was draining away.*

"We're watching the game?" she said devilishly as she slipped into the bed half an hour later. The Chinese had been delivered, sat cooling on his counter.

"Ivan would know if I'd missed it."

"You're worse than my mother."

"It's an uncommonly important game."

"Oh?"

He tried to explain. She kept goosing him, verbally and otherwise, reminding him she was no Mets neophyte. It wasn't that she didn't understand, she had him know. It was that she understood enough, more than enough, to be certain she didn't care. At Ivan's insistence, she'd given the Mets a fair chance.

Pedro looked his craftiest, if not his strongest, through the first three. Meanwhile, Beltran and Floyd strung together hits for a run, and Castro hit one out. Two–zip. A promising beginning. Between innings, they found The Treasure of the Sierra Madre on PBS. It was tempting to see the Mets and Phillies as Humphrey Bogart and Tim Holt, panning for their fortune.

They made love—Harris's preferred term, he'd never admit to Ivan—in the fourth, with the sound muted. Nevertheless, Harris spotted, in replay, the cheap-shot homer Pedro gave up to Ryan Howard, a minor-league call-up to replace the injured Jim Thome. Howard was hitting home runs routinely; he might be the Phillies' reply to Mike Jacobs. Another solo homer in the sixth, to Chase Utley (another name, Harris thought, who ought to be playing for the Red Sox). Tie game. On the commercial break Gena trundled into the kitchen in his sheet, neatly stepping over the stretched cable, and rounded up dinner. She put it on plates, though, and rummaged in his drawers for silverware, explaining how she had always felt bullied by her parents into using chopsticks, and thereby dispelling the *image borrowed from the Allen film. Just as well. They flipped back to the Bogart film, for just as long as Harris could stand the uncertainty. Then back, in time to see Kenny Lofton reel in two Floyd and Diaz drives that would have been out in most ballparks. Ah, Shea, it had robbed Harris Conklin's heart like it stole home runs.*

From there the script soured. Pedro disintegrated in the seventh. Another two Phillie homers. Conklin, in dismay, spilled lobster sauce down his chest as he groped for the remote to restore the volume. The announcer explained how rare a disaster they'd witnessed: Pedro hadn't given up four home runs in a game since 1998, when as an Expo he'd done it the only two times in his career. Once to the Braves and once, poignantly enough, to the Mets. Harris wondered absently who. Bernard Gilkey came to mind. Was Gilkey still in baseball, even? This was the sort of Met-genealogical distraction Harris resorted to when the Met present moment failed him.

Sheets of rain begin to fall, on the screen at Shea, and rattling against the windows and at the top of his apartment's disabled air conditioner. Willie Randolph yanked Pedro, for Heath Bell. The rain, weirdly, shut off, like a faucet. Heath Bell, it seemed to Harris, pitched in a strange style, his leggings worn high, he appeared to be prancing on the mound, like the rabbit from Disney's version of Alice in Wonderland—*he's late, he's late, for a very important date. Against him the Phils added three insurance runs, just in case Conklin was expecting any sort of, ahem, miracle. Among other complaints, fuck Heath Bell. The whole revolving-door bullpen. Hadn't Felt compared Braden Looper to the Cheshire cat? Send these guys back to Won-*

derland, then, and bring on Tweedledee and the Mock Turtle. Now the rain returned, again sudden like a faucet. It should have been romantic, the almost tribal drumming against the old pebbled-glass skylight in his apartment's bathroom. Harris knew, though, that the grout had vulnerabilities, that in a wind this high he'd likely find a puddle on the tiles when he next went in to urinate.

In a near fury—the rallying of his own testosterone lately terrified him—he seized hold of the remote and switched back to PBS. Bogart, with a six-day beard, staggered into a watering hole, pulling his half-dead burro by a rope.

"Sorry, Harris."

"I thought you didn't care."

"I'm expressing sympathy. Your caring so much stirs me."

"I don't welcome pity. I'd prefer you Believe."

"It hurts to Believe," said Gena. "Don't make me go there."

He realized he could say the same to her, in a different context.

6

[*September*]

September 1

Dear Ivan,

Sorry in advance if you've been ringing today. I took my phone off the hook. Hangover. Tuned in the game on "mute" (actually, the television had been running all night on mute—long story) for the one a.m. rubber match against Philadelphia. So we stumbled last night. Yet if we took two of three against Philly, we'd resume our drive for the Wild Card, right? Meaningful games, here we were playing one, in September.

Glavine looked about like Glavine: elegant after the first inning, but in the first he walked two, allowed two hits, and spotted the Phils two runs. On the mound for Philadelphia, Jon Lieber, the sort of pitcher, with good control and a fair sinker, that our lineup has the ability to make look like Greg Maddux in his prime. So the game drifted into the fifth inning in this drab manner: two–nothing Phils, easy as pie.

Disconcertingly, there was another new fellow warming up in the bullpen. A rookie, his first day in "The Show." Tim

Hamulack. A reddish-blond, he resembled, to my eye, Wayne Garrett. Baseball is always doing this to me: reminding me that I don't know my team, not really, that the young are a creeping invasion like mammals pickpocketing dinosaurs' eggs; and simultaneously triggering from the recesses of my brain some doddering recollection of a Met face or batting stance from eons past, a name the current broadcasters haven't uttered aloud in years, might not even know. Hey, whatever: maybe we'll get a look at Hamulack, find out what he lacks, whether he's a hack or a ham or whether he's got any luck. Or is on the lam. Doesn't Hamulack sound like one of those '60s "New Theater" leftist revamps of Shakespeare?

In the sixth, Reyes led off with a triple and immediately scored on a Matsui groundout. Shea erupted. Reyes, god bless him, really is bottled electricity. Have you noticed he runs out from under his helmet à la Willie Mays? I think it was Willie who confessed that he arranged his helmet just so, in order that he'd be able to showily shake it off rounding first.

Glavine was still on the mound, 120 pitches his highest-ever pitch count (as a Met). Yet he finally began to labor. Since the All-Star game Glavine's lost two games 2–1, and another one 2–0. He left this one losing 2–1 in the eighth, for Roberto Hernandez. I can only imagine he sat in the dugout thinking: Hall of Fame: You Can't Get There from Here. As Hernandez drifted into trouble, the camera located another new reliever warming up, Takatsu. Ted Robinson mentioned that only two pitchers have stayed in the bullpen all season— Looper and Hernandez. Everyone else has been "modular" with our triple-A team. The bullpen is like a clown car, Ivan.

No saying who'll tumble out. Leashed dogs, even, with Renaissance Faire ruffs around their necks, and sparkly hats.

We wobbled into the ninth down one run, to face, again, Ugueth Urbina (I love typing that name). This was the rubber match of the set with the Phils, but also with Urbina, who we beat on Tuesday, and who beat us yesterday. Short answer: the rubber match went to Urbina. We brought in Looper to pitch the ninth, perhaps trying to hypnotize ourselves into believing we have a lead. What does Looper do? Give up a solo homer to Ryan Howard, the phenom. Another knife in the heart, Looper, thanks a million. And then he allows two more singles, lonely as ever. If coffee is for closers, Looper gets lemonade. Hamulack was even warming up again! Yet Looper wriggled through the jam, exiting to boos I can't argue with. So, on into the ninth needing "only" a two-run rally against Billy Wagner.

You know the sole and inevitable outcome: we've blown the series, Ives. Somebody go get Billy Wagner a cup of coffee.

Dressed in black, no sugar,
Harris

September 5

Dear Harris,

The Tar Baby, aka Steve Trachsel, starts again. The umps seem to hurry him along, as if they speed up the game not merely in the late innings but late in the season as well.

Let's get the hell out of here, they're saying, let's get some golf in before it starts raining.

A sort of predictable little game. One–one tie evolves into a two–two tie. With the Braves there's rarely a feeling of close-game tension. It's just a question of who's going to get to us, and when. This time it's the Man Called Chipper. Two-run homer. Ah, if I could save time in a bottle.

Beltran strikes out with a man on to end the game. The spendthrift's blown just about all the goodwill he earned knocking himself silly against Mike Cameron's face. We left eleven men on.

What can I say? Another September, another series against the Braves. I'm holding out some hope, Harris, genuinely I am. I think I've mastered my fear of this team. Nobody who comes in first five hundred and twelve times in a row while winning the Series only once can be all that scary. We can take two more from them. Listen: let's hit a bar tomorrow and watch Pedro. I know a place you'll like. It has plenty of intimate corners where we can commiserate with each other and fellow hopeless causers. And if you aren't "pinned" yet, then maybe we can try to meet someone, though from the way you've been acting I have a feeling you'll demur. That's fine; you know I approve. But carve out a little time for me. I'll start calling you around eleven o'clock tomorrow morning, will telephone repeatedly through four PM until you agree to grant me this audience.

Until tomorrow then,
Ivan

September 6, midnight

Dearest G.,

You can begin, please—I mean to say, I beg you to begin—by deleting my last four cell-phone messages. Delete them incurious, unheard, if you will (if you still can!), as you've said to me you frequently do with your mother's voice mails. There's not one shred in those blurted, thwarted utterances of Harris Conklin's heart, nor of my gift—nothing you'll regret never hearing if you'll only delete, oh please, delete. Cell phone's not my medium. And the backdrop of that damned bar Ivan—your father—insisted on selecting, hellacious with its beery hooligan clientele; with its maddening hip-hop jukebox (you would have slid in my five-dollar bill and punched in a whole evening's worth of listenable numbers, I've seen you do it before, you miracle worker, you redeemer); with its competing televisions—Yankees, urgh, on four of them—and not least with those whirring, chortling video-trivia games ("Who Played Lindsay Lohan's Evil Twin Sister in *My Night at Maud's*?") lining the wall where I kept sneaking off to try to speak with you, to appease you, to re-insinuate myself into your forgiving graces. Ivan somehow thinks that my having a television at home means I've got his endurance for the multimedia realms he negotiates so brilliantly. Has no idea how easily baffled I can be. How frequent my recourse to mute. No, the scent of my gift was not to be detected in those cell calls, let alone in the messages that followed. And my heart was nowhere to be found, being left behind with you. Forgive the banality. It's simply the case. Delete, delete, delete, delete, four times, and we'll both be glad.

I had no choice, sweet. Ivan left me none. Pedro was

pitching. You don't realize how he and I have pined for these moments, for a Met like *that* Met, bootstrapping the team into September with a chance to attain a thing that matters, a thing that could restore us to ourselves. And against *Atlanta*. (Never mind that you've so suddenly given me what I'd increasingly feared only victory could.) I've bruised your father with all my cowardly evasions, he knows me too well. This was a bottom line, then: I had to meet his call. And (if only!) it could have been so healing between myself and your father, such a promise for the future (I swear I'll tell him soon, soon, yes, and before the holidays, you keep reminding me it must be before the holidays, why must your tribe's holidays come so unexpectedly soon, they seem so terribly out of place while the city still swelters and the Mets still strive!), if only Pedro hadn't faltered. In damnable Atlanta. A wretched night it turned out to be, Pedro laboring and in trouble from the start, bleeding a run in the first. And we wasted a leadoff double from the Mink in the second. Then in the third Matsui tripled, and we managed to waste that, too, Floyd hitting into a double play. Darling, we're one-for-sixteen with runners in scoring position in this series so far. I emphasize this so you'll understand how strained were my hopes for the evening, how the chance you've urged me to take was drowned in the gulf between myself and your father. Even so, I sat swearing to myself that any moment I'd confide our secret, secure Ivan's blessings, bring him into the light only you and I know. I simply needed a turn in the game, a moment of Met grace, to open the way. Not a lead, that was by this point asking perhaps too much. But a hit. A sweet double play, perhaps.

Furcal, in the very next frame, hits one of those lucky-ass swinging bunts that just can't be fielded. What is it about our visitations to Atlanta? Their ballpark is a Theater of Blood and Chipper is Vincent Price. Andruw Jones drove him in, and the Braves had a two–nothing lead. And so on, from there. Ivan and I sitting in wretched attempted silence in that establishment which robbed us of even our silence with its clangor, tumult, bogus bonhomie. I cannot even begin to explain. He noticed me slipping away for the calls, too, I know he did. Things are worse now, not better, I'm sorry to say. I'm sorry for so much. Pedro surrendered another run in the seventh. We got on the board, too late, though the Wright double was elegant and I nearly broached the impossible matter. No. And then Kyle Farnsworth on to finish us, one-two-three in the ninth. The mechanical efficiency of the Braves. Ghastly foam hatchets. Silence. Ivan condemning my failure with his knowing, unknowing eyes.

Forgive me. And call. On a real, not ersatz telephone, please. I'm sitting up tonight staring at both of mine, real and ersatz, in case either of them rings, or vibrates, or disintegrates.

> With all of an old poet's love,
> H.

September 7

Dear Harris,

For some reason I've felt the need throughout the season to preserve the appearance of conflict, tension, and suspense when writing, even though I've always known that you have merely to reach over, or behind you if I correctly recall the current layout of your media-swaddled cocoon, and switch on WFAN for the latest rabid outburst about our team and its failings. I don't know why. Perhaps it's because you're a poet, and I thought you'd appreciate the sense of plot, pacing, and structure I bring to these things. Well, not this time. The season's lost, Harris. I take no pleasure in reconstructing the way in which we thrust it away from us. Glavine on the mound; his luck against Atlanta historically bad at 1–8.

In the first, we managed to scratch out a lead: Reyes hits, steals (his fiftieth stolen base of the year) and we've scored on an error and two groundouts. Nothing for the highlight reel, but we're on the board, and when Wright gets a hit with two out, we're up two–zip. How's Tommy going to do tonight?

Glavine looks pretty sharp for the first four innings, gives up a well-hit double in the second but otherwise is perfect. But in the fifth the Braves rap out two singles and it's 2–1. Meanwhile, Tim Hudson (aka a naked opportunist from an Anthony Mann western, as I characterized him back in May) has settled in and we're not making a peep.

I'm sitting, for this one, at a different bar. I took to heart what you said last night. All I can say in my own defense is that I remember Stumblebum's as a quiet and meditative place to watch a crucial ballgame. I didn't know that they'd added nine flat-screen televisions to each corner and alcove of the premises, or that it would be quite so loud. I don't blame you in the least for needing to go out for air—eight times seemed a little excessive to me, I admit, but we're all built differently, and I'm happy to have had the chance to spend some time with you, with your dance card as full as it's been and things going so well, even if you're not in the least forthcoming about what, exactly, is going so well, or with who. As I said, we're all built differently.

One of the announcers on Beltran: "He's turning over the top hand, and you just can't get any lift on anything." The whole fucking league knows what's wrong with this guy.

Glavine still on the hill into the seventh. Gives up a lead-off single, but then gets out of it with a couple of strikeouts. It's still 2–1. But how long can a team live scoring one or two runs a night? Not too long. In the seventh, Beltran squibs one through the middle with one out, Floyd draws a walk, but then, with Wright at the plate, Beltran gets thrown out trying to steal third. Motherfucker!

Hudson takes advantage of the free out and so the rally fades. Palpable dread here in the Sazerac House. You'd like it; it's suffused with good ol' Greenwich Village poetical type history. W. H. Auden is reputed to have given someone a hand job in the back room, or something. America's Artistic Disneyland. Plus they serve a great jambalaya.

Glavine, still hanging on into the eighth, gets one out. Trying to pull together the horses for a complete game; the poor guy doesn't trust the bullpen. But after he walks Chipper on four pitches (not the most inadvisable thing I've ever seen a pitcher do, I might add), Willie yanks him for Hernandez—hey, he's been delivering all year, right? And, sure enough, the other of the Jones Boys, Andruw, flies out. Julio Franco comes up—forty-year-old vs. forty-seven-year-old—and Hernandez makes him pop it up.

It's the Braves' half of the ninth inning, and our "closer," Braden Looper, comes in to do whatever it is that he's supposed to be doing for, or to, the New York Mets. Looper's life story, for *Parade* magazine: "The Pitcher Batters Love." Sounds like a line from Mayakovski. Not that I'd know. Looper delivers what the cynics among us expect; a big booming leadoff double on the first goddamned pitch. Dead silence in the Sazerac House. "And, as they say, the incident is closed/Love's boat has smashed against the daily grind." Captain Looper, meet Mr. Mayakovski. "Why bother then/to balance mutual pains, hurts, and sorrows."

On the other hand, the jukebox is playing "All I Want to Do Is Have Some Fun." I got a feeling I'm not the only one.

Question: How much, in the final reckoning, has this entire blown season (I use the word "blown" advisedly here) come down to the mistaken proposition that this man is a CLOSER? From opening day onward, the crushing lie we've told ourselves, eating away at our hearts. For you, McConklin, like unconfessed sin.

A talented individual named Ryan Langerhans (*Ryan Langerhans?*) singles, scoring the run, and it's a tie, 2–2. If I were Glavine I'd be dying inside. The Hall of Fame: you can't get there from here. The director shows Bobby Cox in the dugout, and I remember him, first as a shitty utility infielder on shitty Yankee teams, and then as the button-pusher guiding these implacable, clockwork squads, remembering the Terry Pendleton, Fred McGriff, David Justice teams, one long unvariegated smear of flavorless, oppressive domination, "America's Team," never changing in its fundamental deep anonymity. What's Orwell's line? "The heel of a boot smashing a human face for a thousand years"?

Looper worms out of it. Tenth inning. Matsui grounds out (a low *boooooo* resounds throughout the Sazerac House, thrums, from the moment he is shown walking from the on-deck circle to the moment he sharply breaks off from the run to first to trot back to the dugout), Beltran singles, Floyd walks, Wright singles. The Braves keep changing pitchers (Reitsma, Brower, Foster—I was going to call these kids "cannon fodder" but realized how laughable that sounds in this connection), so all of this takes thirteen years and about sixty-five commercials for pickup trucks that are going to change everything, apparently, for the people wise enough to buy them. All these breaks start to get expensive for the solitary drinker. I wish I had one of those hollow canes you can surreptitiously sip Scotch from. Outside, on Hudson Street, I watch a taxicab rear-end some car with Jersey plates. There's the usual posturing, sigh; god forbid you shouldn't be "New York" enough. *Time Out* or the *Voice* probably ran a feature explaining how savvy New Yorkers behave after fender benders. The woman in the cab hops out and then hauls her cell phone out of her purse, now *she's* gesturing; someone waiting at the Soho Hotel or the Gansevoort is going to get an earful about this one. Woodward comes up, singles on the first pitch—holy shit!—Beltran runs home like a man about to miss the last bus. We're up 3–2, but Castro lines into a double play and so we're playing to preserve the one-run lead, with Chipper, Andruw, and Julio Franco coming up.

Speaking of cell phones, did I hear you *chirping* last night? I thought you were opposed to the devices.

Looper's first pitch: Chipper rifles a single.

Looper hits Andruw. Two on, nobody out.

In some fucked-up way I'm not even rooting for this man anymore; I'm rooting against him, no matter what colors he's wearing. It's a sort of exquisite pleasure to turn to the guy at the next table and say, authoritatively, "He's going to walk the next guy."

He walks Franco. Bases loaded, nobody out.

Can a man be credited with two blown saves in one game? Why not? I think Looper's done it here. Well, at least we're through the big bats. HA HA HA.

Here comes Willie, walking like a man cashing in a season. Now pitching for the New York Mets, Shingo Takatsu. Exactly: Who? Why, another team's washed-out closer. Actually, a nation's washed-out closer: he's the all-time saves leader in the history of Japanese baseball.

The camera pans over the Braves dugout. They look bored. It occurs to me to wonder: Why do they even want to beat us? Completing this sweep couldn't be more incidental to their long-standing master plan to win the division and then lose in the first round of the playoffs to, who? The Padres? The Giants? Takatsu's a stoical submarine pitcher; looks like the Eighth Samurai. After the game, after he's outlived his usefulness, Mets fans will expel him and his Ronin ways from the once-again-peaceful village. He actually gets a pop-up—one out. And another. Two down. Then he goes to 3–1 on the potential third and winning out. (That we're actually in danger of winning this game now seems insane.) A strike—3–2. Pretty good drama now, I'll grudgingly admit. On 3–2 the motherfucking rookie, yes, *Langerhans*, hits a single and Atlanta wins, and I do believe that's the nail in our coffin. To their credit the Braves do run out on the field and jump up and down as if they've clinched something.

So there you have it. What's left is what's left. Three weeks of anticlimax. I wish you'd been there. You would have liked the Sazerac House, not least of all for its eponymous drink specialty. Another time. Possibly another season.

Dying hard,
Ivan

September 10

Ivan,

Here in the aftermath of the ritual season immolation in Atlanta—crushing, definitive failure, change-the-name-of-the-franchise shame—we've crowned it by dropping the first three in St. Louis: whipped-cur obeisance to the class of the Senior Circuit. Hard not to think the Cards will be our champion. La Russa's upright men may poop out in the World Series but he gets them there, he does. Who's bitter? Let these Redbirds massacre the Braves, that's all I ask. I want to see Atlanta blood dripping from their beaks and talons. A hollow-eyed Leo Mazzone rocking like Lily Tomlin in the dugout.

It was Friday's loss that occasions a poem. Yes, incidentally, we're back to five hundred. Fuck me.

Sylvia Plath Homage of the Five-Hundred Team

Innings
Into whose blackness double plays tumble
And the boos!
Boos echoing
Off the upper deck like shrikes.

The out
Rising like smoke, like a
Wrapper swirling
Mustard-stained, to the foot
Of the Whitestone.

Failed bunts
Third strikes
Nerve-flaying blown saves.
Years later I
Encounter them in the stats—

Stats dry and bodiless,
Yet hold the book at arm's length
See the shape?
They reveal the shadow of a skull.
A Met grins.

> Yours from inside The Ball Jar,
> H.

September 11

Ivan,

What's a Sylvia Plath poem meant to be if not final? Yet I should have known better, for Sunday's game was in Pedro's hands. Facing the risk of the four-game Cardinal sweep, and wearing FDNY caps (nobody knocked down the St. Louis Arch, so the Cardinals played au naturel), El Metro pitched a gem. Even Beltran woke up and slugged one out. Recall that early-season complaint, that Beltran "only" hits home runs in Pedro's starts? Hell, Ivan, if he'd hit a homer in every one of Pedro's starts he'd be the National League MVP, most likely. And we'd have a pennant. Diaz added a three-run shot to clinch it, the seven runs our first respectable score of the month.

Scratching the mosquito bite,
Harris

- -

September 15

Dear Harris,

The season is running on sentiment alone: on Tuesday I marveled, nostalgically, as I watched (I tried a joint called Shenanigans this time—Stumblebum's, with old license plates on the wall) Frank Robinson come out of the dugout to pitch a classic fit, protesting the umpire's refusal to call a strike on Diaz's blatantly late attempt to check a swing. Robinson built up a head of steam only gradually, descending from reason to near violence in stages, as captured on camera; three umpires, finally, restraining him from attacking a fourth. He's a scary man, but as he ages there's also a Redd Foxx quality beginning to peek through, and I felt a small gratitude, as the Mets trudge to season's conclusion, that Frank has left baseball's executive offices, returned to the field, where he belongs, to assume the stewardship of expansion's biggest economic failure (for moral and aesthetic failures see: Padres, San Diego, among others) and give the twenty-five or thirty fans who care about such things a regular glimpse of him, as befits a genuine institution.

Not much to say about Tuesday. I'm tempted to say: Saturday, with old license plates on the wall. That we should continue to lose to the Nationals—ugh. Glavine starting his 600th game, fifth most in NL history. The Expos, meanwhile, started a relief pitcher. I mean Nationals, whatever. The most interesting aspect of their team, here in mid-September, is that they have in Jon Rauch the tallest player, at 6'11", in Major League history. Fran Healy says, "Unlike Randy Johnson, this guy's thick." The broadcasters also embody the sense of diminished expectations that now lies loosely draped over the season, like a satin robe over the shoulders of a punch-drunk fighter: they're talking about finishing above .500. Note to Fred Wilpon: the idea isn't merely to play meaningful games in September, though that's a perfectly good jumping-off point. The idea is to win them. Glavine singled home Jacobs in the second—I guess when you've given up five runs in your last three starts, total, and don't have a victory to show for it, you concentrate on your at bats.

Oh, cut to the chase, Felt: we never recover from the three runs the Nats score in the third. Looper comes in in the ninth. Gives up his customary hit, and then an error, and a this-a, and a that-a, and it's 4–2, boos all around for the loneliest closer.

In our half of the ninth, the Mink comes in to pinch-hit. Apparently he was quoted as saying he had "the best batting practice he's had all year" tonight. He grounds out. We go one, two, three. Perhaps beating the Nats in the tent-folding competition. Audrey, behind the bar at Shenanigans: "Can I finally turn this thing off now?"

I have to confess that I don't even listen to more than one inning of the Wednesday game. The guilt that steals over me as I reach for the dial the instant Cohen thinks to give me the score—5–3 Nats, in the fifth—is brief and painless, much like Braden Looper's moments of introspection.

Two artifacts from the September 15 game: lots of press beforehand, a sort of damage control. Willie having one-on-ones, Beltran offering we-won't-quit-we're-professional isms. But the Mink—ah, how I'll miss this sort of self-abrading candor—the Mink, regarding his loss of playing time to Mike Jacobs, said, "I knew it was going to happen as soon as we fell out of the race. This ain't my first rodeo."

Artifact two: Looper enters with a lead (Floyd's grand slam in the fifth, following Beltran's we-won't-quit pop-up [boooo]), after Willie pulls Heilman—very reluctantly, no doubt—for a pinch-hitter. Looper: allows a hit. Man reaches third with one out. Looper: hits the pinch-hitter. First and third. Looper: on the twelfth pitch of the at bat, allows a single. We lose. Let's get out of here. I went to Shea for this one: the place was a sepulcher. Pierrot and I barely exchanged nods through the misery (though he asked after you and your young[!] friend). Mesch had no one to ush, and was not in evidence. No wait for the polish sausage.

Less is more,
Ivan

September 18

Ivan,

Tonight I say nothing about our plummet from contention, our appalling September. Tonight I'll flinch from what's finally only another failed Mets season, one to which we've perhaps paid far, far too much attention. (Has it been worth it, being a Believenik? What are we achieving by gazing so deeply into the team? Do we know more than we'd learn by a cursory attention, a bar-fan's fatuous received impressions? Might all received baseball wisdom be more or less *correct*? What have we concluded that we wouldn't learn from the average *Post*-reading loudmouth—that Wright is righteous; Beltran struggling with the pressure; the bullpen shameful; Randolph stout of heart; Pedro crazy like a fox; Reyes a glamour-puss, etc.) No, tonight we'll only shed a tear for Donn "Big Train" Clendenon, MVP of the '69 Series, the right Met at the right time, a snazzy dresser (I'll never forget him arriving on *Kiner's Korner* not drenched in sweat like the usual postgame interviewee but showered and garbed in Al Green–worthy double-breasted peach-and-tan magnificence), a lawyer, if I remember correctly, in the employ of the Coca-Cola Co., and a slugger whose homers had a McCoveyian authority, deceased yesterday at the age of seventy.

Tonight, between Clendenon's death and the death of the season's hopes, I feel up against the bitterest lie that baseball tells: that time is somehow therein suspended, that the difference between it and other sports is its clocklessness, its elastic frame of innings, its sprawl of months. In truth, the season is a clock, ticking with the thunder of days and nights. And when the clock reasserts itself it is truly a savage disenchantment to suffer: we've been gulled again, lulled again by our own pastoral bullshit.

Enough. Or: not quite enough. I want to admit to you that it's partly my ear that's always adored Clendenon. Have you ever dwelled on the sheer beauty of the *names* of the '69 Miracle team? I know, you'll tell me it's subjective, a retrospective projective affective effect, or some such. But I don't believe it is. The Miracle Mets were and always will be the most beautifully named team of all time, the veritable "cellar door" of rosters (no jokes, Ivan).

In Donn's memory, then, a poem, nothing to do with five hundredness, for once:

Seaver, Swoboda, Clendenon

Seaver Swoboda Clendenon,
Agee Gaspar, Otis Frisella,
Gentry, Gentry—
Koonce Shamsky, Koosman McGraw.

Nolan Cleon, Duffy Grote,
Bud Tug Pfeil.
Gaspar Garrett, Gaspar Gosger,
Boswell, Cardwell, Kranepool.

Seaver Swoboda Clendenon,
Frisella, McAndrew McGraw
Agee, Dyer—
Clendenon. Clendenon. Clendenon.

Good night,
Harris

September 19
(postcard)

H.

No, no jokes from me this time. Only the suggestion that *cellar doors* may be used to depart cellars, as well as to enter them.

I.

September 22

Ivan,

Going for the sweep against the Marlins, having already pretty well wrecked their Wild Card chances with the last two nights' victories, each so stirring—the twelfth-inning heroics on Monday by Diaz and Wright (the future is, if not now, at least real), and the veterans' heroics last night, Piazza and Cairo taking their turn. We're also taking a look now at Anderson Hernandez, potentially the final piece of the all-youth infield mosaic—he's a sharp-looking twenty-two-year-old, a very neat complement to Wright-Reyes-Jacobs. Maybe someday they'll be writing songs about these four.

Tonight could have been such a fine capper, with the glamour matchup: Pedro versus Dontrelle Willis. Having played spoiler for Washington, I was ready to repeat the feat against Florida. The Marlins had Willis batting seventh, in a lineup utterly ragged with injury. We're informed that no pitcher has batted so high in a lineup since 1973, presumably because it would be too severe an indignity for the "every-day" players batting eighth and ninth below a pitcher ever to endure from their manager. (How "everyday" these Marlins scrubs and September call-ups will ever be is another story. Mere cups of coffee shouldn't mouth off to a skipper as old and odd as Jack McKeon. And Willis is a good hitter, no insult there! Since when, Ivan, did pitchers become non-players? I recall plenty who could hit their weight and more, back in the good old blah blah blah.) This wretched condi-tion of the Marlins lineup leads, of course, to a fantasy of this being the night when Pedro throws a no-hitter. Which in turn dissipates quickly, when Delgado doubled in the first inning. But Pedro pitched around it, and both hurlers looked sharp in the early going. A duel—lovely. I settled in. Pen and paper in hand, ready to deliver a poem. I like writing these things when we hit five hundred on the upswing, Ivan, with Pedro on the mound, with our boot on the throat of the Marlins—

The moral of the story is the same as its punch line. I jumped the gun. Jinxed the team. Wrote a five-hundred poem in the fifth inning. Pedro immediately began to labor. Ran-dolph took him out for Padilla. (Somehow my eyes glaze over with Padilla on the mound—I suppose that's his effect on hitters as well.) I'll spare you the dowdy details of this wallflower game: failed Met at bats, cheap Florida runs. Two teams going nowhere, not even each other's spoilers. Pedro didn't dance. Nobody danced. The big difference this night: Pedro's old, Dontrelle's young.

Herewith, the freebie:

John Ashbery Homage of the Five-Hundred Team

Some men never learn to bunt well, it's a thing
that seems petty to them. What if someone erected a
papier-mâché apple from a hat, to no occasion?
    Inimitably,
they come from Norfolk, in pairs or threes, saying,
This is what I can do, here is my hapless position.
Or: Show me to your charming mound. I want to
    play
meaningful games. Mr. Met once had his head
reduced. But I'm getting ahead of myself.

Loving the Mets is such an American
and hectic thing to do, even
through dense acres of losing. All of us who do
were busy at it before we understood we wished
    to be.
You say to me, Let's trade Kaz Matsui.
I consent entirely. But trade him for what?
Our city's other team, the team we try not to
    think of,
has a player who shares Matsui's name
and nation. He was drawn across the sea and is
    known
as Godzilla. Our guy? He's Mothra.

    Yours,

    Harris

September 23

Dear, oh dear, Harris:

Meaningfully fighting for fourth—and against the other suitor vying for that particular crest (a waffle, rampant, against a field of broken bats) of unevenness, the Washington Nationals. Yowza. I trek down to the Ear Inn for this one, figuring, what?, that I can jump in the river afterward? Nearly a need for that, as it turns out, though Trachsel cruises at first, throwing strikes, giving up five hits, shutting them out over six innings. We're starting Jacobs, Reyes, Wright, Diaz, and, at second, Anderson Hernandez. Welcome to 2006, though I suppose it's possible we could trade half the infield for Jeremy Giambi and a bag of scuffed balls.

Oddly, the Ear Inn's picked up the Washington feed of the game, so I get to listen to (i.e., watch the closed-captioning of) the Nationals' broadcasters, including Ron Darling. Never felt this close to Ron when he was a Met. I was a Fat Sid Fernandez man, myself, after Doc. But he's a thoughtful commentator, a fine guy (for a Yale man).

Trachsel is working at his usual fly-in-amber pace. Or, La Brea tar pits, anyone? You could spend a fine afternoon coming up with colorfully serviceable comparisons. The infielders shift from foot to foot. The King of Boredom. And he's not even having trouble, which itself always increases the viscosity. Everything philistines say about baseball is suddenly true when he pitches, a line that could easily make it into some Encyclopedia Metsiana under his name. The Human Rain Delay. There are three barmaids here, Conklin, who could break your heart into little jagged fragments. Any one of them, suitably dressed, would look perfectly at home waiting in Philip Marlowe's outer office. I'd like to take them away from all this. And turn them into porn stars.

I suppose that's already happened with Mme. Felt IV. I'm feeling randy, and contemplating those partnerships that seem as if they should have been more durable. Mantle and Maris. Gould and Sutherland. Arden and Crawford. Kiner, Murphy, and Nelson. Culp and Cosby. Poitier and Cosby. Fat Albert and Cosby. Arkin and Caan. Arkin and Falk (doesn't it seem as if Alan Arkin is a man perpetually in search of a sidekick?). Lana Turner and anybody. Doubleday and Wllpon. Lennon and—oh fuck that. How about John and Taupin? Redford and Newman. Leopold and Loeb. Conklin and Felt? One thing I can assure you, Harris, is that you would enjoy the Ear Inn.

Anderson Hernandez is wearing #1. Always seems to me to come with a set of unmatchable expectations. So much so that you always end up with a light-hitting utility man. Give him 24. Or 44. Now there's a number for a slugger who chugs milk shakes and signs autographs for hours after the game. Give him #2. Look at Jeter—he tries harder.

We get three ground-ball hits—Reyes, Diaz, Beltran—in the sixth, to put ducks on the pond for Floyd, who sees ten pitches, getting it to 3–2, then singles off the wall. 2–0 Mets. Until the ninth.

No more Looper (!). Where is Looper? The Washington announcers don't know enough, aren't intimate enough with the details, to comment knowledgeably. Here comes Hernandez, in the closer's role. Wily old pro, chugs milk shakes (lots of them, from the looks of things), etc. But some tenacious spirochete of Looper's must have escaped the purge and infected Hernandez, because as sure as shit, as sure as *Forty*

Stories is the world's greatest bathroom book, as sure as Ritz Crackers haven't tasted the same since they took the recipe for Mock Apple Pie off the box, with two out and one on, Carlos Baerga—that Carlos Baerga, the one who sought throughout his tenure with the Mets to prove the accuracy of the rumors regarding the degradation of his skills—slugs it out, tying the game. I'll say it again: Carlos Baerga.

This one has a happy ending, though. Beltran, now that things are useless, is looking comfortable behind the plate, and he jacks one out, driving in Marlon Anderson and Reyes, both of whom singled to take first and third. Heilman comes in for the bottom, gets the save (or whatever they call it), and just in time, too: Carmen Sternwood flips to a show called *Hope and Faith.* Yes, exactly.

Hope, Faith, and the Long Goodbye
Ivan Felt signing off

September 24

Harris Conklin lay atop the bedspread, fully dressed, in twilight that leaked through heavy, nicotine-infused drapes, his neck propped against the wood-grain linoleum headboard as he absently flipped through the motel's crappy cable package, expecting nothing yet still disappointed: no Mets. No baseball, indeed, apart from the Cubs and Braves, those overexposed teams with their blandly oppressive national broadcasts, like Pravda, like Big Brother. Fuck Ted Turner. Conklin mused on a conceit to do with "colorized" movies and "colonized" native populations, i.e., the Braves and their unwarrantable Tomahawk Chop, then discarded it: to harp on the nativist-mascot theme verged on the injury-mongering of the politically correct, motifs worthy only of spoken-word poetry slams. The friend of my enemy is my enemy: colleagues brandishing similar agendas had attempted to invade the syllabus of his Postwar American Poetry class—heavy with Berryman, Lowell, Koch, Levine, Pinsky—seeking, ironically, to colonize it, with Sexton, Hacker, Lourde, and Harper. No, let Braves be Braves, Red-skins Redskins, Pirates Pirates, Gypsies, Polacks, Fags, etc.; the trouble wasn't with their name or heritage—Conklin could even resurrect a residual fondness for the early At-lanta teams: the gallant and gracious Hank Aaron's ascent, fatherly Phil Niekro knuckling through nine frames. The trouble was a recent history of complacent, untormented overdogs on the most underachieving dynasty of all time, men like Greg Maddux and David Justice and Chipper Jones, handsome, golfing men, who'd settled for dominance over Conklin's adored team for nearly fifteen years now, yet hardly ever achieved more. How much more honorable it would be, truly, if the Braves had run the table in the post-season a few times, glommed three or four championships— but no. What they preferred to do was break the Mets' hearts, then fold their own tepees and go home. Fuck CNN, fuck Ted Turner. Conklin clicked past C-Span and Country Music Television and several Schwarzenegger vehicles to SportsCenter, there to follow the Mets' fortunes on the crawl of schematic updates at the screen's lower margin.

Lord, the girl took long showers.

Could she, regretting everything, have perhaps left the

spray running for camouflage and squirmed through the motel bathroom window?

Conklin glanced at the bedside table, made certain the rental car's key was still there beneath the lamp with the change and gas-station receipts he'd dumped from his pockets. It was. So at the very worst she'd be a mile into the White Mountains' woods, not coursing back to civilization in the white Ford Taurus.

At 7:14, by the digital readout on the motel clock, the first score slugged past on the SportsCenter *screen: New York 1, Washington 0. Glavine starting against Livan Hernandez. A quick first-inning run, nice. Conklin's team could sweep the Nationals this weekend, why not? It might even be that the Mets could swap places with the team from the capital, send the Nationals to the division's basement, and thereby avoid the ignominy of finishing below a quasi-expansion franchise, one owned and operated by the commissioner's office, no less.*

Conklin and his young lover had come to New Hampshire for what the secretary of Conklin's department at Queens College had advertised to him as a "leaf tour," though he suspected they were at least a week early for any autumnal glories—mercifully, Conklin secretly felt. Route 2's dense green hills remained merely brushed with the colors by which Conklin was privately only reminded of ailment, squalor, taint. The trip's point, for him, was the abscondment from Queens, from the orbit of family, employers, rooting interests (though look at him now, scouring the television for updates—so much for leaving attachment behind), and, for Conklin, from the emptiness of his mailbox, from the unreplies growing more ominous with each passing day.

Signing them into the motel, he'd thought for a humorous instant to ask whether Gena had ever read Vladimir Nabokov's great book; hesitated; thought better of it. Then, as he carted their small luggage across the gravel lot toward the door of their boxy, ground-level hovel, Conklin felt his prudency corrupt into furtiveness and shame, as he realized now he could never ask her, could never bring the name of that novel—nor of the Stanley Kubrick film adaptation—anywhere into their talk, unless she pronounced it first. And even then he'd have to falsify surprise.

Yet, speaking of injury-mongering, why (presuming, of course, that the girl really was still in the shower, not fleeing down the highway with a hiker's thumb upraised) did he lay here rehearsing overfamiliar injuries, slights, and fears? Why couldn't he simply relish what had delivered itself to him: consummate, improbable happiness, and coming so late in his season of self, like the 1973 team's abrupt September salvaging of a National League pennant from the dregs of a long summer's mediocrity?

At 7:19, another SportsCenter *update: New York 5, Washington 0. This score came with an explanation: D. Wright, grand slam HR. Still in the first inning. Some sporting deity was indeed trying to rectify his mood. Though if the Mets won this game, he'd have to write a poem to fulfill an old promise. Now was hardly the time to lapse in that duty.*

Conklin and Gena's drive north had been nothing less than jubilant, revelatory, life-altering. Conklin at the wheel, she pushing compact disks into the car's player, "DJ-ing," she called it. The names of the bands she auditioned for his pleasure evaded his comprehension utterly, except as fragments of limp imagist poetry—Neutral Milk Hotel? The Arcade Fire? The Rain Injuries?—though their sounds, while pleasant enough, were more or less encompassed, it seemed to him, by a handful of innovations perfected by the Band and Moby Grape, in a time previous to the girl's coming into the world. He didn't share the thought. She pointed out and sang along to moments in the songs that she particularly admired and groped Conklin's leg and they barreled in the Taurus up the New England Thruway, and then across Vermont. And they talked. Not, as so often before, about the difficulties in her life or his, or about the resonances between the two. Now they talked of the stuff of their own feelings, the text of themselves: their history, their secret and its uncovering, how it felt to be Harris loving Gena and Gena loving Harris. The answer being: different, marvelously different, each day.

Then, outside St. Johnsbury, where they'd eaten Chinese buffet at the Jade Pagoda on High Street—cold sesame noodle and moo shu pork that Conklin kept belching up during the subsequent conversation, Chinese still the only food they could agree on, Felt had certainly been right in predicting that difficulty—they pulled over at a strange contemporary sculpture or monument, portraying two people walking leashed dogs. A monument to pet ownership? Well, it led to a bizarre ornamental garden, laced with pathways intended for, yes, the walking of dogs. Conklin and Gena walked without dogs, giddy in the sunlight (whatever you felt about foliage turned or not turned to glamorous colors, this was a sensational afternoon to be out of doors) and in their bliss. That they had no dogs on leashes seemed conspiratorially hilarious, beyond explanation to anyone else, though in the privacy of his thoughts Conklin kept explaining it, helplessly, to Ivan Felt—we had no dogs, Ivan, that was the thing. And it was there, walking no dogs, that between them a certain question was framed, and there that between them a certain answer hovered into view. By the time the two were back in the car the decision was secure enough not to need speaking of. Or else it had been a hallucination native to the bee-drenched honeysuckle arbor, which would make it equally unmentionable. Conklin wasn't superstitious, just struck dumb.

She came out of the bathroom, in a towel. Conklin had now to reassemble himself into the happy wise man she took him to be. It was this imperative, and how it overrode his hesitation, that was in fact her gift to him: she rendered him other than himself.

Flopping onto the bed, she took the remote from his hand and immediately switched the channel. He wasn't about to explain that he was waiting for the NL scores to update.

"What's on?"

She surfed, landing on TCM—Ted Turner again, though the footage was black and white. Perhaps Conklin's information was out-of-date. Garbo, plainly dressed, ascending the stair of the Eiffel Tower.

"Ninotchka," he said.

"Sorry?"

"Ninotchka, that's the name of this movie."

"Who are those two?"

In this, at least, her confidence in him wasn't mis-

placed. *"Greta Garbo and Melvyn Douglas. The screenplay's by Billy Wilder."*

"I've never seen Greta Garbo before."

"They promoted this film with the slogan 'Garbo laughs.'" Conklin wondered, as he said it, what it could possibly mean to Gena.

"Oh, wow . . ."

"Melvyn Douglas, what a strange career he had. Never really a big star, but he goes from romancing Greta Garbo to three decades later playing the aging rancher in Martin Ritt's Hud *. . . already seems like an old man at that point . . . then he ends up as a really old man playing the senator married to Shirley MacLaine in* Being There.*"*

"Being there?"

"Jerzy Kosinski . . . Hal Ashby . . . Peter Sellers . . ." He thought: Neutral Milk Hotel . . . Arcade Fire . . .

"Sounds great," she said noncommittally.

They fell to silence, watching Garbo and Douglas flirt. Gena clutched the knot of towel at her breastbone with one hand, draping the other lightly on his clothed knee. Conklin, incongruously miserable, wondered about the game. What if Glavine was throwing a no-hitter? Conklin felt his selfishness as never before in his preference that such a thing shouldn't happen when he wasn't there to witness it.

"Don't you want to get cleaned up?" she asked.

"I guess so."

"What's the matter?"

"What we talked about, before—it's real?"

"Crazily, beautifully real, Harris."

"You know I haven't gotten a letter from Ivan for a week."

"Lots of people don't write letters for two weeks."

"You don't understand." The season, and so much else, was slipping away. Or was it gone already? *"He should have answered mine."*

"He's waiting for you to explain."

"You think so?"

"You imagine because you love us both he automatically understands. But we're not one person, Harris."

"You don't need to tell me that."

"Send another letter. You're a writer, win him over. Bring him into our shiny new world."

"We mostly talk about the Mets."

"I know, Harris. I grew up hearing."

Five orgasms later (none of them Conklin's, but never mind), Gena snoring, a web of drool at her mouth's corner, Conklin relocated the remote. They'd never switched the television off, only muted the sound. He flipped from Grand Hotel—*Turner's network, archivally impressive, was seemingly engaged in a Garbo marathon—and checked the final results. The Mets, typically, hadn't scored after Wright's first-inning blast. They'd held on, though, for a 5–2 win, another increment in Glavine's trudge to Cooperstown. Conklin was relieved it wasn't a no-hitter.*

September 26

Mon Frere Felt,

I write you on return from a leaf tour, needing to bare the branches of my heart to you, needing to exfoliate. With Gena, your daughter—a woman, Ivan, a grown and delightful and giving woman—I spent the weekend driving in New England, through Vermont and as far as the Rangeley Lakes of Maine. Everywhere I kept Believenik faith: when we stopped so that Gena could pee or browse trail-mix options at a 7-Eleven or Cumberland Farms, I hurriedly tuned the car's radio to whatever local sports broadcast I could find with the "seek" button—stations out of Burlington, Vermont, out of Keene, New Hampshire, out of Bangor, Maine, and once, I swear, as we topped the Green Mountains, out of Montreal, Quebec, where they still, God help them, give two hoots about the Nationals-née-Expos (and why, I ask you, was this not Filthy Pierrot's team all these years?). So, I caught by a series of audio glimpses our weekend series sweep of the Nats—the second of the Wild Card vampires into whose heart we've plunged a stake, in successive series. We're playing well, Ivan! Beltran's hitting three-run homers in tenth innings! Piazza's going out with a flourish, with multi-homer games! Jacobs and Wright are pounding the ball! Braden Looper's not the closer anymore! We're back over five hundred, even out of the cellar! This is good!

Of course, in searching for the updates of the games I was therefore forced to bear a lot of call-in sports talk radio, and I tell you, Ivan, those Red Sox fans have consciences that are gnarled in ways undreamt of in our philosophy. I don't think winning was good for them. Now their bad faith has bad faith. All across the region, in four or perhaps five states, ostensibly stolid men are worrying aloud, in tones of rage and despair, over the definition of "Valuable." They're all afraid David Ortiz won't win the MVP Award, and that Alex Rodriguez will—a displacement, needless to say, of the fear they cannot name: that the Yankees will consummate their present revival by knocking the Sox from the playoffs. So, the radio talk-show hosts are plunging, led by their tremulous constituency, into semantical and baseball-historical thickets: Can a Designated Hitter ever be regarded as a league's most valuable man? Shouldn't an MVP also field? What, pray tell, is "value"? Anyway, is A-Rod even the most valuable on his team, let alone in the league? What about Mariano Rivera? But can a man who not only pitches but pitches for a mere fifty innings in a season possibly rival someone standing near a base with his glove on, day after day? Ah, but has anyone ever won an MVP award for their fielding? Nay. Shouldn't it be more honestly termed the Most Valuable Hitter? Hence, Ortiz, the clutchest of the clutch, with his dozens of game-winning home runs—he's their man! And anyway, isn't A-Rod an overpaid prima donna? A pussy, in fact? So the cry goes up in favor of "Big Popeye," or whatever it is these Bostonians have nicknamed their reincarnation of Cecil Cooper.

Well, you know me well enough, Ivan, to know this aggrieves my old complaint about the format of the postseason awards. I've always adored that pitchers win it, or used to— I mean, they're on the team, aren't they? Isn't Pedro, for one, plainly the Mets MVP this year? And I like it, too, when they give it to a master fielder and clutch hitter like Keith Hernandez, or a spark plug like Rickey Henderson. Yet again and again this award is debated as though it ought to be sheerly measured in hitting stats, a number crunch of home runs, RBIs, and average: triple-crown stuff. Well, this points to the deficit only I seem to notice: there really needs to be a hitter's award with the same profile and prestige as the Cy Young. Call it the Ted Williams Award, the Splendid Splinter being the best sheer hitter in baseball history not distinguished for attaining championships or necessarily for being a "team guy." Fix this, and the MVP takes beautiful care of itself. Each year one pitcher gets the Cy Young for pitcherly dominance, one hitter gets the Ted Williams for most closely approximating that hitting ideal. And a third player takes the MVP, which is now freed to go to a pitcher, leadoff man, sterling fielder, clubhouse leader, whatever. Listen—many years the Ted and the MVP might be the same person. Fair enough. Other years it might duplicate the Cy Young. Also fine. But at last we'd be free of these eternal debates as to whether "valuable" adjudges intangibles, presence, clutchness, leadership, a good smile, etc., or whether it is reserved for the guy on a division-winning team who drives in the most runs—such a dull, mechanical operation, don't you think (I mean the bean-counting, of course, not the driving-runs-in, which is glorious)? In this new world I'm imagining, just for instance, in 1988, when Kirk Gibson got his "white-guy-with-heart" MVP, Darryl Strawberry would at least have had the consolation of the Ted. (Will I ever recover from 1988, Ivan?)

By the way, I'd give the American League MVP this year to closer Derrick Turnbow, who's single-handedly restored the Brewers to respectability. Oh, that's right, Milwaukee's in the National League now.

I'm trying to make you laugh, I.

This train of thought—awards—brings me to another of my pet subjects, one in which I know I've tried to interest you before: foul balls. Bear with me, Ivan, this is all going somewhere. Doesn't every broadcaster, and every fan, hold their breath in delighted suspension when a hitter works a pitcher to a 3–2 count and then deeper, running an at bat to eight or ten or fifteen pitches? Don't we all feel certain this is some kind of accomplishment, one that often leads to a free pass, or to the pitcher's will sagging, so that he grooves one and the hitter doubles or knocks it over the wall? Even just to tire the pitcher thus is a kind of moral victory, and a strategy now, in this era of pitch counts. And of course it is often the most talented hitter who pushes an at bat into the extraordinary. Yet the admiration remains local, circumscribed; however stat-obsessed baseball fans may be, no one ever wonders who might be the leading hitter of foul balls in a given season, or the greatest hitter of foul balls of all time. No one but me. I've dwelled extensively on this seeming chimera. You know my long-standing interest in wastage, byproduct, chaff, fallen leaves, forgotten men, and as well my corresponding contempt for those who mistakenly overvalue the immaculate or obvious—in other words, it is my assertion generally that men left on base, far from being regrettable, are an inevitable consequence of profitable innings; that foul balls are a symptom of a thriving hitter; that soil on the jersey is evidence of commitment; that injuries to the hamstring, rotator cuff, or heart are corollaries of being alive on this mound of dirt called earth in this stadium called the universe. Ahem.

So, herewith my suggestion: an award, legislated by you and I, named for Keith Hernandez, given to the player at the end of the season who has amassed the greatest number of fouls. I name it for Hernandez because he was an exemplar of the "tough at bat," aka the foul ball—I feel certain Keith would have won his own award a few times. (Of course, a purist would insist that a truer statistic would be "fouls per at bat," or "foul-to-called-strike ratio," but screw 'em.) In fact, in this pursuit I arranged a surprise for you, comrade: earlier this year I enrolled us both in the Society for Baseball Research, in hopes of discovering some way of counting fouls. Then conquered my distaste for online chat rooms and bulletin boards in order to join a forum called SABR Research Questions (in case you'd like to sign on, try username: IFELT; password: jerrygrote), where I posted this most innocuous and tantalizing query: "Which player hits the most foul balls? How can I find out?" You'd think fellows in an organization like that would be interested in such a fundamental question, right? Wrong. Day after day I returned to my post to see what interest it had stirred up, yet it garnered "0 replies," as weeks, then months, passed. Meanwhile, subsequent topics such as "Need help with Babe Herman fielding percentages 1926–34" and "After John Montgomery Ward, who were the greatest teenage pitchers of the nineteenth century?" and "Inventor of the delayed steal?" rapidly garnered strings of a dozen or more replies. Now, is it just me, or is this the equivalent of claiming an interest in the periodic table of elements but spurning a conversation about oxygen in favor of ones about osmium or rhenium? Foul balls are the very stuff of each game, each at bat, each career. They are the binding that holds the greatness together, the very ocean in which hits and outs swim.

Stat nerds, bah. May they congregate again only in Hades.

"But what," you ask, "does all this have to do with foliage in New Hampshire, or my daughter?" Patience, Ivan.

Somewhere, driving home yesterday with your daughter asleep in the passenger seat beside me (she's a champion snoozer, by the way), my foul-ball fugue gave way to a suppressed memory, of a storybook, a novel for teenage boys, one I'd loved as a ten- or eleven-year-old, called *The Kid Who Batted a Thousand*. It was a sports-morality fable, masked, as usual, in a tale of wish-fulfillment. The main character was a rookie on his high-school baseball team, who'd learned the trick of somehow fouling off any pitch thrown to him: he never hit it fair, but also never whiffed. So by this tenacious method the boy had become the greatest on-base-percentage player ever, since a pitcher facing him inevitably faltered, and issued a walk. (This book must have been written in the fifties, Ivan, long before the on-base-percentage fad.) In this capacity he was a kind of oddball star for his team—reliably on base, though he'd never once had a hit. A nice kid, I should mention, well liked by his friends and teammates, not some odd egotist. At the story's climax, of course, a situation arises—his team behind, with two outs and a man on third, it must have been something like that—in which the boy must throw over his tendency and risk swinging to put the ball in play for once. I'm certain he succeeded, though those details I don't exactly remember. What I remember instead is my slight feeling of loss at his surrendering his distinctively perverse you-can't-fire-me-I-quit approach to the game—being who I was, I liked the kid better as the master of foul balls than I did when he capitulated to normative baseball.

You think I'm still stalling, Ivan, avoiding the difficult main topic, I know you do.

But here's the main topic: I may, in my life, have been guilty of loving foul balls too much. That's the realization that Gena has led me to. In my preference for the underrated, the autodidactical, the three-corner shot, the refused and benighted and hapless ("Harris Conklin, America's foremost neglected poet"), I may not have heeded the lesson of *The Kid Who Batted a Thousand*. For, to bat a thousand is also to bat .000, to never have put the horsehide in play.

This is a filibuster, my friend. I'm trying to fill in the silence that has opened between us, to fill it with the new love I've discovered. I need you to forgive me. More than that: I need your blessing. I won't quit until I hear from you again. I won't take action, won't do anything without your consent, the consent I so desperately need, but I promise you, Ivan, neither will I shut up. If you ignore this letter it's not the last you'll hear from me.

Friday afternoon, in Vermont, I asked Gena to marry me, and she said yes.

I took a swing, not foul for once. The ball went over the first-base bag, landed on the fair side of the line, and I rounded first never thinking of settling for one base, or even two. That's me you see standing out there, ninety feet away on third base, panting heavily, my uniform scuffed, but safe, and near home. And that's you, next in the lineup, now standing at the plate. I need you to drive me in, Ivan. I need you to be my MVP.

It's late in the season, yes. But not too late to come out of this thing, like our Mets, with a winning record. Here's what I discovered on my leaf tour, Ivan. What is a baseball season, after all is said and done, but a May–September romance?

The Mets are at home against Colorado the last four days of the schedule. They've earned a cheer or two more from us, don't you think? Let's go, and sit in section 101, the three of us now.

And please keep in mind: unlike you, and unlike the Mink, this is my first rodeo.

Hoping,

Harris

P.S.

Villanelle of the Five-Hundred Team

Half my life I've given to this team.
Like Stendhal, I'm in both red and black.
To win by losing days, a fannish dream.

I wish I'd saved the tickets to redeem,
Though never claim that I got nothing back
For half my life, now given to this team.

Losing's every gambler's secret theme.
Roulette wheels all anchored to time's track.
To win by losing days, a fannish dream.

Wins and losses, a sort of tidal stream.
I'd love to think I'm slightly in the black.
Half my life I've given to this team.

Losers, winners, all melded in my esteem.
And in merciful Lethe's waters, I've lost track.
To win by losing days, a Met fan's dream.

Grapes overhead I've declared sour cream.
No bitterness to taste in winning's lack.
Half my life I've given to this team.
To win by losing days, a lover's dream.

September 27

Harris,

A traveling salesman's car becomes hopelessly stuck in a snowbank during a blizzard. In a matter of minutes he realizes that he's unlikely to be rescued where he is, so he decides to take his chances, and he strikes out to look for shelter. Several hours later, nearly frozen and after numerous brushes with death, he makes it to the nearest farmhouse, and hammers on the door. An old farmer answers his knock, and studies the salesman, shivering in his soaking suit and limp fedora, as he pleads for a place to spend the night.

"Sure, young man. I reckon you can stay overnight," says the farmer hospitably, "but I ain't got no daughter for you to fuck, like you hear about in them jokes." The salesman pauses for a moment, running his finger across his pencil mustache as he thinks. "Well," he responds, "just how far is it to the next farm?"

How often do you get to hear a farmer's daughter joke nowadays? They're like Chinese waiter jokes. Hmm.

An old, damned fool goes to a Chinese restaurant every single day, because this is an old fool who's inclined to the repetitious habits of the vacuum-packed introvert, the tortured aesthete—oh, pick your caricature. At this restaurant he's always waited on by the same waiter, who always asks after his young—very, very young—and beautiful wife, extolling her for her looks, grace, charm, and kindness. One day the old fool, who's been summarily and possibly quite justifiably dumped by his bride, regrets to inform his waiter that his wife has, alas, departed for greener, or at any rate less gray, pastures. "Oh," says the waiter, without missing a beat, "you betta off."

Ba-da-bump.

The big problem with you, Conklin, is that you're so fucking flabby and out of shape when it comes to impropriety; so totally convinced of the value of what you think of as your essential probity and rectitude. Easy to hang on to those qualities when you spend your life in a crummy imitation of Boo Radley. But when the occasion of sin presents itself . . .

So you're schtupping my daughter. Don't try to sneak it in the back door without my noticing. You're human like the rest of us. Don't think I'm going to be fooled that you're getting hard because she's grown, delightful, and giving. I was experimenting with these euphemisms back in the days when Jolie LaRita was going down on me in the stairwell at Our Lady of Pompeii. This was two years before *Portnoy*, buddy! I told myself that she was a nice person, an interesting person, a sort of head-giving friend. But it was all bullshit. I put my dick in her mouth a lot more readily than I would have held her hand walking down Carmine Street, believe it. Roth had it right: the thrill was in a Jew boy like me getting my cock sucked by an Italian girl right on the premises of a Catholic school. Hot stuff!

I'll remind you that this usually occurred after the broadcast of night games. Mets games used to begin around 8:05, if I remember correctly, so these would have been lambent summer evenings around about 10:30. 1967. The year of Seaver's First Coming. I wasn't really interested before that. My father gave up on baseball once the Dodgers had gone. More plutocrats fucking around with the workers, that's what baseball was to him. Fuck the Whitneys and the Paysons and the DeRoulets and all the other bluebloods with their multimillion-dollar playthings, was his attitude. I think he might have felt more kindly toward a Brooklyn boy like Fred Wilpon, but perhaps not: Albert Felt above all others would have recalled Plato's teaching concerning the self-made man as opposed to the heir: the former was a real fucking tightwad, Plato had it, if I remember my Philo 101 correctly. So there was no cute Dodgers lore that I learned at my father's knee. No trips with Dad to the Polo Grounds to see the infant team and its traveling comedy act. But when Seaver came, the Mets became irresistible to me. Never went in for the lovable loser jazz. Tom Terrific blew into town and I was in love. So I associate the Mets with that big goyish boy from Fresno with the rising fastball, and with sweet fumbling experimental sex.

Maybe because of these pleasurable associations, I've never lost my appetite for the Mets. I wouldn't call it passion, exactly. I'm suspicious of sports-related passion. That to me is groups of men in sweaters sitting camped behind beer-can towers and heaping bowls of Doritos—a snack whose only redeeming virtue is that it makes your hands smell pretty much the same as your feet—ready to leap into the air and shout at the top of their lungs at a "touchdown," while their wives cower fearfully in the kitchen. And maybe that's why I am rejecting so entirely—while acknowledging how much it has to do with who you so enchantingly and adorably are— your foul-ball analogy. In the corners and interstices of base-ball where you see foul-ball tallies and Keith Hernandez awards for us to administer and bestow, I see the promise of the strangely familiar. Foul balls? For one thing, this is an ex-ample of the power of the anecdotal. An actual verifiable sta-tistic would just ruin things. "Joe Morgan fouled off eighteen pitches against Kent Tekulve in 1981." No, you want to hear about an at bat that went on for *hours*. Thirty-five, forty pitches. Switch-hitters growing so tired they switched sides of the plate halfway through the at bat. Talismanic. Baseball is voodoo. That's why record-breakers get murder threats. Besides, pal, once you get into that you get into the deep dark woods of esoteric calculations. Who holds the record, pitcher or batter, for first-pitch outs? Strike-to-first-pitch-take ratio? Hit-to-first-pitch-swing ratio? And then there's the Ron Hunt factor. You know that once they—*they*? You're saying *we*—gave prizes for that sort of thing, there'd be some specific class of asshole who'd attempt to win them.

Considering such matters makes my head ache. Feel free to consult the online statisticians all you like in my name,

Conk. I like my statistics big and broad. Wins, losses, that's all that matters. Did I ever mention to you that one of my favorite all-time teams, the 1970 Pittsburgh Pirates, had a starting rotation (Veale/Blass/Ellis/Moose) that went 44–47? They took the East that year. Just how much does that atomize the validity of statistics? Or statistical conventional wisdom?

This is all by way of saying that I completely agree with you, Conk. You *are* guilty of loving foul balls too much. I may similarly confess to loving back-stairwell blow jobs (in the guise of serial marriages) too much, in good time, but what's at issue is you and the particularly veiled way you've chosen to go about your life. It's all up to you. Gena's a big girl. I'm afraid I'm going to have to strand you at third, champ. You want to make a run for it, I'll be the first to greet you at the plate to high-five you or pull your jersey out of your pants or slam my chest into yours, whatever these guys are doing this year, I promise. Go ahead, try to make me laugh. You seem like a very nice boy. Though, please, open-minded as I am, when it comes to my daughter I'd appreciate it if you'd try to avoid pleas that require me to "drive you home." And don't call me Dad. And, listen: I love that kid. But I never had to marry her. Don't you ever once come to me, rending garments and tearing flesh, and tell me that I didn't warn you that—my daughter or no, love her or no—it's still a woman you're marrying.

Felt

September 28

Felt,

Never in all our years. Not when go-betweening for myself and Teresa Frundisch in tenth grade you reworked my first-ever mash note (a rescue, I knew even then, and I've ever since kept clutched to my bosom your proscription against adverbial gerunds, with the exceptions of "charmingly," "seemingly," "winningly," and "Mattingly"), not when you quit allowing me to do anything apart from ride shotgun in the VW Bug on our sophomore-summer Kerouac to Boulder after the little fender bender on the Akron off-ramp, not when we acquired Viola and Saberhagen and I gushed that we had a rotation of four Cy Youngs and you pointed out that not only hadn't Cone actually captured the award but that the other three, Gooden included, would be lucky ever again to glean so much as a second-place vote, not those or a thousand other times. Never. I'm not speaking of you (imperious, monumental, beloved), Ivan Felt, tossing cold water on the parade of me (moist, faltering, well-intentioned), Harris Conklin. Your cold water I'll take every time, it's the cold water I've come to know, the cold water I crave. You've kept me cold and awake and fighting all these years. But now this. Something other. Never before. Never.

Ivan: Though your profession, your avocation, was evident the day I first met you, in the periodicals section of the Bronx Science Library, illicitly annotating the school's run of *Commentary*, never once previously had you treated me the way, I suppose, you must always have been tempted to: as a critic typically treats a poet, in this degraded and bristling cultural surround of ours.

That's how you sound today; like a critic with a poet's neck in his teeth.

I brought you something living, something beautiful. You returned a dissected specimen. For shame, Ivan.

Losingly,
Harris Conklin

P.S. Seo spectacular last night, after the rain delay. Impossible not to take note, even under present, ahem, conditions. What a splendid comeback, to stun the Phils that way. Kept ourselves from mathematical elimination, and me from a poem, too. Lovely, odd game to watch, for those several dozen of us who stayed up until one to do so. (At least two that I'm aware of.) Ishii—back from the dead! And sterling in relief! Graves—back from the dead! And, well, fairly adequate in relief. From those three, to Takatsu, for the save. Four Asian-born pitchers in sequence, first time in (American) baseball history. (You hadn't forgotten, had you, that Graves is born of a Vietnamese mother, out of an American G.I.?) That's baseball for you: always showing you something you've never seen before, even if it feels mildly racist to have pointed it out.

September 30

Ivan Felt,

I write you in disarray, sir. While you and I go on losing (you won't even answer my letters now), the team goes on win-

ning. Now that it doesn't matter. Except somehow it does.
Reyes single-handedly destroyed Philadelphia, a one-man
team. We seem to be, at the last minute, the Reyes Mets: jubilant, charismatic, sharp. Doing to the Phils what we did to the
Fish and Nats: knocking them out of the Wild Card race
(thereby delivering the goods to Houston, but hey: someone
has to win it). In the process, almost absentmindedly, clamber-
ing out of the basement. Is it spiritually putrid that I take so
much satisfaction in this? Or in the fact that Braden Looper's at
last been buried, anonymous, in the bullpen? Heilman's our
closer, at least for the team's final week. Home to Shea for the
cakewalk series against the Colorado Rockies, we've ensured
ourselves already a third-place finish, and no risk of sinking below five hundred (no more poems this year, whew). Every
chance of finishing with a record superior to the "division-
winning" Padres. Winning and losing, inextricably mingled
again. As in my relations with the Felt family. I think I'm apolo-
gizing now, sir. Realize the crux is neither the fact of my
"schtupping" the woman I now call my fiancée nor in your jarring use of the term "schtupping," but in my evasions of your
gruff yet honest inquiries. I never lied, I remind you. Only
stalled. Yet I grasp, typing the word, that this is essentially
what you've been telling me not to do—stall—for forty years.
I'm sorry. I'm not now. Not not sorry, I am that. But not stalling.
Time's running out. Just two games left, in a season with a
miraculous tang of youth at its close. Have you gotten a load of
Anderson Hernandez? I haven't seen him actually hit anything
yet. But he looks really lovely out there at second base.

Fully,
Harris Conklin

October 1

Harris Conklin:

Oh, I can't keep a straight face, addressing you that way. Do you remember that man, Lirtzman I think his name was, who used to keep watch over study hall at Bronx Sci? Like most New York City public-school teachers, he sooner or later disabused kids of any idea they might have held that a classroom was anything other than the secret kingdom of a misshapen, frustrated individual. His special technique, you'll doubtless recall, was to take attendance spottily, jumping around the alphabet, and intermittently, stopping and starting at various times throughout the forty-five-minute period. In that manner, all cutters were to be discovered and brought to justice! So we'd sit, unless we could con someone into answering "here" when our names were called, watching the motes of dust silvering lazily in the afternoon sunlight that poured through the tall mullioned windows of the auditorium, "studying." But do you remember how you stymied him, with your strangely reversed last name? Not so common as it is nowadays, when America is full of little Madisons and Taylors and Jacksons, the gift of an ersatz pedigree just a few keystrokes away at the Bureau of Vital Statistics. No, we were the well-adjusted Stephens and Pauls, Phillips and Peters, with the occasional self-confident reach back into the Old Testament or the shtetl for a name such as my own—we had been named, after all, by the children and grandchildren of immigrants, 100 percent assimilated and comfortable with their American identity. As night followed day, Cohen followed Michael, Sheehan followed Francis, Sanguinetti followed John. And then there was Harris Conklin. We would delight when, two or three times a season, Captain Kirk would have to destroy the computer with illogic, or with a logical and self-annihilating proposition that the computer would have to accept. Instead of simply going dark, of refusing to do anything at all (the tendency of the device on which I'm now typing), these *Star Trek* computers would begin spewing smoke and sparks; their dry automaton voices rising hysterically in pitch, becoming panicky, as they considered the perfect logic, or defective unsoundness, of what Kirk was telling them. And so it was with Mr. Lirtzman and the simple proposition of your name: "Harris, Conklin. Conklin, *Harris?* Conklin Harris. Harris *Conklin?* Conklin, Harris Conklin." So it was each and every time with Lirtzman, Mister, attempting from the trochaic pair of words in your name to determine order, emphasis, meaning itself.

I feel a little like Lirtzman. Harris Conklin Harris Conklin Harris Conklin Harris—there are only two places to stop and I'm not sure I'll be arriving at the real you either way. It's not your loving my daughter. That's fine. Surprising, a little. But this is like Shakespearean comedy: the worldly-wise man advises his lovelorn and innocent friend in worldly matters, yet providence—and, unwittingly, Mr. Worldly himself—thrusts upon the innocent friend the responsibility of chaperoning and advising the worldly man's daughter, with romance ensuing. The play's comic tension is derived from the innocent man finding within himself untapped reserves of those putatively worldly (and in the worldly man's previous opinion, estimable) qualities, dissemblance and guile. I'm tempted to say lesser Shakespeare, *All's Well That Ends Well* (one hopes). But I won't: I love that play. And Falstaff has nothing on you.

I don't know if it ever occurred to you, but my protective impulse is toward *you*. Now, how do I protect you (a) from my own daughter, and (b) from precisely that which I've been urging upon you for forty years? I won't even try. I issued my sole warning; I shan't repeat it. Mazel tov. Tell the kid to give me a call. Not that I think she's been avoiding me; that was all you, I know it, I understand, don't worry.

A better idea. We're still playing in October. Semi-meaningful. Two in a row from the Rockies, and I'm listening to the third right now: Anderson Hernandez is starting; I still haven't seen him do anything notable but I'm in favor of him in principle. Castro/Jacobs/Hernandez/Wright/Reyes. All the way in 2006! And with Jacobs we have a nice Jewish boy. As if in answer, Wright hits his twenty-seventh homer, a two-run shot that puts us up 3–1. A better idea: meet me there, the both of you, tomorrow afternoon, 12:30, at Game Day Ticket Sales. The three of us will watch the game. I'll see firsthand exactly what an old man can learn from a youngster. We're winning it . . . The kids are winning it . . . We win it, 3–1, finally.

> Cras amet qui nunquam amavit;
> Quique amavit, cras amet
> Ivan

October 2, last game of the season
View from an airplane window: a blue stadium, its
circular exterior housing a ball field in the shape of a Vicks
cough drop, its sprawl of half-filled parking lots wedged be-

tween a marina and an expressway, and threaded by an elevated subway line, the whole scene an island in a sea of World's Fair wreckage, on an early autumn afternoon.

Closer: the field is still strewn with stretching ballplayers in their white home uniforms, the stands are filling: this game's yet to begin. Closer again: the upper deck. A haggard usher, brandishing a filthy chamois, rubs at three seats in section 101, then grudgingly gestures to a group of three standing uneasily to one side. Closer still: the group of three includes two middle-aged men and a strikingly attractive woman in her twenties. The stouter of the two men, one Harris Conklin of East Flushing, New York, stops the usher from departing with a gentle hand on his elbow, then ostentatiously offers him a balled five-dollar bill.

"Trying to impress your daughter?" grumbles Mesch.

"No," says Ivan Felt, the thinner of the two men, before Harris Conklin can manage a response. "Trying to impress his father-in-law, I'd say."

To this Mesch offers no reply, turning sullenly away.

"The gall," says Conklin.

"You deserve it," says Felt. "I thought you'd sworn never to tip him, after that seat he sold you in the so-called 'lower boxes.' "

"Pierrot looks happy to see you guys," says Gena Felt, the young woman. She waves at the Frenchman. "Look, guys, he's got a samovar! And a toque!"

"I suppose he thinks it's autumn," says Conklin.

"It doesn't look like a winter toque," says Felt.

These men are fans. Having suffered the highs and lows of their team's season, they've taken more sustenance from the last-minute winning streak than either would like to acknowledge. Arguably, the past ten days have been the healthiest and most promising baseball the New York Mets have played in 2005. So Conklin and Felt have come to this final game of the season very much banking on victory. The opponent, the Colorado Rockies, has shown no resistance whatsoever in losing the first three games of this series. Conklin and Felt are hardly alone in this wish, needless to say. Many have come here today yearning for the grace note of a sweep, as well as to celebrate Mike Piazza's likely last day in a Mets uniform.

"Randolph's done the fine thing," says Conklin. "Penciling Piazza into the cleanup spot in the lineup, to gratify our sentiment today."

"At twenty thousand dollars an at bat," replies Felt, "he'd better get a hit."

"I could wish for better than Zambrano on the mound," says Conklin.

"Today's your no-hitter," says Felt. "You heard it here first."

"I've never seen a Met no-hitter in person," says Conklin, expansively, to his young fiancée.

"That's because there's never been one, you idiot," says Felt.

Though Piazza's delivered nothing, and Zambrano has already failed to no-hit the Rockies—in fact he gives up two runs in the first—in the second inning things are feeling rather celebratory. Mike Jacobs, the Mets' late-September call-up par excellence, hits a magnificent home run. Victor Diaz follows with a home run of his own, tying the game. Pierrot has poured wine, a cabernet franc, and is beginning to delve with a long-handled ladle into the steamy depths of his samovar, to produce delectable-smelling serv-ings of some as-yet-unspecified fricassee.

"I love these young Mets!" says Conklin.

"Yes," replies Felt. "Young is good. And that Jacobs is of the faith gives me a certain stirring of tribal pride. Though he's no Hank Greenberg—I noticed he played yesterday, on a Saturday."

"Excuse moi," says the man they know only as Pierrot. "Why should Jacob not play on zee Saturday?"

"He's Jewish," says Felt, as though this fact is self-evident.

"Oh, I am zorry . . . I was reading in zee media guide . . . Jacobs is, how you say—Protestant?"

"No!" says Felt, sounding violently out of sorts, yet just as quick to cover this impression. "He must have con-verted."

"I am zorry. More wine?"

In the third, however, Zambrano surrenders two more runs, quickly souring the mood, however delicious the meal the three of them are enjoying. Gena Felt, a professed vegan (though she certainly seems to enjoy Chinese takeout), has declined Pierrot's offering.

"Zambrano's confused," says Conklin. "He doesn't un-derstand the script. This is Piazza's farewell. Last game of the season. The three of us—oh, sorry, Pierrot, the four of us—together at last. We're supposed to beat *these guys.*"

"Fuckhead," says Felt. "I want him off the team. Here's my 2006 rotation: Pedro, Glavine, Benson, Seo, Heilman. Though by the season's end I'd wager they'll be ordered Pe-dro, Heilman, Glavine, Seo, Benson."

In the sixth, Cliff Floyd leads off with a home run, and

then Piazza, to much cheering, grounds out for the third consecutive time. Anderson Hernandez comes to the plate, providing some distraction from an all-too-drab ballgame.

"He looks great in the field," says Conklin.

"Still haven't seen what he can do with the bat," says Felt.

"Zed for dix-sept," says Pierrot.

"Really!" says Conklin. He's obviously not been paying close enough attention.

"Yeah, but he's Hispanic, Pierrot," says Felt. "Not French."

"Wait," says Gena. "What does that mean, what Pierrot said?"

"It means Anderson Hernandez is zero-for-September," says Felt. "The guy is still looking for his first major-league hit."

"Sometimes it happens that way," says Conklin sympathetically. "Some of the very best players have been late bloomers. When Willie Mays was first called up he went oh-for-twenty-four!"

"But this is the last game of the season," says Gena.

A silence fell over the group.

"What's this delicious and tender meat?" says Conklin. "Is it veal? Lamb?"

"Pork, I'd say," ventures Felt.

"Porc foetal," says Pierrot.

"What's that?" says Gena.

"Just unborn pig," explains Felt. "Falls right off the bone."

By the seventh, the game has become hopeless, the Mets bullpen, in the form of Heath Bell and Danny Graves, giv-

ing up bushels of runs, climaxing in a Todd Helton two-run homer.

"The Rockies are hitting as if they're at Coors Field," says Conklin, not a little morose.

"Yet we're hitting as if we're at Shea," adds Felt.

At the seventh-inning stretch, the game is halted for a scoreboard video-montage tribute to Mike Piazza—essentially a series of clips of Piazza clouting home runs—that lasts nearly fifteen minutes.

"Feels great, sort of," says Conklin.

"What's this heavy metal song they've edited this thing to?" says Felt.

Both men turn to Gena, who shrugs.

"The title of zee song is 'You Zet Me Free,' " says Pierrot. "It ees by a band called Zee Rain Injuries."

"You set me free?" asks Felt.

"Oui."

"We certainly will."

After the montage Piazza emerges from the dugout and endures—even appears to slightly enjoy—five minutes of sentimental cheering.

"It's genuinely heart wrenching," says Conklin. "Amazing the way baseball gets under your skin. I didn't even like this guy when he was a Dodger."

"That's the point," says Felt. "He's not a Dodger. He's a Met."

In the last of the ninth in a hopelessly out-of-reach game, the final Mets of the season begin to come to the plate. The first is Jacobs, who obligingly slaps a single. Next is Diaz, who drives the right fielder almost to the track: one out, but a fun one. This brings up Anderson Hernandez, at *bat with one last chance before the long winter. Hernandez slips a grounder between the first and second basemen. As the young man arrives at first base the Mets can be seen celebrating, semi-ironically, in the dugout. There's nothing as endearing as a rookie's long-awaited first hit, especially in his very last opportunity.*

"Appropriate," muses Felt, "should that turn out to be the last hit of the campaign."

"Or," counters Conklin, "should we perhaps think of it as the first Met hit of 2006?"

It is at that very moment that Jose Offerman hits into the season-ending double play.

—fin—

- - - - - - - - - - - - - - - - - -

Coda

TIME WARNER CABLE

"The Power of You™"

120 East 23rd St.

New York, NY 10010

OCTOBER 3, 2005

Mr. Ivan Felt

20 Perry St., Apt. 2F

New York, NY 10014

Dear Mr. Felt,

Time Warner Cable welcomes you to its family of satis-
fied customers! As a Time Warner subscriber you'll have full
access to the best of both cable and broadcast television, including pay-per-view events, first-run Hollywood movies, the
award-winning offerings of such premium channels as HBO
and Cinemax, and of course nonstop sports action.

We're pleased and delighted to welcome you as a customer, Mr. Felt. Within a few days a package will arrive in your mailbox detailing the many services and options available to you as a Time Warner subscriber. In the meantime, please accept these free adhesive channel guides with our compliments!

Again, welcome, and happy viewing!

Sincerely,
Angela Marciano
Customer Service Supervisor

Bold = 2005 roster

Abner, Shawn (never played a game in a Mets uniform): The
    outstanding prospect of the '80s—the white Darryl
    Strawberry—Abner rhymes with bust. Played a few games
    for the Padres.

Agee, Tommie (1968–72): Let Us Now Praise Famous Catches.

Alfonzo, Edgardo (1995–2002): For a couple of years at the end
    of the century, a truly great Met. Pushed around the infield
    by the arrivals of Carlos Baerga and Robin Ventura, he
    probably ought to have been installed at second base for a
    decade and allowed to flourish. Lost his power stroke, and
    a step or two, to injuries, around the time he was shipped
    to San Francisco.

Allen, Neil (1979–83): Trade bait. Got us Keith Hernandez, so
    all is forgiven.

Alomar, Roberto (2002–03): One of the great second basemen
    in baseball history, until he reached the Mets. We turned
    him into an old man. Grouped with Mo Vaughn and

Jeromy Burnitz in a cluster as the second-most contemptible gathering of failed Mets—after Bobby Bonilla, Vince Coleman, and Bret Saberhagen in the early '90s—in both cases not for failing to win but for failing to be lovable.

Anderson, Marlon (2005–?): Seemingly destined to destroy the single-year pinch-hit record in June; the Mets instead destroyed his chances by inserting him, mostly, into the everyday lineup.

Astacio, Pedro (2002–03): We Believeniks always had a weakness for Astacio, a pitcher who gave his all to terrible Mets teams. Born in 1969, which may explain something.

Baerga, Carlos (1996–98): Never let it be said that ghosts do not walk this earth. Another All-Star second baseman who seemed to come to the Mets to end his career, he was still to be seen in 2005, getting key hits for a team that didn't exist when his career was in its bloom.

Beauchamp, Jim (1972–73): The quintessential utility man. Often confused with Jim Gosger. Never confused with Bobby Grich.

Benson, Kris (2004–?) The least Tri-State Met, with the most Tri-State wife. Benson looks like Minneapolis, Minnesota; talks like Menlo Park, California; pitches like a Kansas City Royal. His wife is pure Long Island–New Jersey tabloid. One senses a True Crime fable in the making.

Berra, Yogi (1965): The greatest hitter/catcher before Mike Piazza, Yogi had nine at bats for the Mets before calling it quits. Did some other stuff for us too. And for some other team.

Boisclair, Bruce (1974–79): Led Mets in stolen bases with nine in 1976.

Bonilla, Bobby (1992–95, 1999): See Alomar, Roberto.

Buchek, Jerry (1967–68): Traded for Napoleon and Bressoud.

Cairo, Miguel (2005–god help us): Stalwart and versatile former Cardinal and Yankee, and a pet of manager Randolph, a sturdy and professional player, and the first of Egyptian extraction in the history of the major leagues. It was said of Cairo, in the *Baseball Prospectus 2005*, that he formed the very definition of a player who, if he is starting for your team rather than filling in, your team could be seen to be ipso facto unserious about contending for a title. Cairo, acquired for the bench, through May and June increasingly appeared on Randolph's lineup cards as the team's starting second baseman. Mets fans saw nothing to object to in this. In fact, they had been chanting his name.

Cameron, Mike (2004–?): A major leaguer.

Cedeno, Roger (1999, 2002–03): Base stealer, and son of a great man. Became a cynosure of Met-fan hatred—a precursor to Kaz Matsui, in this respect.

Clendenon, Donn (1969–71): Attorney and executive with the Scripto Mechanical Pencil Co., Donn didn't need baseball for a paycheck. World Series MVP of the Miracle 1969 team.

Coleman, Vince (1991–93): See Alomar, Roberto. Arguably the worst free-agent signing in Mets history. Unfortunately, behind that word "arguably" lies more than a dozen arguments.

Cone, David (1987–92, 2003): Traded to the Yankees. Bitten by a dog.

Darling, Ron (1983–91): A little something for the ladies.

Diaz, Victor (2004–?): "Little Manny," "Totebag," "The Wood
Duck," "Dial Z for Diaz," "Hoppy," "Tequila 'n' Titties,"
"The Rose Tattoo," "Sirius," "The Kneaded Eraser," etc.

Dykstra, Lenny (1985–89): Displaced Mookie Wilson from
center field, which seemed dubious at the time. By the
time he finished growing into his career, he'd lead the
Phillies to the World Series.

Everett, Carl (1995–97): Claims that man did not walk on the
moon. A denial of 1969 that should have given Mets
executives pause. Would not make a good babysitter.
Presently in a White Sox uniform, Everett, as of this
writing (October 24), threatens to be "The Last Met
Standing" in the World Series. His competition for this:
Jose Vizcaino of the Houston Astros.

Foster, George (1982–86): The former "Big Red Machine"
MVP; we suffered with George's decline and
eccentricities just long enough to jettison him from the
glories of '86.

Foy, Joe (1970): Trading Amos Otis for Joe Foy is one of the
heartbreaking crucial mistakes made in the wake of the
'69 Miracle—the dynastic possibilities fading so quickly
from view.

Franco, John (1990–2004): The 1990s version of Ed
Kranepool, a New York boy, son of a waste-removal
engineer. For twelve years, our closer. For two more
years, our mascot.

Fregosi, Jim (1972–73): Received from the California Angels in
return for Nolan Ryan, his 1973 baseball card depicts him
popping out to the catcher.

Garrett, Wayne (1969–76): Mets' answer to Harry Carey Jr., the carrot-topped Garrett was a mildly charismatic nonsolution to third base in the early seventies, once the Fregosi balloon collapsed. Number eleven was the inexplicable favorite player of a befuddled young fan in Brooklyn.

Gentry, Gary (1969–72): A Miracle Met pitcher, started and won a game in the '69 Series. Grew a handlebar mustache and was traded for Felix Millan.

Glavine, Tom (2003–?): A run-support nightmare, out of Craig Swan's old playbook. Don't forget to buckle the seat belt in your taxicab.

Gooden, Dwight (1984–94): Done in by his addiction to driving in Tampa.

Grote, Jerry (1966–77): A survivor, the Mets ur-catcher. Played in two World Series and two All-Star games for his trouble. A real player.

Harrelson, Bud (1965–77): A Miracle Met who remembered the bad years, unlike kids like Seaver and Koosman. And then, as manager, made some bad years of his own.

Heilman, Aaron (2003–please don't trade him): Not a setup man.

Hernandez, Anderson (2005–?): Second baseman. Possibly the fourth—and weakest?—link in a 2006 Met "all-youth" infield, with Wright, Reyes, and Jacobs.

Hernandez, Keith (1983–89): Retire this man's number, right away.

Hernandez, Roberto (2005–?): Had he been the Mets closer beginning in April, this book would have another chapter. The same could be said of a hundred men.

Ishii, Kaz (2005–?): The Remains of the Day.

Isringhausen, Jason (1995–97, 1999): Along with Paul Wilson
and Bill Pulsipher, Isringhausen was part of a trio of
pitchers who formed the Mets' future ca. 1994.

Jacobs, Mike (2005–?): A catching prospect who filled in at
first base late in the season. Beginning with a three-run
homer in his first at bat, he assembled one of the most
confoundingly productive debuts in the history of baseball.
Will still be eligible for Rookie of the Year in 2006.

Johnson, Howard (1985–93): Got no respect. The greatest third
baseman in the history of the franchise. Deal with it.

Jones, Bobby (1993–2000): A bland starter who'll always have
the fourth game of the 2000 NLDS, a one-hitter.

Jones, Cleon (1963–75): A true Met. Was made an example in a
moral purge by M. Donald Grant, who, somewhere, should
be ashamed.

Kazmir, Scott (never played a game in a Mets uniform): The
future ca. 2003, was traded to Tampa Bay for Victor
Zambrano in a move many found inexplicable at the time.
Many more find it inexplicable now.

Kingman, Dave (1975–77, 1981–83): The paradigm of steroids,
before steroids; everybody agreed he just oughtn't be
hitting all those home runs. It simply wasn't jake. We
smelled a rat, and then he offered one. The least popular
white star of his generation was rumored to have roused a
conspiracy among the general managers of baseball not to
sign him for an additional year out of the shame and
confusion it would bring the pastime should he attain the
golden circle of players who'd hit more than 500 dingers—
that threshold now "tainted" by McGwire, Palmeiro,
Bonds, et al.

Kranepool, Ed (1962–76): The "original" Met of longest service. Currently employed as the actor inside the Mr. Met mascot. From *Faith and Fear in Flushing*: "The story of Krane is not what he accomplished but over how long a period he accomplished it."

Matlack, Jon (1972–77): Rookie of the Year in 1972, Matlack was the latest-arriving player to feel like a part of the Founding Mythos of Metdom (with Felix Millan and Rusty Staub, he forms the second wave of quasi-excellence).

Matsui, Kaz (2004–?) Puzzlingly dysfunctional Japanese shortstop, converted to second baseman in deference to Jose Reyes's superior arm and status as farm-system ornament. Having hit a home run in his first at bat of each of his first two seasons, Matsui exemplified "peaking early" in each case, and rapidly became a fan unfavorite for his panicky fielding, ill-timed bunting, and semiconscious unfavorable comparisons to his countrymen in other uniforms, some even sharing his surname. Injury gave a plainly disgusted Willie Randolph the excuse needed to "disappear" Matsui, who sat out for six weeks with a bruise—a rare instance of managerially imposed malingering. Matsui would do anything for his team.

Mazzilli, Lee (1976–81, 1986–89): Another instance of Kranepoolism; however, less reconciled with Met identity, as befitting his era of service.

McGraw, Tug (1965–74): You Gotta Believe.

Millan, Felix (1973–77): Felix the Cat. Choked up on the bat. One of the greatest trades in Mets history. After breaking his collarbone went to Japan, where he won two batting titles.

Milledge, Lastings (2006–28): The first Met to win a batting title, in 2008; an RBI title, in 2010; and a triple crown, the following year. League MVP in '10 and '11, and the linchpin of the '07, '11, and '15 championships.

Mitchell, Kevin (1984, 1986): Another morals exile. Genuinely a rough customer (see: cat anecdote), Mitchell was also a strangely touching figure. Won an MVP award in San Francisco.

Mora, Melvin (1999–2000): Spark plug of the 1999 postseason run; traded in 2000 for Orioles shortstop Mike Bordick, and currently a perennial candidate for the AL batting championship.

Offerman, Jose (2005): Who does he remind me of? Shawon Dunston? Darryl Hamilton? Kevin Bass? Alex Ochoa?

Perez, Timo (2000–04): You knew the Mets had to trade this guy to get the trauma of his not running out a drive to the fence in game one of the 2000 World Series behind them (had Perez run it out, Subway Series history would be altered). So what did they do? Made him a regular in 2001.

Piazza, Mike (1998–2005): Straight catcher for the Mets and Dodgers.

Pratt, Todd (1997–2001): A gamer. He was the guy who carried Robin Ventura off the field before he touched second base running out his "grand-slam single."

Ryan, Nolan (1966–71): He'll never get control of that stuff.

Saberhagen, Bret (1992–95): Led Mets in sacrifice hits two seasons in a row.

Seaver, Tom (1967–77, 1983): Current Mets broadcaster.

Seo, Jae (2002–05): A slow-cooking prospect, Seo brings his own cheering section to Shea.

Staub, Rusty (1972–75, 1981–85): Le Grande Orange. Born in New Orleans, played in Montreal, the most cosmopolitan and worldly of Mets, despite his folksy nickname, and his freckles.

Strawberry, Darryl (1983–90): You Can't Go Home Again.

Swan, Craig (1973–84): The lost great pitcher of Mets history. A high-grade guy. Modeled his delivery on Seaver's, credibly. The ace of the worst years, he amassed a record of 59–71. Now working as a Rolfing instructor, helping others avoid the rotator-cuff traumas he endured.

Theodore, George (1973–74): The Stork.

Thompson, Ryan (1992–95): Another version of "the future." Thompson, known for his appearances at the openings of shopping malls, owns the single most glorious moment of the '93 season: he scored the winning run in Anthony Young's first victory after Young's immortal twenty-seven-game loss streak as a pitcher. Thompson arrived at home plate as if consecrating a pennant, stamping with both feet and awaiting the bench's emptying to greet him and hoist him to their shoulders. He wasn't waiting for nothing: they did.

Trachsel, Steve (2001–?): The human rain delay (there is no better joke). The King of Boredom. Everything philistines say about baseball is suddenly true when he pitches.

Vaughn, Mo (2002–03): See Alomar, Roberto. Signed by Steve Phillips after the infamous "batting cage workout." The problem being that his legs didn't work.

Ventura, Robin (1999–2001): Briefly, but unmistakably, a true Met. The P.A. system always played the opening bars of Dylan's "Positively Fourth Street" when he came to bat: "You've got a lotta nerve, to say you are my friend . . ."

Viola, Frank (1989–91): You Can't Go Home Again, vol. 2. He
said his favorite restaurant was Borelli's in East Meadow
on Hempstead Turnpike.

Zachry, Pat (1977–82): Bob Murphy: "Pat Zachry has the unique
ability to make the opposition hit the ball to the deepest
part of the ballpark without it going out."

Zambrano, Victor (2004–?): We see a "Fear Strikes Out"–type
biopic in this young man's future.

ACKNOWLEDGMENTS
- -

I. F.: No book of this nature would be complete without a full accounting of those without whose contributions the book would not be complete—the *sine quibus non*. First and foremost, my writing partner, lifelong friend, and son-in-law, Harris A. Conklin, long America's foremost neglected poet. May this book bring to him a small measure of the success he so richly deserves.

For his constant aid, patience, and unstinting help, I'd like to thank Ron Swoboda—surely the most contemplative of Mets alumni.

The Stieglitz of the camera lens, she of the sensuous diastema, Maude Mossimound took unforgettably rich photos, both in connection with this project and in certain more private contexts.

For aid, and comfort, I can't forget Adrienne Muscovy, Cultural Studies Department secretary at Hunter College, CUNY. Her long hours spent bent over the copy machine will not soon be forgotten.

My editor, Bill Thomas, for his unswerving faith and belief in this project—despite his being a fan of that other team in the Bronx.

My old friend Russell Banks, for sharing his artistry and skill, as well as his collection of baseball memorabilia.

H.C.: To Ivan, to whom I cannot even begin to express my very most heartFelt thanks.

To our agent, Felipa Muskrat, at Muskrat & Seltzen, who Believed in this project when no one else would.

To John Berryman and James Agee, totemic instructors from beyond the realm of the living.

To Bob Pinsky, generous colleague and tutor, so fortunately in the realm of the real.

And to Aloysius and Gena, who made me and made my life worth living, respectively; if this book were not dedicated to Jerry Koosman (a promise made in a hasty moment, forgive me for keeping it), it would most certainly be dedicated to both of you.